THE SOCIOLOGY PROJECT

Introducing the Sociological Imagination

THE SOCIOLOGY PROJECT

Introducing the Sociological Imagination

FROM THE
NEW YORK UNIVERSITY DEPARTMENT OF SOCIOLOGY

JEFF MANZA	COLIN JEROLMACK
RICHARD ARUM	ERIC KLINENBERG
LYNNE HANEY	STEVEN LUKES
VIVEK CHIBBER	GERALD MARWELL
TROY DUSTER	HARVEY MOLOTCH
PAULA ENGLAND	ANN MORNING
KATHLEEN GERSON	CAROLINE H. PERSELL
JEFF GOODWIN	PATRICK SHARKEY
GUILLERMINA JASSO	FLORENCIA TORCHE
JENNIFER L. JENNINGS	LAWRENCE L. WU

PEARSON

Boston   Columbus   Indianapolis   New York   San Francisco   Upper Saddle River   Amsterdam
Cape Town   Dubai   London   Madrid   Milan   Munich   Paris   Montréal   Toronto   Delhi
Mexico City   São Paulo   Sydney   Hong Kong   Seoul   Singapore   Taipei   Tokyo

Editorial Director: Craig Campanella
Editor in Chief: Dickson Musslewhite
Acquisitions Editor: Brita Mess
Assistant Editor: Seanna Breen
Editorial Assistant: Joseph Jantas
Director of Development: Sharon Geary
Senior Development Editor: Lisa McLellan
Senior Development Editor: Deb Hartwell
Director of Marketing: Brandy Dawson
Marketing Manager: Jessica Lasda
Marketing Assistant: Frank Alarcon
Managing Editor: Denise Forlow
Production Liaison: Barbara Reilly
Senior Manufacturing and Operations
   Manager for Arts and Sciences: Mary Fischer
Operations Specialist: Alan Fischer
Interior and Cover Design / Design Manager:
   John Christiana
Cover Illustrator: Max-o-matic/Máximo Truja

Cover Photo: Background wall: Jon Helgason/Alamy;
Sidewalk background: Mary Rice/Shutterstock;
Soccer player: Aflo Foto Agency/Alamy; Man with
cane: Paul Maguire/Alamy; Tai Chi man: Robert
Harding Picture Library Ltd./Alamy; Young
rockers: rgbstudio/Alamy; Asian couple: TongRo
Images/Alamy; Doctors: Image Source/Glow Images;
Yoga woman: Edvard March/Corbis/Glow Images;
Woman in striped shirt: Bill Sykes/Cultura/Glow
Images; Male couple: Kablonk/Glow Images
Digital Acquisitions Editor: Debbie Coniglio
Digital Media Director: Brian Hyland
Digital Media Editor: Rachel Comerford
Digital Media Project Manager: Nikhil Bramhavar
Full-Service Project Management: PreMediaGlobal
Printer/Binder: Courier Kendallville
Cover Printer: Courier Kendallville
Text Font: Adobe Caslon Pro 10.5/13

Credits and acknowledgments borrowed from other sources and reproduced, with permission, in this textbook
appear on appropriate page within text (or on page C-1).

Library of Congress Cataloging-in-Publication Data

Manza, Jeff.
   The Sociology Project : Introducing the Sociological Imagination / From the New York University
      Department of Sociology ; Jeff Manza [and nineteen others].—1st edition.
      pages cm
   Includes bibliographical references and index.
   ISBN-13: 978-0-205-09382-3
   ISBN-10: 0-205-09382-5
   1. Sociology.   I. New York University. Dept. of Sociology.   II. Title.
   HM585.M3456 2013
   301—dc23   2012026698

10 9 8 7 6 5 4 3 2

ISBN 10: 0-205-09482-1
ISBN 13: 978-0-205-09482-0

BRIEF CONTENTS

CONTENTS

3 SOCIAL INTERACTION

Harvey Molotch

4 SOCIAL STRUCTURE

Jeff Manza with Harel Shapira

*5 CULTURE, MEDIA, AND COMMUNICATION 110

Eric Klinenberg with David Wachsmuth

6 POWER AND POLITICS

Steven Lukes and Jeff Manza

THE BIG QUESTIONS

1 What Are the Distinct Forms of Power?

THE THREE DIMENSIONS OF POWER

The One-Dimensional View of Power   •   The Two-Dimensional View of Power   •   The Three-Dimensional View of Power

A Sociological Perspective: **Is power everywhere?**

2 How Does the State Distribute Power in a Society?

THE INSTITUTIONS OF POWER

What Is the "State"?   •   Why States Matter in the Distribution of Power   •   Promoting the Interests of the Powerful

3 Who Has Power in the United States Today?

POWER IN AMERICA

Who Wins? Policy and Politics in the First Dimension   •   Who Sets the Agenda? Politics in the Second Dimension

■ **INFOGRAPHIC Money and Politics**

The Third Dimension: Do Americans Believe in Policies Benefiting the Powerful?

CONCLUSION: THOUGHTS AND QUESTIONS FOR FURTHER INVESTIGATION

THE BIG QUESTIONS REVISITED

7 MARKETS, ORGANIZATIONS, AND WORK

Richard Arum and Jeff Manza, with Abby Larson, Michael McCarthy, and Christine Baker-Smith

THE BIG QUESTIONS

1 How Do Social Factors Impact Markets?

THE CREATION AND FUNCTIONING OF MARKETS

Defining Markets   •   Three Key Social Factors in Markets: Networks, Power, and Culture

2 Why Are Organizations Important for Social and Economic Life?

ORGANIZATIONS IN THE MODERN WORLD

Organizational Persistence   •   From Start-Up to Bureaucratic Firm: The Case of Apple   •   The Downside of Bureaucracy

3 What Is the Relationship between Organizations and Their Environment?

ORGANIZATIONS AND THEIR ENVIRONMENTS

Organizational Structure   •   Organizational Similarity

4 How Are Jobs Structured?

THE DIVISION OF LABOR IN MODERN SOCIETIES

Increasing Specialization in the Division of Labor   •   The Labor Process

A Sociological Perspective: **How have work organizations changed?**

5 What Makes a Good Job?

GOOD JOBS, BAD JOBS, NO JOBS: WORK IN AMERICA

Work Satisfaction

✳ 10 RACE AND ETHNICITY 260

Ann Morning, with Nandi E. Dill, Rachel Garver, and John Halushka

16 CRIME, DEVIANCE, AND SOCIAL CONTROL

Troy Duster and Jeff Manza

19 POPULATION, AGING, AND HEALTH

Lawrence L. Wu and Jennifer L. Jennings

20 GLOBALIZATION

Vivek Chibber

THE BIG QUESTIONS

PREFACE

In *The Structure of Scientific Revolutions*, his famous study of the history of science, Thomas Kuhn argued that introductory textbooks are inevitably the most backward part of any scientific field. He suggested that because they seek to appeal to the lowest common denominator to maximize their audience, they reproduce out-of-date ideas and findings far removed from the cutting-edge of knowledge. Even worse, Kuhn argued, they tend to reinforce popular but out-of-date dogmas that stand in the way of progress. Worst of all, they provide beginning students an entirely misleading view of the discipline. When it comes to sociology textbooks, Kuhn's claim is reinforced because of the simple fact that sociology is such a wide-ranging discipline, with many rich subfields of scholarship and knowledge. No one author (or small team of authors), however well-meaning and determined, can possibly attain mastery of the whole discipline and convey that knowledge to students.

We created this new introductory book in the hopes of overcoming the problem Kuhn so famously identified, and offer up to our beginning students a new kind of textbook. Our aim is nothing less than to reinvent the introductory sociology textbook. We envision an entirely new kind of introduction to the discipline, one that draws on the collective wisdom of a large, successful sociology department and its faculty to bring to our students and readers the real excitement of each of the main subfields of sociology. Rather than reproducing what is said in existing textbooks, as so often happens, the chapters in this book are freshly authored by one or more faculty members from the New York University sociology department who write and teach in the area. In this way, we seek to bring together the best of sociology as a discipline with the challenge of reaching our students.

At the center of this book is a set of tools for learning how to ask hard questions about the world around us. These tools are what we call, following C. Wright Mills, the "sociological imagination." In every chapter, we draw upon contemporary research findings, those of our colleagues and in many cases our own, to puzzle through how individuals are shaped by the contexts in which they live and act. We treat social norms, organizations, institutions, and global dynamics as a linked set of puzzles to explore. Rather than simply giving answers, we suggest a set of questions that sociological research poses. We do not suggest that all of the answers are at hand, but we show how and in what ways sociologists and other social scientists struggle to answer them. If nothing else, we hope that our readers will take away from this book a new determination to question things

The proceeds from this book will be reinvested in the graduate and undergraduate sociology programs at NYU, and used to support minority graduate student fellowships. We have deliberately entitled the book *The Sociology Project* both to reflect our commitment to a collective agenda of our field as an evolving project, and to signal our intention to continue to develop the book in future editions as sociology itself evolves. New findings, theories, and ideas are constantly being developed. Our book will evolve as that research develops in new directions, and we look forward to revising our ideas and questions as the evidence suggests we should. But perhaps most importantly, we think of *The Sociology Project* as a dialogue with our readers – including both our students and our colleagues around the country. We invite you to engage and challenge us where we come up short, tell us what we are doing wrong, and share ideas you have for the presentation of sociology as a field.

Jeff Manza for the NYU Sociology Department
New York City
August 2012

Acknowledgements

Writing a textbook takes a village, as they say, and we have been blessed with a strong and committed team of colleagues, friends, graduate students and editors to pull the book together. Our first and most important debt is to the truly wonderful team at Pearson Education, who have thrown themselves into a new and untested project with conviction and determination. Our image of corporate publishers has been completely transformed by this experience. In particular, Dickson Musslewhite and Brita Mess, the Editor-in-Chief and Acquisitions Editor for Sociology at Pearson, respectively, embraced our project from the beginning, got if off the ground, and stayed in good spirits as we progressed, unevenly, towards completion. They were wonderfully supportive and helpful at every stage. Our development editors Lisa McLellan and Deb Hartwell have done a masterful job, wrestling 20 different chapters written by different authors, into a coherent whole. Often working under considerable time pressure, they kept track of and resolved an endless array of problems and issues as we moved along. The rest of the Pearson team also deserves our gratitude: Sharon Geary, Seanna Breen, Rachel Comerford, Kelly May, Jessica Lasda, Denise Forlow, Barbara Reilly, Blair Brown, John Christiana, Kathie Foot, Karen Noferi, Ben Ferrini, Martha Shethar, and Joe Jantas. We are also thankful for the help of Melissa Sacco, Jen Nonenmacher, Liz Kincaid, and the rest of the team at PreMediaGlobal.

At NYU, we have a number of debts to acknowledge. Joe Juliano, formerly the Dean of Business Affairs at the College of Arts and Sciences, now the Vice Provost for Strategic Planning, connected us to Pearson through a personal relationship with Tim Bozik, the CEO of Pearson US Higher Ed. Joe also provided early advice on the project in a number of ways. In the Sociology Department, several wonderful staff members played key roles in the book. The extraordinary Chloe Anderson served as the Managing Editor of the project and ran it to perfection, turning the impossible to the possible with hard work and subtle organizational acumen. As we were nearing completion, Chloe left for graduate school at Columbia, but we had the good fortune to be able to replace her with the brilliant Poulami Roychowdhury, a PhD student in Sociology who will soon make her own mark on the discipline. In addition to co-authoring a couple of chapters, Harel Shapira provided critical help and advice on many of the chapters while managing to finish his own important book on immigration politics. Writing a book in the way that we did, with the full involvement of the faculty of the Sociology Department, allowed us to draw on the great wealth of intellectual resources of a first-rate group of undergraduate and graduate students. A number of them co-authored chapters and are identified there. Others did critical work behind the scenes, and we can only thank them here: Jonah Birch, Mark Cohen, Nandi E. Dill, Francesco Findeison, Jennifer Heerwig, Julian Jurgenmeyer, Noah McClain, Joshua Musoulf, Ihsan Sadi, Harel Shapira, David Wachsmuth, Christine Baker-Smith, Abby Larson, Michael McCarthy, Max Besbris, Rachel Garver, John Halushka, Leslie-Ann Bolden, Carse Ramos, Stacy Torres, Abigail Weitzman, Shelly Ronen, Adam Murphree, Julia Mendoza, Rene Rojas, Catherine G. Cochran, Emily Rauscher, Eyal Press, Albert Yin, and Madhavi Cherian.

As drafts of the book began to appear, we received exceptional help and guidance from an editorial board assembled by Pearson. Most authors find the "advice" of external reviewers to be more of a pain in the neck than useful feedback, but in this case the final book was genuinely and often critically improved by the generous help we received from our anonymous editors. Often working on short deadlines, every chapter benefitted from their feedback, and we thank them all of them for their help: Angie Beeman, Borough of Manhattan Community College; Karen Bradley, University of Central Missouri; Jim Castleberry, University of South Dakota; Karen Done, Coahoma Community College; Richard Jones, Marquette University; Hence Parson, Hutchinson Community College; Janice Purk, Mansfield University; Rachel Schneider, University of Akron; David Townsend, Ivy Tech Community College; and Thomas Waller, Tallahassee Community College.

THE SOCIOLOGY PROJECT

Introducing the Sociological Imagination

By Jeff Manza, Richard Arum, Lynne Haney,
and members of the Sociology faculty at New York University

Do you recall the first time your sociological imagination was ignited—that moment when the connections between an event or circumstance in your own life and the society in which you live first became clear?

I think it is excellent! It is creative, innovative, collaborative, cutting-edge, interesting, forward-thinking and well-written. I also like the idea of a collaborative book drawing on experts in their fields.

—Bernadette Barton,
Moorehead State University

As sociology instructors, we struggle to convey the power of that insight to our students. How can we get our students to engage, to view and question the world around them, through a sociological lens?

Our challenge as instructors is to help beginning students learn to ask new and hard questions about their worlds; this is the heart of the sociological imagination and the central agenda of *The Sociology Project*.

—Jeff Manza, New York University

I think it is great. Teaching sociological imagination in my mind should be the most important objective in an introduction to sociology course.

—Moshen Mobasher,
University of Houston

I think it is brilliant. Using experts in each area of sociology to write the chapters is a wonderful idea.

—Jan Schall,
Riverside Community College

Fresh, insightful and engaging. By far the most interesting strategy that I have seen in a long time. It is so needed and timely.

—David Townsend,
Ivy Tech Community College

What is the best way to show my students that sociology is not a collection of facts, but rather a process of inquiry?

THE BIG QUESTIONS

👁 Watch the Big Question Videos in **MySocLab**

To understand why and how the institution of education has become so important in our lives, we need to consider the following five big questions:

1 **What are the major functions of schooling?** We will examine the various purposes of schooling in this section, from socialization to preparation for work as well as for citizenship and community life.

2 **How is education related to important life outcomes?** Education is strongly related to many important life outcomes, including work and economic opportunities, health and life expectancy, and marital success and happiness.

3 **Is education equally available to all?** Is education the great equalizer in U.S. society, or does it reproduce existing inequalities? Here we examine the sociological research that investigates whether educational access, experiences, and outcomes are similar for persons of different social classes, races, and genders.

4 **How do educational systems differ?** How can there be such wide variations in the quality and types of schooling, particularly by social class and race? To address this question, we examine differences in educational systems around the world and the various ways that U.S. schools are organized.

5 **How do digital technologies affect education?** We examine how digital systems of monitoring and control may transform teaching and learning, the impact that substituting digital media for live contact between teachers and learners may have, and the effect that the spread of technology may have on inequality in education.

Rather than presenting a broad array of concepts and findings for students to memorize, we instead pose students a set of **BIG QUESTIONS** in each of the subfields and topics in the book. Students will discover the many different ways sociologists have employed creative, and sometimes unconventional, approaches in their efforts to answer those questions and better understand and investigate the social world.

Because each major section in the chapter is tied to a big question, the questions serve as a road map for students and form the basis of the learning objectives for the chapter.

- Each chapter is organized around 3-6 Big Questions that tackle the main points of sociological inquiry for that subfield. The Big Questions help guide students in understanding what's most important.

- Students are introduced to the theories, concepts, and research that are central to investigating each Big Question in the context of sociological inquiry.

"My greatest challenge is to find a compelling textbook that pulls students into the world of sociology. I spend a lot of time looking for textbooks in general, but particularly Introduction to Sociology since there are so many to choose from. It is difficult to find a text that fascinates students while seeing the world through sociological eyes. Most introductory texts are too traditional; they focus on three main theories and many different topics."

—Kim Mac Innis,
Bridgewater State University

- Each Big Question is accompanied by a **BIG QUESTIONS VIDEO** on MySocLab that provides students with an overview of the major theories, concepts, and ideas that are explored in that section.

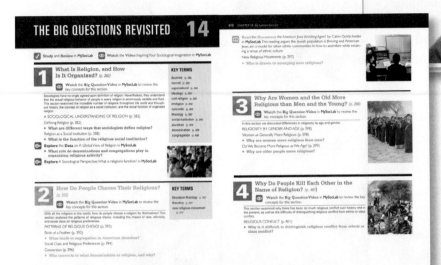

- Each chapter concludes with a section called **REVISITING THE BIG QUESTIONS**. Here, students can see the Big Questions along with short summaries of the main points and a clearly articulated learning pathway through MySocLab.

"My goal is to help students develop their sociological imagination and the biggest challenge is to find the right content and amount of readings that help do that while at the same time introduce students to the basic concepts and theories of the discipline. Students are definitely interested in the topics sociologists study, but I find it a challenge for them to fully comprehend a sociological framework."

—Rhonda Levine,
Colgate University

- The entire instructor's resource program is tagged to the Big Questions so you can organize, lecture, and assess student's understanding of each of the major points of sociological inquiry.

ow can I engage each student's sociological imagination?

Every aspect of *The Sociology Project* encourages students to develop and utilize their own sociological imaginations. Throughout each chapter, compelling examples and critical thinking questions engage students. Videos, interactive maps and charts, and dynamic visualizations make the program a window into a wider world of discovery.

The coast of northwestern Alaska is crumbling into the sea as global warming melts the frozen earth that glues the landscape together. Shown here, a home destroyed by beach erosion tips over in the the Alaskan village of Shishmaref.

Watch the Video in **MySocLab**
Inspiring Your Sociological Imagination

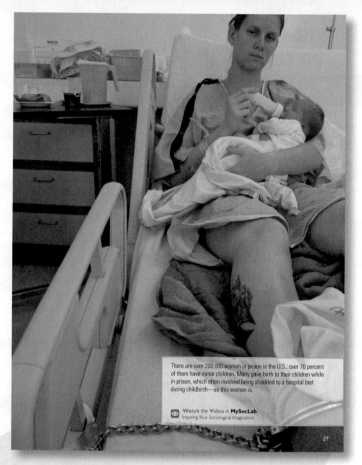

There are over 200,000 women in prison in the U.S., over 70 percent of them have minor children. Many gave birth to their children while in prison, which often involved being shackled to a hospital bed during childbirth—as this woman is.

Watch the Video in **MySocLab**
Inspiring Your Sociological Imagination

27

■ MySocLab features documentary-style videos in each chapter, beginning with **INSPIRING YOUR SOCIOLOGICAL IMAGINATION** videos that illustrate the chapter opening story and provide a preview of the exploration to come.

|| 00:48 ▬▬▬▬▬▬▬▬▬▬▬▬▬▬▬▬▬ 01:52 ◀))) ▬▬▬ ⬚

MY SOCIOLOGICAL IMAGINATION
Ann Morning

My sociological imagination developed from my experiences growing up with people from many different cultural backgrounds. I was raised in Harlem, the famous African American neighborhood in New York City. But even though my home community was very ethnically homogeneous at the time (it isn't anymore), I was exposed every day to people from all over the globe because I studied at the United Nations International School. The contrast between those two worlds really got me curious about how social environments shape our thinking. As a sociologist today, my research focuses precisely on how people from different social backgrounds think differently about some of the things that seem most natural or objective to us, like racial identities or scientific knowledge. My research connecting these areas was recently published in my first book, *The Nature of Race: How Scientists Think and Teach about Human Difference* (2011).

■ **AUTHORS** provide insight into their own sociological imaginations at the beginning of the chapter, discussing what drew them to the discipline and how their sociological imaginations have evolved over time.

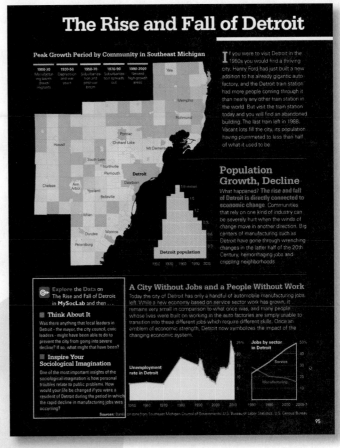

■ **APPLYING YOUR SOCIOLOGICAL IMAGINATION** videos conclude each chapter, illustrating key concepts with real-world examples. Each Applying Your Sociological Imagination video is accompanied by an activity that allows students to upload their own videos or submit a short essay illustrating how these concepts apply to their own lives.

■ **INFOGRAPHICS** visually highlight complex data, information, and concepts. These graphic representations target particularly difficult or complex concepts that would be unwieldy to present in text form.

Each Infographic comes to life in MySocLab with a **SOCIAL EXPLORER** activity that expands on the topic and allows students to actively explore the data, compare change over time, and see what's happening in their own communities.

A SOCIOLOGICAL PERSPECTIVE
What is the quality of healthcare around the world?

There are many factors that determine quality of healthcare. At an elementary level, physician density—the ratio of medical doctors to people in a given population—greatly affects how many patients can visit the doctor and how much time doctors can devote to each individual patient. Physician density varies greatly across the globe and provides some insight to the way medical care differs from country to country. According to the World Health Organization, there must be a minimum of 2.3 health workers—meaning medical doctors, nurses, and midwives—per 1,000 people in order to sufficiently meet the healthcare needs of a population (World Health Organization 2008).

In the United States there are approximately 2.7 physicians per 1,000 people (2004), slightly lower than that of other Western nations. In many developing countries, particularly in Africa, a lack of medical professionals is a major obstacle to adequate healthcare. In Sierra Leone, for example, there are only 0.016 physicians per 1,000 people (2008)—even fewer in Ghana, indicating that healthcare needs of people in these countries are far from being met. On the other hand, Cuba has one of the highest physician-to-population ratios at about 6.4 physicians per 1,000 people (2007), indicating that the wealth of a nation it is not the sole determinant of the healthcare resources available to its people (TCIA World Factbook).

How do countries like Cuba and Venezuela make the healthcare needs of their people a top priority (per capita) over Western countries when they don't have the same financial resources to draw from?

Women wait in a Tillaberi hospital for their children to be seen by medical staff. Facing food shortages and drought, a cholera outbreak threatens the people of several villages. Would a cholera outbreak in the U.S. pose the same or less of a deadly threat to our cities?

Emergency rooms and clinics in the U.S. are often crowded and overflowing with people needing medical attention. What are some of the social and economic issues related to this reality that go beyond the immediate healthcare issue of the individual?

Explore A Sociological Perspective in **MySocLab** and then . . .

Think About It
Why do Americans have worse health outcomes, even though we spend more on healthcare than other countries around the world?

Inspire Your Sociological Imagination
How would the healthcare you receive be different if you were born in Africa?

556

- **A SOCIOLOGICAL PERSPECTIVE** engages students' sociological imaginations visually through photographs. Each chapter features an annotated walkthrough of a social scene with insights into questions and observations that a sociologist might make while doing research.

Students broaden their sociological perspective on MySocLab through a dynamic tour of more photos to fully complete the story. Here students engage their sociological imaginations and are encouraged to make connections with the world around them.

A SOCIOLOGICAL PERSPECTIVE
Can environmental damage be reversed?

Agriculture is responsible for 15-30 percent of global greenhouse gas emissions. Yet agriculture is also one of the areas where the most can be done to reverse environmental damage and to enhance people's standard of living. One example of sustainable and equitable agriculture is the fair trade and organic foods movement, where communities producing goods like chocolate or coffee band together to increase their wages and improve their working conditions, while growing food in ways that promote the health of the surrounding ecosystem.

The Movimento sem Terra (MST) of Brazil was formed by peasants who were evicted from their leased farms by corporations. By protesting and occupying private land, the MST has become a global symbol of peasant farmers' efforts to produce food in a way that sustains both their land and their communities. In the United States, there has been an explosion of urban farming and community gardens. Such lifestyle choices reduce the carbon emissions associated with long-distance transportation and factory farming, and they enable people to take back control of their food supply.

What similarities or differences are there between the Brazilian farmers' efforts to produce sustainable food and take care of their land and U.S. farmers producing food within government subsidizing programs?

What impact does a public or personal produce garden have on the local environment and community health?

How can local supermarkets take advantage of locally grown food and what long-term impact can this partnership have on the environment?

How does the fair trade movement protect farmers and lands throughout the world?

Explore A Sociological Perspective in **MySocLab** and then . . .

Think About It
More and more people are demanding locally grown and organic produce. In what ways are such food choices more sustainable and healthy than fast food?

Inspire Your Sociological Imagination
As people become increasingly concerned about the contents and origins of what they eat, many are questioning the safety of genetically modified produce and consuming fewer processed foods. What changes in the environment and society do you think are responsible for this consumer movement? Can you think of examples of popular foods that have come under scrutiny because they are now considered unhealthy or unsustainable? Why do you think it might be harder for poor people to have access to healthy food?

"I want students to 'engage in' sociology. I tell my students, 'Life is sociology, sociology is life.' If they can leave my course with a better understanding of the world including their own personal lives, I feel like I have accomplished something important."

–Margaret Preble,
Thomas Nelson Community College

Explore A Sociological Perspective in **MySocLab** and then . . .

Think About It
More and more people are demanding locally grown and organic produce. In what ways are such food choices more sustainable and healthy than fast food?

Inspire Your Sociological Imagination
As people become increasingly concerned about the contents and origins of what they eat, many are questioning the safety of genetically modified produce and consuming fewer processed foods. What changes in the environment and society do you think are responsible for this consumer movement? Can you think of examples of popular foods that have come under scrutiny because they are now considered unhealthy or unsustainable? Why do you think it might be harder for poor people to have access to healthy food?

- **THINK ABOUT IT** and **INSPIRE YOUR SOCIOLOGICAL IMAGINATION** prompts accompany the Infographics and A Sociological Perspective photo essays to get students immediately connecting to the data and concepts illustrated.

What are the benefits of a book authored collaboratively by specialists from each sociological subfield?

Standard Introductory Sociology textbooks typically cover 18-20 complicated topics and subfields and are written by one or two scholars with expertise and teaching experience in only a small subset of those topics. *The Sociology Project*, in contrast, is authored collaboratively by the members of the NYU Sociology Department, and coordinated by an editorial team of Jeff Manza, Lynne Haney, and Richard Arum.

Each chapter is prepared by faculty members who teach and do research in the area. The content of each chapter grew out of a challenge the editors posed to each of their colleagues: What are the most important things undergraduates should understand about this topic, especially if they never take another sociology course? How can this be conveyed without jargon or the excessive use of complicated concepts?

This program is a truly collaborative project, one in which authors have created their chapters based on detailed feedback from both other department faculty and their undergraduates, as well as students and colleagues at institutions around the country with different student populations.

MY SOCIOLOGICAL IMAGINATION
Eric Klinenberg

I grew up in the center of Chicago, and my interest in the sociology of culture and cities grew out of my experiences there. I lived in a bohemian but rapidly gentrifying neighborhood called Old Town, a place that was long famous for its vibrant street life and for its blues clubs, jazz bars, cafés, and counterculture scenes. Chicago is a segregated city, and Old Town is wedged between two of the city's most affluent areas, the Gold Coast and Lincoln Park, and Cabrini Green, a housing project (recently demolished) where most of the residents were African American and poor. I was always puzzled by this arrangement, and trying to understand it as a child was the beginning of my sociology career.

My research examines cities, culture, climate, and communications. My first book, *Heat Wave: A Social Autopsy of Disaster in Chicago*, explores the two questions, Why did so many people die during a short heat spell in 1995? And why was this disastrous event so easy to deny, overlook, and forget? My second book, *Fighting for Air: The Battle to Control America's Media*, examines how media consolidation has affected newspapers, radio stations, television news, and the Internet and tracks the emergence of the global media reform movement. My latest book, *Going Solo: The Extraordinary Rise and Surprising Appeal of Living Alone*, analyzes the incredible social experiment in solo living that began in the 1950s and is now ubiquitous in developed nations throughout the world.

How can I encourage students to interact with sociological data to see what's happening in the world, the nation, and in their own communities?

The new Social Explorer allows students to easily engage with sociological data to see concepts in action, change over time, and local statistics.

"I ask the students to understand how to calculate basic descriptive statistics. They are also expected to be able to read graphs and charts that display statistical data."

–Romney Norwood, Georgia Perimeter College

"I like the idea that students can use the data to see trends in their communities because I think that it helps them to develop their sociological imagination and see how sociological concepts can be applied to their own lives and communities."

–Tara Hardinge, San Jose State University

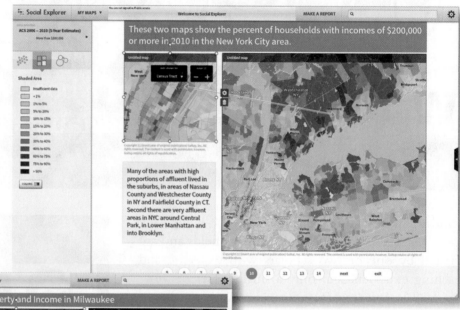

- 90% of instructors surveyed say that quantitative literacy is important to their course.

- 87% say it's important to explore change over time.

- 87% say it's important for students to be able to localize data to see social trends in their own communities.

Working with data starting in 1790 up until today, Social Explorer employs information from the U.S. Census, American Community Survey, General Social Survey, CIA World Factbook, and more.

Students are just as excited about the new Social Explorer as instructors:

"It's fantastic that it's all in one spot. I think it will be huge for citing in papers... it's awesome."

"The fact that we don't have to extrapolate all of the Census data, that that's compiled for us, that's amazing."

Useful as a presentation tool in the classroom and a homework tool after class, Social Explorer includes a number of assignments that introduce students to important concepts in sociology using real-world data.

THE SOCIOLOGY PROJECT includes 40 assignments unique to this program that draw from The Big Questions and infographics in each chapter.

Instructors and students can build their own presentations in Social Explorer utilizing interactive maps, charts, and graphs. Full presentations as well as individual maps and graphs can be exported to PowerPoint or image files.

"To me, quantitative literacy is very important; I tell my students that if they leave the class with anything, I hope they leave it with a healthy skepticism about statistics and how statistics can be presented, while at the same time understanding how to interpret legitimate information."

—Joyce Clapp,
University of North Caroline at Greensboro

"Students are definitely interested in the topics sociologists study, but I find it a challenge for them to fully comprehend a sociological framework."

—Rhonda Levine,
Colgate University

How can MySocLab help my students better prepare and engage with course material outside the classroom?

MySocLab for *The Sociology Project* provides all the tools you need to engage each student's sociological imagination before, during, and after class. An assignment calendar and gradebook allow you to assign specific activities with deadlines and to measure your students' progress throughout the semester.

"(My greatest challenge) is making the material accessible to students with a wide variety of academic abilities in a large course that doesn't allow for lots of one-on-one attention."

—Jason Crockett,
Kutztown University of Pennsylvania

"(My greatest challenge) is getting students to come to class prepared (having completed readings, home-work, etc.)."

—Robyn White,
Cuyahoga Community College

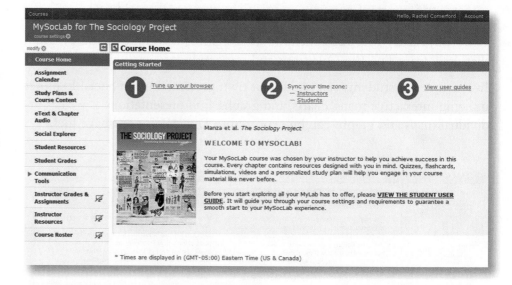

■ The **PEARSON eTEXT** lets students access their textbook anytime, anywhere, and any way they want, including listening online.

- A **PERSONALIZED STUDY PLAN** for each student, based on Bloom's Taxonomy, arranges content from less complex thinking—like remembering and understanding—to more complex critical thinking—like applying and analyzing. This layered approach promotes better critical-thinking skills, and helps students succeed in the course and beyond.

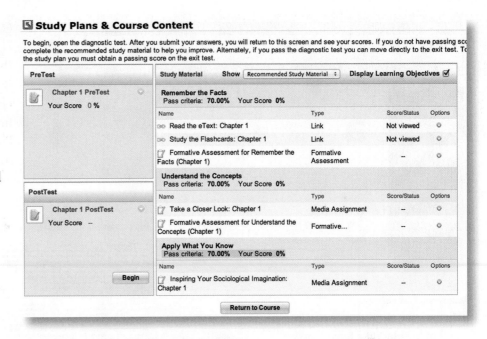

- **SOCIAL EXPLORER** activities connect to the chapter infographics as well as to broad sociological topics, engaging students with data visualizations, comparisons of change over time, and data localized to their own communities.

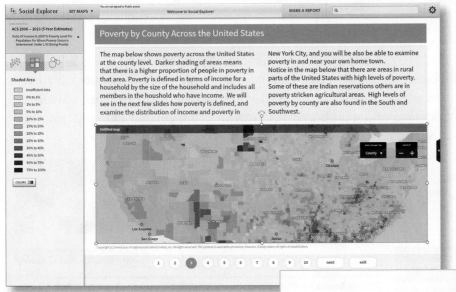

- **INSPIRING YOUR SOCIOLOGICAL IMAGINATION, APPLYING YOUR SOCIOLOGICAL IMAGINATION,** and **BIG QUESTIONS VIDEO ACTIVITIES** quiz students on the concepts covered in each video and provide opportunities for students to upload and share their own videos.

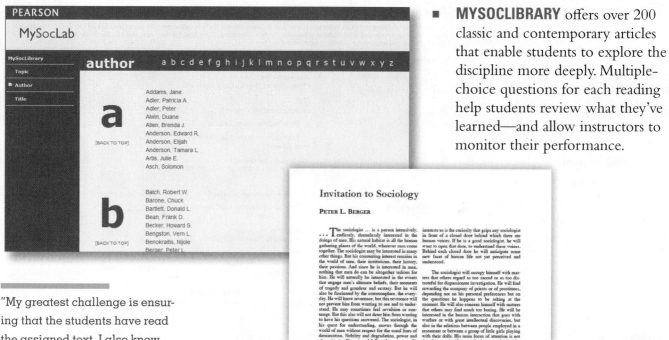

- **MYSOCLIBRARY** offers over 200 classic and contemporary articles that enable students to explore the discipline more deeply. Multiple-choice questions for each reading help students review what they've learned—and allow instructors to monitor their performance.

"My greatest challenge is ensuring that the students have read the assigned text. I also know that I am teaching this computer generation, so I face the challenge of trying to incorporate as much multimedia information in my class as possible."

–Karen Done,
Coahoma Community College

- **SOCIOLOGY IN FOCUS (www.sociologyinfocus.com)** is a blog by sociologists for students that highlights a sociological perspective on current events, pop culture, and everyday life. Updated at least twice a week, Sociology in Focus is a terrific way to bring current examples into the classroom.

"My greatest challenge is adapting the course to a fully online environment."

–Jennifer Brennom,
Kirkwood Community College

How can I encourage and assess critical thinking with a variety of student skill levels and enrollments?

Richard Arum, coeditor of *The Sociology Project*, is also the coauthor of *Academically Adrift: Limited Learning on College Campuses.* In a study that followed 2,300 students at 24 universities over four years, Arum measured critical-thinking and writing skills. Arum found that more than a third of students showed no improvement in their critical-thinking skills after four years at college.

We know that the more students write, the more they strengthen their critical-thinking skills. Now, MySocLab allows you to introduce or augment a strong writing component in your Introduction to Sociology course. Pathbreaking innovations now make possible automated scoring and feedback of student essays.

> "Our country today is part of a global economic system, where we no longer have the luxury to put large numbers of kids through college and university and not demand of them that they are developing these higher order skills that are necessary not just for them, but for our society as a whole."
>
> —Richard Arum, New York University

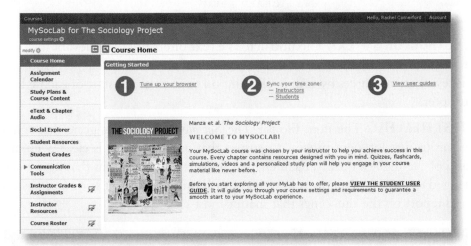

> "My greatest challenge is getting students to do projects and papers with sufficient analytical content."
>
> —Pamela Forman, University of Wisconsin–Eau Claire

Writing prompts, developed by Richard Arum, encourage students to think critically on key topics. Prompts connect key sociological concepts to contemporary and historical issues. Student essays receive feedback on several traits. A detailed scoring rubric sets criteria for substantive traits like development of ideas, focus, and coherence, as well as writing traits like conventions and voice. Students are scored and receive instant feedback on each trait.

This substantive feedback promotes critical thinking about sociology. As the instructor, you can utilize the feedback to facilitate independent revision, peer review, writing workshops, or as a first pass for your own assessment.

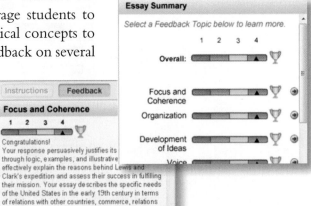

How can I make the most of my time in the classroom?

The **INSTRUCTOR SUPPORT PROGRAM** for *The Sociology Project* is designed to help you engage your students' sociological imaginations from the first day of class and throughout the entire term. Each component offers maximum flexibility so you can customize to meet your needs and goals.

You can instantly access these materials and more in your MySocLab account under Instructor Resources.

> "In the past I have found it difficult to choose from among an enormous possible range of topics and approaches to cover in one semester."
>
> –Kevin McElmurry, Indiana University Northwest

INSTRUCTOR'S eTEXT: The instructor's eText offers links to relevant instructor resources and student activities in MySocLab for each chapter. You can access these resources by simply clicking on an icon at the start of each eText chapter.

TEST ITEM FILE: The item file for *The Sociology Project* has gone through a rigorous development process to ensure that each question is clear, accurate, and of the highest quality. Each chapter features 125 questions that have been tagged to the Big Questions, as well as to Bloom's Taxonomy, so you can assess and report on the outcomes that matter most to you.

> "I usually pick and choose which chapters to present, as I feel there just isn't enough time in 16 weeks to properly teach all of the information in the book."
>
> –Steve O'Boyle, Kutztown University

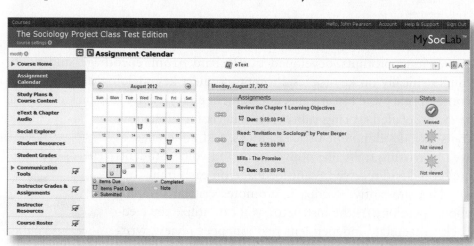

MYTEST The test item file is available through MyTest, a powerful assessment-generation program that helps instructors easily create and print quizzes and exams. Questions and tests can be authored online, giving you ultimate flexibility and the ability to efficiently manage assessments anytime and anywhere.

POWERPOINT LECTURE SLIDES: A variety of PowerPoint lecture slides are available to enhance your experience in front of the class. PowerPoint slides are organized around the Big Questions and feature images, chart, graphs, and maps from the text. The following formats are available:

- MySocLab enhanced with video and Social Explorer links embedded
- Traditional image, art, and text
- Image and art only
- Text only

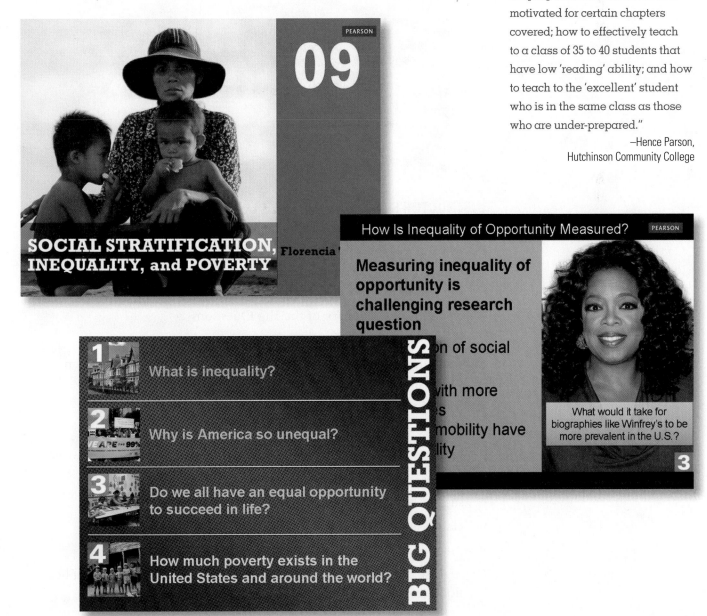

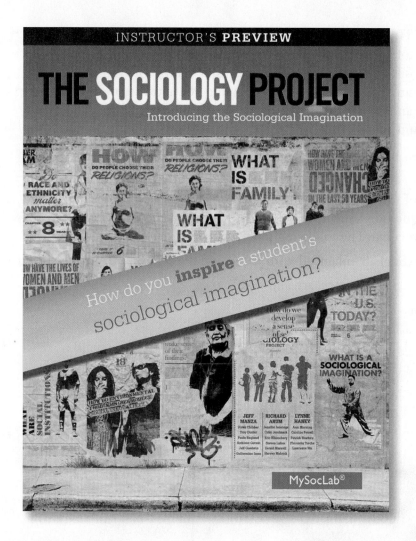

INSTRUCTOR'S MANUAL: Authored by members of the Sociology Department at NYU, the Instructor's Manual has been developed to support a variety of teaching styles and course goals. For each chapter, you'll find:

- sample syllabi from *The Sociology Project* authors and instructors around the country from a variety of institutions

- an annotated summary of the Big Questions

- key terms and definitions

- teaching tips and presentation ideas drawn from the authors' own experiences teaching the topic

- learning outcomes

- detailed chapter outline

- overview of the Infographic and A Sociological Perspective photo essay

- MySocLab learning pathway overview

- suggestions for teaching theory

- classroom discussion questions

- short essay questions and exercises

- suggested supplemental lecture materials including websites, publications, resources on highered.org, and films

Your Course, Your Book

Create custom books with Pearson Custom Library to give your students a more engaging and affordable education.

- You can delete chapters you don't use; rearrange the chapters to suit your syllabus; and add outside readings and content for students.
- Students give high marks to professors who use all of their required course materials.
- Your syllabus will run chronologically with the text, making it easier for students to follow.
- With a custom text, the students are only paying for what they use. When you control the content, you control the price.

How do I build a custom text?
You have two options to get started.

1. Go to www.pearsoncustomlibrary.com to begin building the book yourself.

2. Contact your Pearson representative at www. pearsonhighered.com. Click on the Educator tab, and then click on "Find my Representative."

I'd like to include primary source readings in addition to the text.

You can add readings to your custom text. Place the readings at the end of each chapter, or create an appendix of readings. Following this section is a list of our most popular primary source readings. These are also available on MySocLab so students can read in print or online.

In addition, we have hundreds of primary source readings in the Pearson Custom Library for you to choose from.

Can I use MySocLab with my custom text?

Yes! MySocLab can be packaged with your custom text. Your representative will provide you with the package ISBN.

TIPS and IDEAS for Customizing Your Book

You can add:

- your syllabus.
- a "Where are They Now?" page with photos and stories from recent Sociology grads in your department to show students what you can do with a degree in Sociology.
- a photo and or name of a department member next to the table of contents that discusses that professor's areas of expertise, along with a description of their work.
- MLA, APA, and/or Chicago guidelines.
- your own commonly assigned worksheets to the text. Place them exactly where you want them at the end of specific chapters or create an appendix of worksheets.
- your department's plagiarism policy.
- your school's code of conduct.
- a chapter from a different Pearson text.
- your MySocLab assignment directions at the beginning or end of each chapter.
- a study guide of your own making.
- your PowerPoint lecture slides.
- our PowerPoint lecture slides.
- self-quizzing for students.
- notes pages at the end of each chapter. This way the student brings the book to class and takes notes directly inside of it. See a template on the following page.

Am I obligated to use the Pearson custom book once I build it?

We will send you a hard copy of your custom text in the mail to review with no obligations. If you like it, your representative will provide you with an ordering ISBN. If you want to make further edits, you can do so online or your representative can help you. We will then send you another copy to review.

When do I have to give my bookstore my custom text ISBN?

Printing custom texts takes approximately four weeks. Make sure your bookstore orders your custom text at least that far in advance of the start of classes.

Need a template for adding your own note taking sheets at the end of each chapter? Feel free to use ours. Tweak it, modify it, and or use it just as it is.

Notes Page Example

Your Name: _____

Date: _____

Course Name: _____

Topic of today's class/lecture is: _____

_____

_____

Main Point 1: _____

_____

_____

Supporting Evidence: _____

_____

_____

Supporting Evidence: _____

_____

_____

Questions I have about this main point and/or supporting evidence: _____

_____

_____

Main Point 2: _____

_____

_____

Supporting Evidence:_____

_____

_____

Supporting Evidence: _____

_____

_____

Questions I have about this main point and/or supporting evidence:_____

_____

_____

Summary of Class: _____

_____

_____

Primary Source Readings from Pearson Custom Library

The readings below are the most commonly included primary source readings for sociology. All of the readings below are also available in MySocLibrary on MySocLab so students can read online or in print.
Go to **www.pearsoncustomlibrary.com** to search or browse the complete list including hundreds of readings in sociology.

1

THE SOCIOLOGICAL IMAGINATION

((o Listen to the **Chapter Audio** in **MySocLab**

by JEFF MANZA, LYNNE HANEY, and RICHARD ARUM

Who are we? When we are asked to describe ourselves, we tend to think in terms of our individuality: our likes and dislikes, our interests and skills. But what about the time and place we live in or the family we were born into? We are also products of these contexts, as well as of the relationships we had growing up, our neighborhoods and communities, the schools we attended, the jobs we've had, the organizations we belong to, and so forth. We are individuals, but we are also *social* individuals, connected to other people in a variety of different ways.

The social nature of our lives is becoming increasingly clear in recent years. In 2004, Harvard undergraduate Marc Zuckerberg created a website originally intended for students at Harvard to make such social connections with each other. The idea caught on like wildfire, and the social networking site Facebook was born. Facebook is a worldwide phenomenon with hundreds of millions of registered users that allows us to link to and communicate with "friends" (actual or "virtual" friends) and create or join communities of users. Through these networks, individuals become linked together.

Facebook is extremely popular in part because of its wide variety of uses. As the TV show *Entertainment Weekly* jokingly put it, "How on earth did we stalk our exes, remember our co-workers' birthdays, bug our friends, and play a rousing game of Scrabulous before Facebook?" But Facebook is much more than that. Although the Facebook founders were not

MY SOCIOLOGICAL IMAGINATION
Richard Arum

I grew up as a white privileged Jewish kid in the suburbs of New York, but in a manner a little different than the norm. While my friends were surrounded with adult role models who were in professional fields such as law and medicine, I grew up connected to a broader set of individuals, including cultural icons and civil rights heroes such as Muhammad Ali. This early personal exposure shaped who I was and the choices I would end up later making as an adult.

In the years following, I received a teaching certificate from Harvard University and subsequently worked as a teacher in a segregated public high school in Oakland, California. In that institutional setting, in order to make sense of the dysfunction of the school as an organization as well as the impact that the school was having on the lives of the students, I increasingly was drawn to asking sociological questions of the world. In order to move beyond simply asking these questions, I enrolled at the University of California, Berkeley—coincidentally joining my coauthors on this chapter, Lynne and Jeff, who were also training in the Department of Sociology there—with the objective of developing sociological tools and skills to better understand the problems around schooling in America. Developing a sociological imagination for me was an attempt to develop a set of analytical competencies to participate actively in policy discussions that could substantively improve the outcomes of youth.

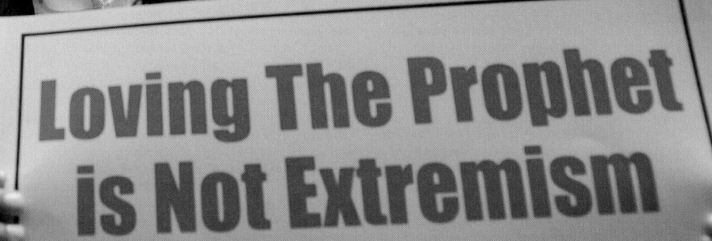

Facebook is controversial in some parts of the world for its ability to allow people of different beliefs to find each other. Why is social media so powerful?

Inspiring Your Sociological Imagination *videos illustrate the chapter opening story and provide a preview of the exploration to come.*

 Watch the **Video** in **MySocLab**
Inspiring Your Sociological Imagination

sociologists and probably didn't realize it, in developing the initial idea for the program they drew upon some very basic sociological ideas about how **social networks**, or the ties between people, groups, and organizations, work. Facebook and its many spin-offs draw from the sociological idea that human beings are not simply individuals with a few close friends and family members who otherwise only randomly bump into strangers in the course of their daily lives. Rather, we all are part of otherwise hidden social networks in which we know people who know other people we don't know but who share some important traits with us (like common interests, backgrounds, areas of expertise, and so forth). Facebook uses an algorithm that makes these normally hidden connections between people suddenly visible. Your friends' friends can now become your "friends" as well. If you identify a particular interest, say in an obscure band, religion, TV show, or political group, you will be prompted to connect to other individuals with similar interests.

Facebook's success in connecting networks of like-minded people has been sufficiently powerful that some governments and citizens around the world have attempted to curtail its use out of fear that it can help people create and spread antigovernment ideas or mobilize groups of citizens to protest in the streets. In the last couple of years, for example, Facebook has been blocked in countries such as China, Syria, Pakistan, and Iran. In other, less threatening but still critical ways, Facebook appears to change the nature of relationships, making it much easier to develop new contacts as well as to keep in touch with old friendships even after people geographically drift apart.

The entire social networking phenomena, of which Facebook is but one part, exemplifies one way in which learning sociological ideas can help us better understand some of the ways that our own existence is dependent on our relationships with others. Hidden in our individual biographies is a story about **society**, a large group of people who live in the same area and participate in a common culture. **Sociology**— the study of societies and the social worlds that individuals inhabit within them—faces the specific challenge of trying to uncover and analyze the patterns that lie beneath the surface of these social worlds for individual lives.

Sociologists are keen to explore phenomena like Facebook, which raises fundamental issues about the social aspect of our lives, but the insights of sociologists do not end there. Sociologists are also asking hard questions about the future of social networking and its implications for how individuals and societies relate to one another. These include: How has new technology changed the form, content, and character of friendship? How has the emergence of online dating changed the nature of intimate relationships? How has technology changed the way work is organized, how we find employment, and what kinds of jobs are likely to be available in the future? Is the new technology helping governments spy on their citizens or helping citizens better monitor their governments and exercise their democratic rights?

The digital revolution has facilitated and deepened long-standing patterns of global interaction. In recent decades, sociologists have begun to think about how what happens in any one society is influenced by the rest of the world. Sociology has always drawn upon cross-national comparisons and explored how societies differ, but theories of **globalization**—the increased flow of goods, money, ideas, and people across national borders—have raised a host of new questions. Sociology provides a set of tools to understand the patterns of globalization, and their impact, on societies and individuals. You won't get a high-paying job in international finance simply because you took a course in introductory sociology (or read this book!), but you *will* have the tools to think hard about how and why our world is the way it is and how you can make decisions to navigate its challenges. We have titled this book *The Sociology Project* to reflect the idea that constant changes in the world around us make life, and the study of sociology, an ongoing project. We invite you to explore sociological ideas with us in this book, to develop your sociological imagination, and to join us and others in participating in this project.

> **The entire social networking phenomena exemplifies one way in which learning sociological ideas can help us better understand some of the ways that our own existence is dependent on our relationships with others.**

THE BIG QUESTIONS

Each chapter is organized around three to six Big Questions that tackle the main points of sociological inquiry for that subfield.

Each Big Question is accompanied by a **Big Questions Video** on MySocLab that provides students with an overview of the major theories, concepts, and ideas that are explored in that section.

👁 **Watch** the **Big Question Videos** in **MySocLab**

Each chapter in this book identifies a set of questions that have defined the research and teaching puzzles of that topic. These questions organize each chapter and provide a lens for exploring sociological thinking about each topic we cover. In starting from questions, not answers, and puzzling together in the search for answers, you will learn to think sociologically. In this first chapter, we will explore the following questions:

How can a sociological imagination help you better understand your world? In this section we introduce the concept of the sociological imagination and explore how it helps us learn to ask hard questions.

Why do social contexts matter? Sociology is fundamentally concerned with how we are influenced by society. All of us are situated in an array of social contexts. How do these influence us and our behavior?

Where did sociology come from, and how is it different from the other social sciences? Here we examine the context in which sociology began to develop and explore the question of how sociology "fits" into, and relates to, the other social sciences.

How can this book help you develop a sociological imagination? Our goal for this book is to provide enough background on the key areas and findings of sociological research in foundation for you to develop your own sociological imagination.

Because each major section in the chapter is tied to a Big Question, the questions serve as a road map for students and form the basis of the learning objectives for the chapter.

1 How Can a Sociological Imagination Help You Better Understand Your World?

THE SOCIOLOGICAL IMAGINATION

Students can click on the "watch" icons to see the Big Questions videos directly from the eText.

 Watch the **Big Question** Video in **MySocLab**

Sociology since its inception has puzzled over how we are connected to each other in the world. These relationships shape not only how our individual lives unfold but also how we come to understand them. This book aims to assist you in developing a sociological imagination that will provide you with a scientifically informed understanding of the social aspects of your life. A **sociological imagination** is the capacity to think systematically about how many things we experience as *personal* problems—for example, debt from student loans, competing demands from divorced parents, or an inability to form a rewarding romantic relationship at college—are really *social* issues that are widely shared by others born in a similar time and social location as us. The sociologist C. Wright Mills (1916–1962), who coined the term in 1959, wrote that "the sociological imagination enables us to grasp history and biography and the relations between the two within society" (Mills 1959:6) To understand the world around us, and to begin to think in a deep way about how to improve it, is to recognize the extent to which our individual lives are strongly shaped by where, when, and to whom we were born and the range of experiences we have as a child, an adolescent, and later as an adult. At each stage, we are both individuals and are members of a social world. Our opportunities and potentials are always influenced by the inequalities and injustices we encounter, but understanding these requires that we think about them sociologically. In short, the sociological imagination helps us to ask hard questions and seek answers about the social worlds we inhabit.

☐ Looking through a Sociological Lens

A sociological imagination challenges some very basic impulses all of us have. The human mind wants to make sense of the world around us by seeing aspects of it, and differences in it, as somehow inevitable or natural. If we have grown up in a social context where marriage is defined as a life-long commitment between a man and a woman, we might be quick to conclude that such an arrangement was

The sociologist C. Wright Mills on his motorcycle in a famous photo. Mills coined the phrase "the sociological imagination."

People watching is an enjoyable activity and a way of beginning to exercise our sociological imagination to make guesses about people we don't know. But we may also be tempted to draw on stereotypes in making those guesses.

the way that intimate relationships were meant to be. Observing those relationships across societies and over time shows, however, that marriage is only sometimes a lifetime commitment between a man and a woman. In some contexts, intimate relationships may be between two men, or two women, or among a man and multiple women, or among a changing carousel of romantic partners. A sociological imagination helps us see the diversity of intimate relationships and question our assumptions about a particular form of marriage being natural as opposed to social in its origins.

In a similar fashion, we are also often quick to identify differences across groups of people—men and women, rich and poor, whites and other races—as inherent to characteristics of these groups. When we attach such differences to real people, it is all too easy to develop faulty generalizations, or what are known as stereotypes. **Stereotypes** are beliefs about members of a group that are usually false, or at least exaggerated, but are the basis of assumptions made about individual members of the group. For instance, some people think that older individuals are not good workers. It *is* true that at some point most of us will become too old to perform jobs that they we may have done for many years. But older workers often face active **discrimination**—which refers to any behavior, practice, or policy that harms, excludes, or disadvantages individuals on the basis of their group membership—because of their age long before they are too old to do their jobs. Many employers and fellow employees generalize from conclusions based on *some* older people (who may have reached a point where they can no longer do a certain kind of work) to *all* older workers. This example will apply to almost everyone at some point, even if it seems a long way off for many of us. But if we are reasonable[,] older, and when we do, we may run [ ] about aging.

Focus Questions help students critically examine and think about the Big Questions.

A sociological imagination also challenges such stereotypes by raising questions about where they come from, what they are based on, who stands to benefit from them, and why they are harmful. Sociology not only produces important theories and ideas, it *also* gives us tools to understand and think critically and creatively about our own lives, the times we are living in, and why we are the way we are. Possessed of a sociological imagination, we are able to be more active and effective participants in the world around us.

How can a sociological imagination help us to challenge stereotypes?

Engaging Our Sociological Imaginations: Learning to Ask Good Questions

Everyone has some degree of a sociological imagination. We exercise our sociological imaginations every time we try to make sense of something in the social worlds around us. Walking through a shopping mall or going to a concert or sporting event, we observe lots of people. If we look closely, it is not hard to make educated guesses about many of these people. We can identify their gender and perhaps their age, race or ethnicity, and maybe even their religion (for example, if they are wearing some kind of identifying clothing). The way they dress may also convey something about their income (look closely, for example, at whether someone's jeans are expensive and high-fashion, or cheap knock-offs). If you hear them speak, it is not too difficult to gather even more information about them. Are they well-educated or not? Are they from a particular region of the United States, or from a foreign country, that is suggested by their accent?

When we "people watch" in this way, we are, without necessarily realizing it, beginning to engage our sociological imaginations. We are using information we know about our society to make educated guesses about the individuals we encounter. But how good are these guesses? That depends, in part, on how well we've trained our sociological imagination to look beyond our assumptions and stereotypes to search for deeper understandings. A good sociological imagination goes much further than just making broad generalizations about individuals. The well-developed sociological imagination is rich with ideas and theories about the endless complexity of the very categories in which we assign individuals. Knowing that someone is white or African American or Asian does not necessarily tell us very much about their annual income, the type of job they have, what they like to do in their spare time, whether they are hardworking or lazy, or in fact much else about them. In this sense, then, just looking at people or groups around us and making generalizations is not in and of itself an example of the use of our sociological imaginations. A sociological imagination instead requires one to ask deeper and more meaningful questions. It does not allow us to settle for simple answers in understanding human beings and the worlds they inhabit. *It is our ability to ask hard questions instead of just accepting easily available answers that is the hallmark of a good sociological imagination.*

From Personal Puzzles to Sociological Questions

All professional sociologists, including the authors of this book, have had experiences in their lives, before they began doing sociological research, where a light bulb first went off that ignited their sociological imaginations. For some it was triggered by a particular event, while for others it may have developed more slowly—a combination of things that inspired them to develop a sociological imagination. One situation that often triggers our sociological imaginations occurs when we see some kind of conventional wisdom, or widely shared assumption, as incorrect. That can literally happen at any moment, but when it does and we start to question what we observe around us, we are taking the first step towards developing a sociological imagination.

Forming Sociological Questions What are these questions? They can range from what is right before us to questions about entire societies. Here are a few examples. Consider eating at a restaurant or school cafeteria. If you look around, you probably will notice that there are relatively few, if any, groups that include both whites and blacks. Or visit a bunch of churches; you will rarely find large numbers of blacks and whites worshipping together. Why is it

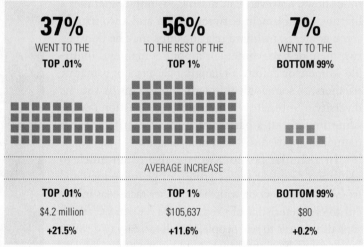

FIGURE 1.1 **THE RICH ARE GETTING RICHER** Income inequality is particularly great in the United States, and the divide between rich and poor is growing. While the rich are getting richer, the majority of Americans are not. In 2010, as the United States continued to recover from an economic recession, a remarkable 93 percent of the additional income created in the country that year went to the top 1 percent of taxpayers, those with at least $352,000 in income, while the bottom 99 percent received a minuscule $80 increase in pay per person.

Of Total Income Increase in 2010 …

37% WENT TO THE TOP .01%	56% TO THE REST OF THE TOP 1%	7% WENT TO THE BOTTOM 99%

AVERAGE INCREASE

TOP .01%	TOP 1%	BOTTOM 99%
$4.2 million	$105,637	$80
+21.5%	+11.6%	+0.2%

Source: The New York Times (2012).

that, long after major civil rights legislation has ended legal discrimination, friendship networks so rarely cross the racial divide? Or think about two-parent families you know (your own or others): How much more housework does the female member of a heterosexual couple perform? Or think about the United States. Why is it that the richest country in the world has so many people living in poverty—far more than other, less wealthy countries (see Figure 1.1)?

Thinking more generally about such questions, it is not a great leap to turn simple observations like these into broader and more profound questions for research. Sociologists have developed a set of **social theories**, or overarching frameworks that suggest certain assumptions and assertions about the way the world works, for posing such questions and evaluating evidence related to those questions. They also have developed **research methods**—ways of systematically studying these questions—in order to develop new evidence that allows new answers to be generated. While we do not just pose questions in our research, learning to ask questions about received wisdom is a key part of learning to think seriously about the world around us.

Asking questions can be dangerous. Governments often do not like it when their citizens begin to ask questions about topics government officials would prefer to keep secret. Large corporations or other organizations often do not like it when workers or members start to ask questions rather than doing what they are told. School authorities often do not like it when students, parents, or outside observers raise questions about the character and quality of student learning. It is true that questioning everything without any foundation for the questions is counterproductive; when a small child starts asking the same question over and over (Why? Why? Why?), it is a game meant to fluster adults, not produce useful knowledge. But hard questions are important, and oftentimes the world becomes a better place only when the authorities are forced to address such questions.

Sociological Questions: An Example

Sociologist Richard Arum, one of the authors of this chapter, has been carrying out a project tracking more than 2,000 young adults as they progressed through 24 diverse colleges and universities and then left college to work, live with friends, move in with romantic partners, or return to live with their parents (Arum and Roksa 2011). The students in the study had quite different college experiences and fared very differently in terms of learning outcomes. Some of these students were in college settings where they were exposed to challenging coursework and successfully moved into well-paying jobs immediately following graduation. Yet many more students did not enjoy such fates. In fact, two years out of college, 24 percent of college graduates in the study were back living at home with their parents or relatives (see Figure 1.2). What explains such differences in outcomes?

Consider the following two students tracked in the project. Maria attended a highly selective, residential liberal arts college in a small Midwestern town. She had come to college with a high SAT score and three high school Advanced Placement course credits. In college, she quickly decided on becoming a social science major after taking a small freshman seminar with a sociologist who did her research on urban youth culture. She spent a semester of her junior year abroad in Europe, and during her semesters at college she reported that she met frequently with her instructors outside of class to discuss her work and that faculty at the school had high expectations for students like her. She also reported that her classmates—many of whom she had come to know well as the college had integrated her academic program with her residential dorm—were equally encouraging of her focus on academic work; on average, she estimated devoting 20 hours per week preparing for classes, many of which in her social science major had significant reading and writing requirements. When we measured her performance on tasks that required critical thinking, complex reasoning, and written communication, her score moved up dramatically from freshman to senior year. Two years out of college, she was living with a friend she had met at college and was working at a job where she made slightly more than $38,000 per year. Although she had assumed a great deal of student debt, she was on a path to adult success.

Contrast Maria's college experiences with Robert's. Robert attended a high school that was predominantly

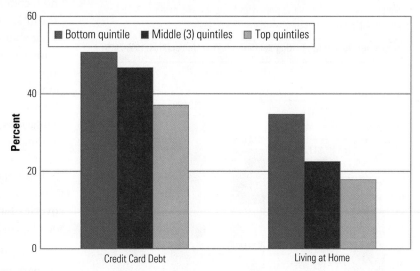

FIGURE 1.2 FORMS OF SUPPORT TWO YEARS AFTER COLLEGE BY TEST PERFORMANCE AT TIME OF GRADUATION

nonwhite before enrolling in a nonselective large public university in his state. Like many of his classmates, he entered college without any Advanced Placement coursework completed and did not score particularly well on the SAT. In college, he reported rarely meeting with his instructors outside of class. When asked about whether faculty had high expectations for students like him, he reported that they largely did not. He muddled through coursework with passing grades but did not finding his coursework either interesting or challenging; he found himself increasingly focused on socializing with his friends and earning spending money to support himself at school. Like many of his peers, he only studied about eight hours per week; when he did prepare for his classes, he often found himself doing so with his friends, who ended up frequently distracting him from really focusing on his work. During his senior year, when we tested his performance on the same tasks that Maria completed, we found no improvement in his performance after attending college for four years. He was not alone. We found slightly more than a third of students in our study demonstrating no significant improvement on a test of general skills. If he had learned subject-specific skills that were not captured well by our assessment indicator, they were not ones that were rewarded in the labor market when he graduated in 2009. Two years after graduation, he was about $30,000 in debt, unemployed, and living back at home with his parents (see Figure 1.3).

How can we understand why these two students had such different college experiences and ended up on such different postcollege paths? There are many ways in which the ideas and research of sociologists give us the tools to understand how Maria's and Robert's lives are unfolding. A sociological view of student experiences in college poses a range of questions about how individuals, institutions, and societies vary. Some of the questions sociologists might ask include: Do Maria and Robert and others like them spend less time

FIGURE 1.3 THE RISE OF STUDENT DEBT Student Debt is on the rise. According to the Project on Student Debt, in 2009, average debt levels for graduating seniors with student loans rose to $24,000, just about double what they were in 1996.

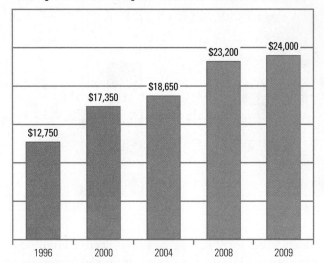

Average Debt of Graduating Seniors at 4-Year Universities, 1996-2009

1996	$12,750
2000	$17,350
2004	$18,650
2008	$23,200
2009	$24,000

Source: The John William Pope Center for Higher Education Policy (2011).

on their studies now than students did a generation ago? And if so, why? Why are certain colleges more focused on academic learning than others? Why do some schools become known as "party schools"? And how has the nature of campus life changed in the past few decades? Are students more or less likely to join organizations or to interact with each other collectively during their college years than at other points in their life? As the ratio of male to female students on college campuses changes, how have dating and courtship patterns been altered? And is the United States alone in these changes in higher education, or are there global shifts underway to change the meaning and experience of college across national borders?

Our sociological questions are different from the questions asked by researchers in other academic disciplines. Psychologists who study cognition, for example, are also interested in what shapes academic achievement. Among other things, they are interested in what affects our ability to concentrate and focus for a sustained amount of time. These interests have led some to study the wiring of our brains—and how things like online media, e-mail, text messages, and Twitter updates can

rewire our brains and cause us to think differently. While these studies are at the cutting edge of research on education and technology, they address questions about how *individuals* think—which does not necessarily tell the whole story. What about the broader *social* factors shaping academic performance and thinking? How do our relationships with each other, as well as our participation in groups and organizations, affect how we learn and experience education? What about the even broader effects of government social policies, regulations, and laws—and the ways they can make education inaccessible or unappealing to certain social groups?

These are the questions that sociologists are particularly well equipped to explore. Because research on higher education is abundant and crosses many fields of study, new discoveries happen all the time. But some of the things that sociologists of higher education conduct research on include:

- How do students' lives *before* college shape their experiences *in* college? We all know that freshmen enter college with quite different backgrounds. But how do those backgrounds shape students' paths through college? For instance, how does your family influence your educational experience? How does your parents' educational background influence your own education—how would being the first in your family to go to college change it? What about your parents' educational expectations of you—do parents expect more from their later children, or from their firstborn? Think back to Maria and Robert: Might Maria's parents have had particularly high expectations for her because she was the first in the family to go to college? Or might Robert have learned to value his friends over his studies well before he stepped onto a college campus—perhaps because his parents expected less from him than from his siblings?

> Students will discover the many different ways sociologists have employed creative, and sometimes unconventional, approaches in their efforts to better understand and investigate the social world.

What types of questions are sociologists particularly well equipped to explore?

The use of new technologies in everyday life raises different issues for psychologists (who are interested in how they are rewiring our brains) than sociologists, who are studying how social media is changing our connections to each other and society as a whole.

How does the social organization of college life shape students' experiences? Universities are organizations. Like other organizations, universities have their own structures, logics, and informal rules. Yet we are only beginning to understand how those structures and rules put students onto different academic paths. College is a time when students form a variety of social, cultural, and political identities. And universities play an important role in those formations—through things like class size, faculty accessibility, and study abroad programs, all of which can give students more opportunity to form academic bonds and support academic focus. Even the physical layout of campus can help or hinder the development of group interaction and identification. Back to Maria and Robert: Perhaps Maria's engagement with professors and other students had less to do with her own internal motivation and more to do with the college context that encouraged such engagement? Perhaps Robert's lackluster academic performance had less to do with his own laziness and more with the lack of supportive academic contexts at his university?

- Does the experience of college benefit everyone equally? We know that the social hierarchies of class, race, and gender shape who goes to what kind of college. But what about students' experiences in college? Are those students with more resources (money, connections, and confidence) better able to take advantage of university opportunities? Does this give them an advantage over other students? Does college life offer more privileges to those who came to school privileged? Or is college the great equalizer, as is often promised? Consider again Maria and Robert: Did their college paths simply reflect advantages they came to college with? Or did those advantages get reversed through their decisions about how to spend time while in college?

- How are students' college paths shaped by the larger labor markets awaiting students upon graduation? The U.S. economy is undergoing massive restructuring as its manufacturing sector continues to transform into service and high-tech sectors. Yet even in these expanding economic sectors, there are changes: Many jobs that once required skilled human intervention have been automated, leading to drastic reductions in the amount of human labor required. There is an international component to this. New information technology now means that many jobs can be performed anywhere in the world, even if their company headquarters remain in rich countries. How have all of these changes affected students' experiences in college? Have they made students more or less motivated in their studies? More or less optimistic about their future? Have they influenced what students major in? The kinds of clubs and organizations they join? The amount of student

FIGURE 1.4 EMPLOYMENT STATUS OF RECENT COLLEGE GRADUATES What kind of jobs are recent college graduates getting? Fifty-six percent are working in fields that require a college degree, but 22 percent are working in fields that don't require a college degree, apparently taking jobs they are overqualified for. And the bad news is that another 22 percent are out of work altogether.

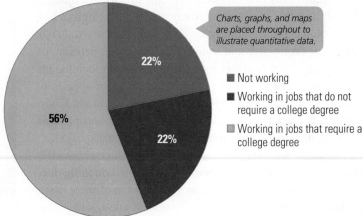

Charts, graphs, and maps are placed throughout to illustrate quantitative data.

- Not working
- Working in jobs that do not require a college degree
- Working in jobs that require a college degree

Source: John J. Heldrich Center for Workforce Development at Rutgers University (2011).

loans they are willing to take out? And once more with respect to Maria and Robert: Has the world of work changed in ways that help explain Maria's ability to secure well-paying work and Robert's postcollege unemployment? See Figure 1.4 for more information about the employment status of recent college graduates.

As these four examples suggest, sociological questions are concerned with a broad canvas of the modern world. Our questions range widely from the basic units of human life—or individuals' relationships with others—to the groups and organizations we are a part of, all the way up to a now rapidly changing global economy that is impacting all of our social relationships.

In short, the project of this book is to outline the big questions in many of the most important topics sociologists investigate. We will also suggest how sociologists and other social scientists are thinking about these but at the same time learning about the world around us. But our first big point is this: Learning how to ask the important questions, and to think hard about how to probe for answers, is the heart of the sociology project.

The Endless Reach of the Sociological Imagination

There are very few areas of life that cannot be studied sociologically. The smallest of particles, say our DNA, would appear to fall outside the sociological imagination. Not so: Sociologists like Troy Duster have studied the discovery of DNA and its political and economic ramifications, such as the idea that there is a genetic foundation to race (Duster 1990). Sociology might appear ill equipped to address the really big issues, like how world economic systems developed across time and space. That, too, has been done—40 years ago by sociologist Immanuel Wallerstein, who created an influential area of research to map the development of a world economy. What about the seemingly frivolous aspects of popular culture, like daytime talk shows? They have been studied. Or toilets? They have already been examined, although in this case only very recently by sociologist Harvey Molotch and his colleagues (Molotch and Noren 2010). Or senior proms, gay and lesbian families, ballet dancing, or street gangs? All have been done. In fact, some sociologists have even moved beyond a narrow focus on our species to study human interactions with the world of animals. Colin Jerolmack has written a book on how humans and pigeons relate to one another around the world (Jerolmack 2013).

The fact that the sociological imagination can be widely stretched to explore many aspects of the human condition does not mean, however, that anything goes. In each of these cases, sociologists draw upon a particular way of asking questions, and a set of theories about where to look for those answers, that have evolved over the past hundred years. Sociologists also deploy a common set of tools for studying those questions. In one way or another, those questions build off a common starting point: How and in what ways do social contexts matter?

Exposure to violence is another topic that has been explored by sociologists: Living in a high-crime neighborhood increases stress levels and is harmful to children in many ways.

📖 **Read** the **Document** *Invitation to Sociology* in **MySocLab**.

Each chapter features a link to a primary source reading from MySocLibrary.

MySocLibrary features over 200 primary source readings that can be assigned in addition to the text.

2 Why Do Social Contexts Matter?

SOCIAL CONTEXTS: FROM INDIVIDUALS TO SOCIETY

👁 Watch the **Big Question** Video in **MySocLab**

Sociology is fundamentally concerned with how individuals are influenced by society. The story of college students Maria and Robert provide one example. We refer to this influence of society on individuals as the **social context**. What is that context? What do we mean when we refer to it?

One way of thinking about the diverse kinds of contexts individuals face is through the following thought experiment. Imagine you are in the maternity ward of a large hospital, looking at a group of newborn babies. They are all helpless and adorable, with a full life ahead of them. In some perfect world, they would all have an equal opportunity to develop their many talents and abilities and succeed in life. In fact, we might look at those cute little creatures and think to ourselves something like "any one of these babies could one day be the president of the United States." But we know that is not really realistic. Why not?

At the core the sociological imagination is the idea that individual lives unfold in contexts—in this case, the social environments, including economic and cultural conditions, that each of these infants will live in. If we could know something about the contexts each of these infants will grow up in, we would be able to make much better-educated guesses about their prospects. What are these contexts? We can immediately identify a variety of factors that are going to influence each baby's life:

How do our families and communities shape our social development?

- the child's immediate family (past and present) and parents' education level, wealth, and income;
- the neighborhood and community the child will grow up in or will live in as an adult;
- the education the child will get (including the quality of the schools he or she will attend);
- the types of organizations (churches, clubs, or groups) the child will join or have access to and the people he or she will meet in these settings; and
- the type of employment he or she will find.

Other contexts of the birth are also important to keep in mind, such as:

- the country he or she is born into (a rich country, a poor country, or a rapidly developing country); and
- the period of history in which he or she is born.

That cute little baby will, in fact, enter a social world that will have a huge impact on where he or she ends up. Let's review these in more detail.

Families and Communities as Context

We are born into families, and generations of sociological research have stressed the importance of family situation as a key to understanding how individuals develop. Our families shape who we are in a variety of ways: by giving us racial, ethnic, and religious identities; by teaching us the basic rules of society and how to behave in society or in particular social settings; through the networks parents provide us and where they have chosen to live (and thus where we grow up); by the financial resources that our parents can invest in our education as well as the emotional and cognitive capacities they have developed in us through life-long interactions; and (possibly) in the extent to which they are willing and able to help out later in life as we become adults and perhaps even attempt to raise a new generation of children of our own.

This brings a second important context into view: the neighborhood and community in which we grow up. Living in a safe neighborhood with good schools, surrounded by families who encourage their children to do well in school and to be ambitious and confident, creates a different set of pathways than that experienced by a child living in an impoverished, high-crime neighborhood with poor schools. The latter environment can have many negative consequences, including not just obvious things like the continual risk of being a victim of crime and the lack of people who can provide positive social networks, but also more subtle things like increased stress levels that may reduce sleep and school performance. Explore *A Sociological Perspective* on page 14.

For instance, in groundbreaking recent research, New York University sociologist Pat Sharkey has discovered a link between neighborhood violence and children's school performance (Sharkey 2010). He discovered that within the week following a homicide in their neighborhood, children in Chicago scored significantly lower on reading and vocabulary tests than they had in the week prior to the homicide. Amazingly, this drop occurred regardless of whether or not the children had actually witnessed or heard about the violence directly. Among other things, Sharkey's research teaches us how violence can be absorbed by and transmitted through neighborhood contexts—and how children, who are perhaps the most vulnerable to such exposure, experience their effects at school as well as home. Aside from our interest in reducing violent crime, Sharkey's work suggests we need to also think about the consequences of neighborhood violence on innocent children.

Organizations and Institutions

From the families that raise us to the neighborhoods we are raised in, contexts then flow outward to the schools we attend, the occupations we enter, and the organizations where we become members. What church, synagogue, or mosque do we go to? What unions or professional associations do we join (or do we have a chance to join a union or professional association in the first place)? What clubs and political groups do we participate in? What bowling leagues, knitting circles, book clubs, or fraternities or sororities do we belong to? The doors to special opportunities that may (or may not) open for us down the road hinge partly on what kinds of groups we place ourselves in and what kinds of contacts we forge—as well as how valuable those contacts become. The same is true of the identities we form for ourselves—both our public identities, like political and religious affiliations, and our personal identities, like our sexual, gender, ethnic, or racial identifications. The organizations we are a part of shape what identities are available to us, how we value them, and why we gravitate to some and not others.

A SOCIOLOGICAL PERSPECTIVE

When you see someone begging for money on the street, what do you think?

A Sociological Perspective *engages students' sociological imaginations visually through photographs. Each chapter features an annotated walkthrough of a social scene with insights into questions and observations that a sociologist might make while conducting research.*

One way to think about this particular unemployed person might be to consider his situation a personal one: He is poor and unemployed, possibly because he is lazy and didn't work hard in school. Maybe he has a bad attitude and his situation is a reflection of his personality. But putting our sociological imaginations into action requires us to look at this situation differently. It asks us to look beyond the individual and uncover this person's larger social situation.

If we use our sociological imagination to think person not as an individual but as part of soci consider poverty not an individual problem bu one. Doing so allows us to reframe the question so we no longer just ask, why is this person in this situation, but why are so many individuals in this situation? And to do this, the sociological imagination asks us to take account of context. Where is this happening? When is this happening?

How does a lack of jobs for all who need them lead to poverty and homelessness?

Where in the U.S. has the housing crisis most affected homeowners and what is the impact on those communities?

What factors cause businesses to lay off workers, or go out of business?

How has globalization affected the U.S. economy and an individual's opportunities to find work?

Students broaden their sociological perspective on MySocLab through a dynamic tour of more photos to fully complete the story.

Think About It *and* **Inspire Your Sociological Imagination** *prompts accompany A Sociological Perspective photo essays to immediately get students connecting to the data and concepts illustrated.*

 Explore A Sociological Perspective in **MySocLab** and then ...

◼ Think About It

Unemployment rises in economic recessions, as do the numbers of families living in poverty, and many people will remain unemployed far longer than normal as a result. Is this a valid reason to support increasing the amount of unemployment insurance the government provides to those in need?

◼ Inspire Your Sociological Imagination

How does the knowledge that being unemployed is frequently due to forces beyond a person's control impact how we view those who live in unemployment and poverty? Why is this alternative view not mentioned in the media? How does its absence influence the way Americans think about poverty and homelessness?

Being in prison can change the way we think of ourselves, including our racial identities.

Sociologists have found that something as fundamental as our racial identity can change according to the kind of institutions where we are connected. For example, serving time in prison (where African Americans are significantly overrepresented) can actually prompt a change in one's racial identification. Sociologists recently discovered that male prisoners were more likely to identity as African American after doing time in prison or jail than before (Saperstein and Penner 2010). What's more, the researchers who interviewed these men were also more likely to define them as African American after learning they had served time—again, even when these same men had earlier been categorized as white prior to incarceration. This is a dramatic case of how deeply our sense of self is tied to the institutions in which we are a part (or, in the case of prison, the institutions from which we cannot escape).

Social and Economic Contexts

Beyond specific organizations and institutions lie the social, economic, and historical contexts of our lives. The state of the world we are born into shapes the opportunities available to us, either limiting or enabling us to pursue different goals and aspirations. An African American male born in the South in 1910 faced a very different environment than the same man would today. A child growing up in a working-class family in Detroit in the 1940s would experience a different set of economic opportunities than the same child growing up in contemporary Detroit (once the center of the automobile industry and home to a large number of high-paying working-class jobs, today the Detroit area has been hard hit by a devastating decline in the U.S. manufacturing sector). Women entering adulthood in the 1950s faced a different set of choices and cultural expectations than women currently entering adulthood. Finally, all of these contexts are influenced by a global environment. We live in an era where events in regions and countries around the world deeply influence the lives of Americans—and vice versa. In particular, many types of jobs once done in the U.S. are now performed by workers in other countries. As jobs, ideas, and technology move around the globe at an unprecedented pace, it is increasingly clear that we are connected to people and places far away. Examples like these highlight how C. Wright Mills' (1959) notion of sociology as the study of where history and biography meet comes to life.

How do the organizations and institutions we are a part of help us form our identities?

Sociology as the Study of Social Contexts

We can now define more fully and clearly what we mean by *sociology:* Sociology is the study of the diverse contexts within which society influences individuals. In order to understand those contexts, sociology ranges widely from how individual attributes (like race, class, gender, education, religion, and so on) are associated with differences in life course outcomes, all the way up to the world of politics, government policies, technology, and the global economy and environment.

At the core of social contexts is a distinction between social interaction and social structure. **Social interaction** refers to the way people act together, including how they modify and alter their behavior in response to the presence of others. Social interaction is governed by a set of **norms**, which are the basic rules of society that help us know what is and is not appropriate to do in any situation. The violation of norms of behavior will cause us all kinds of problems. As we interact with others, we engage in a process of working within those rules and norms to try to present a pleasing version of ourselves to others. Examples include our Facebook and professional website profiles, our business cards, and the different ways we characterize ourselves in social settings when we meet new people or introduce ourselves to a group. For example, the authors of this chapter are sometimes sociologists, sometimes professors, sometimes parents, sometimes politically active citizens, and sometimes various other things depending on the situation. In choosing among these identities, we are engaging with the social world. We always occupy the same body, but who exactly we are (or how we characterize ourselves) depends on the context we are in.

The importance of the "social" part of social interaction becomes most clear to us when we violate societal rules of acceptable behavior (or when we imagine the social sanctions that would follow if we did violate the rules). Consider this example. What would happen if a student in a college classroom were to suddenly stand up on her or his desk and shout profanities at the instructor or fellow students? Even though each of us might occasionally feel like doing this, there are strong and powerful constraints that discourage such action. Without even saying anything, we understand that if we did this our classmates might shun us; the instructor might lower our grade or, perhaps, call campus security to escort us out of the class. So even when we are annoyed or frustrated or bored in our classes, or in similar situations like being in seemingly endless meetings or standing in long lines, we generally know to keep our true feelings to ourselves.

But even if you think there is no chance of any significant consequences, you still "know" it is wrong to be disruptive in that way. How? Sociologists argue that we censor ourselves because of our concern for the social consequences of our action. Societies develop a set of norms that typically govern our behavior. Norms gives us guidelines for our behavior; while they are generally not written down anywhere, we learn and absorb them from our interactions with important others (such as parents, friends, teachers, ministers, or mentors). Knowing what the norms of a situation are is important for avoiding embarrassment and acting appropriately in different contexts, and because most of the time we want to "fit in" wherever we find ourselves. Not knowing, or failing to act in accordance with, the norms governing the situation can be costly in either sense. Something as simple as messing up a handshake or a kiss-on-the-cheek greeting can violate norms. We have various funny phrases for when that happens—we might call it a gaffe, a mishap, a misstep, a *faux pas,* and many others—but whatever name we might use to call it, when we violate social norms we will be embarrassed and possibly sanctioned for our failures.

The complexity of the rules of social interaction has perhaps been most clearly revealed by the limits of artificial intelligence. It was the dream of a generation of computer scientists to build robots that could think and perform like human beings. But trying to program all of the rules and thought processes humans experience, even when doing the simplest of tasks or having relatively simple conversations, proved too difficult. While robots could do some tasks some of the time, they would always and inevitably make some catastrophic misjudgment. So the ambitions of the first generation of artificial intelligence (AI) researchers failed. Later, however, AI research moved on to approaches that have proved remarkably valuable, such as Internet search engines that can predict what we are looking pretty effectively and lead us to information that in the precomputer age was extremely difficult to obtain.

Social structure, the flip side of social interaction, refers to the external forces, most notably in the social hierarchies and institutions of society. A **social hierarchy** is a set of important social relationships that provide individuals and groups with different kinds of status, in which some individuals and groups are elevated above others. The **institutions** of society—those important practices (like marriage, family, and economic markets) as well as the organizations that structure those practices (such as the government, the military, schools, and religion)—provide the frameworks for our daily lives. These external forces confront us in our daily lives and require that we work within them. These social structures are both limiting but also enabling; without them, chaos ensues. Social structures provide both order and organization, but they are often invisible. They are most obvious to us when they are absent or when they break down. In the aftermath of a catastrophic natural disaster—think of a major hurricane, tsunami, or earthquake—social structures can, at least for a period of time, disappear. There are no authorities around to tell people what to do, no police to enforce order. Rules are unclear, and everyone has to improvise. To be sure, some parts of the social structure may be visible in the ways that the poor have a much more difficult time either getting away from danger or surviving after it strikes. But it is in these moments of their absence that the power of social structures becomes most clear.

What exactly, then, is this mysterious thing called social structure? Two distinct components of social structure are, as we noted, hierarchies and institutions. Every society has at its core a set of inequalities (such as those along class, race, or gender lines), and where we stand in those hierarchies impacts who we are and what we can accomplish. Our **roles** in life—our positions within an institution or organization that come with specific rules or expectations about how to behave—are partly determined by our social standing. Institutions matter as well. Because they are not easily changed, institutions are difficult to avoid, and we frequently must answer to them. This is fairly obvious in the case of laws and the legal system but perhaps less so when we think about institutions like economic markets. But even if we try to avoid the formal institutions of the economy (such as a paid job working for a company), we will find that even the underground economy operates according to a set of rules and norms that are often not that different than those of the regular economy. Just because you sell drugs or other illegal goods does not mean that you can escape basic social rules about contracts (for example, in which buyers and sellers each make a promise to the other). Violate the implicit terms of a contract with a conventional business and you may face a lawsuit. Violate the implicit terms of a contract with an underground business and you may face a different (and possibly more dangerous) type of threat. But in either case, contract violations tend to be subject to social enforcement.

> *Students are introduced to the theories, concepts, and research that are central to investigating each Big Question in the context of sociological inquiry.*

What is the distinction between social interaction and social structure?

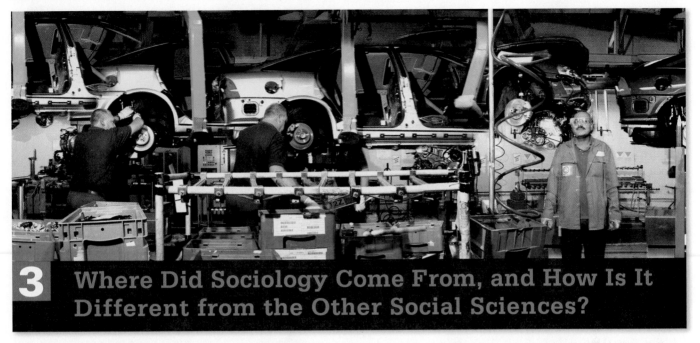

3 Where Did Sociology Come From, and How Is It Different from the Other Social Sciences?

THE SOCIOLOGY OF THE SOCIAL SCIENCES

 Watch the Big Question Video in MySocLab

We can apply the sociological imagination to study many topics, including the development of sociology and the **social sciences**. To do so, we need to ask questions such as: In what context did sociology begin to develop? How does sociology "fit" into, and relate to, the other social sciences?

☐ Sociology and the Industrial Revolution

In general, sociology and other social sciences began to develop when growing numbers of people began to turn from abstract ideas or debates (like "democracy is good" or "racism is bad") to thinking about how things work in the real world and how that world could be systematically investigated. But the sociological imagination was not built overnight. In fact, traces of sociological thinking can be found everywhere people talk or think about their communities or institutions. The desire to answer hard questions about the world with something other than pure speculation lies at the heart of the modern sociological enterprise. This is the point where philosophy crosses over into sociology and social science.

The development of a new way of questioning and seeking answers to issues and problems of the modern world unfolded in fits and starts throughout the nineteenth century, but the idea that the social world could be studied with rigor and scientific methods akin to those that had been applied to nature and the natural world took hold from the 1880s onward.

What was the historical context in which sociology began to develop?

The term *sociology* is typically credited to Auguste Comte (1798–1859), who first used it in 1839. Comte thought that sociology would eventually become the ultimate science of the social world and would include both what he called "social statics" (the study of societies as they are) and "social dynamics" (the processes of social change) (Comte [1839–1853] 2009).

As time went by, a variety of different ways of studying the social world began to emerge. The lines between these social scientific disciplines were very fuzzy at first. Early social scientists often identified with several disciplines. For example, two of the most famous and influential early economists, Thorstein Veblen (1857–1929) and John Commons (1862–1945), held chairs in sociology at one point in their long and storied careers. Similarly, some of the social theorists that later influenced sociology, most notably those of philosophers Adam Smith (1723–1790) and Karl Marx (1818–1883), spent much of their time writing and thinking about the economy and economic relations. As one study of the rise of the social sciences has put it, these early years were characterized by the "chaos of the disciplines" (Abbott 2001). But between 1880 and 1910, however, the social sciences began to settle down into organized bodies of knowledge and distinctive professional profiles.

For sociology, this settling down first occurred in Europe. Indeed, the "father of sociology," Emile Durkheim (1858–1917), founded the first European Sociology Department at the University of Bordeaux in 1895 and the first major European journal of sociology in 1898. On the other side of the

The Chicago School developed many important ideas about society based on detailed studies in the city of Chicago.

Atlantic, a distinctively American tradition of sociology also emerged around this time, centered around the Sociology Department at the University of Chicago, founded in 1895 as the first such department in America. Frequently taking the city of Chicago as its laboratory, the so-called Chicago School intensively studied the problems of cities and the groups of people living in them, developing a body of knowledge that remains influential to this day.

But great thinkers and schools alone cannot explain what makes a set of ideas take off. It is instructive that most of the earliest thinkers we now call sociologists did not train to be sociologists. So what was the social context that made people interested in this new kind of knowledge? Two critical developments spurred the social sciences in general and sociology in particular. The very rapid period of **industrialization**—the growth of factories and large-scale goods production—and **urbanization**—the growth of cities—in the late nineteenth century in the United States, Europe, and elsewhere was especially important. This was a period when new technologies and innovations made possible the growth of large-scale manufacturing of consumer products—transforming economies based primarily in agriculture to those based in the manufacturing of goods. The spread of factory labor in this period of industrialization created jobs that were concentrated in **urban**

areas, which are commonly defined as those with a population density of at least 1,000 people per square mile and all surrounding areas that have an overall density of at least 500 people per square miles). This period of urbanization was marked by growth in the proportion of the population living in urban areas and cities—which grew rapidly in size between 1850 and 1920 (see Figure 1.5). Chicago grew from a population of 29,963 in 1850 to 2.7 million people in 1920. Detroit went from 21,019 in 1850 to just under 1 million in 1920. Philadelphia, the fourth largest city in America in 1850, with 121,000 people, reached 1.8 million inhabitants by 1920. Figure 1.5 summarizes the growth of cities and surrounding metropolitan areas throughout American history. The jobs driving this growth pulled people away from farms and rural communities and provided economic opportunities for wave after wave of immigrants from other countries who arrived in steadily increasing numbers from the 1870s until the early 1920s, but continuing into the 1960s.

The social changes enabled by industrialization were immense. The contexts of both individual lives as well as whole communities were changing rapidly. And it was clear that the natural and biological sciences seemed unable to explain fully what was occurring. While chemistry and physics proved enormously useful in providing the basis for new industrial processes and could be drawn upon to explain the physical effects of the pollution spewing from the newly constructed industrial landscape, they could offer little insight into how working for wages in factories was changing the most basic human relations and group identifications. Similarly, while biology might have been able to predict some of the physical challenges that people faced once they moved to crowded cities,

FIGURE 1.5 GROWTH OF THE URBAN POPULATION IN THE UNITED STATES

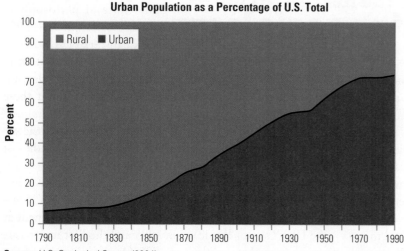

Urban Population as a Percentage of U.S. Total

Source: U.S. Geological Survey (2004).

it could provide little clue as to how city life was altering how politics was practiced, how work was done, or how families were organized. For these kinds of issues, different approaches to the emerging world were needed.

The exploding cities that developed in the United States and Europe from the middle of the nineteenth century onward were teeming with deep problems that were markedly different from the agricultural economies of previous centuries. To begin with, these cities were rife with high levels of poverty. The early factories paid poorly, and living in the expanding cities was often expensive as the housing supply struggled to keep up with the demand. Cities were dirty places—this was before public health and public sanitation measures had become widely implemented—and they were breeding grounds for disease, infant mortality, and early death. They were also places where crime and violence were much more common than in rural communities. Finally, they were places where people could organize themselves to protest unpleasant conditions of life. Instead of tolerating misery alone on one's farm, now it was possible to meet and discuss problems with dozens or hundreds of people in close proximity. This created a new type of political challenge, especially as organized associations of workers (created in order to protect and fight for their rights) called **unions** began to form. Also on the rise during this period were **social movements**, which are marked by collective action aimed at bringing about some kind of change in society.

In the face of these challenges and conditions, sociology found its place in beginning to seek to understand the sources of these emerging social problems. Of course, sociology was not the only academic discipline to emerge from this period of social change; a diverse group of disciplines also emerged right around the same time, in the late nineteenth and early twentieth centuries, concurrent with the rise of the modern research university. It was really quite remarkable how all of the traditional social science disciplines consolidated into coherent, organized, and increasingly distinct fields of study at a similar historical moment. In large part, this was due to important expansions in higher education in both Europe and America in the period. The dates of the founding of the major social science professional associations give some idea of how compacted the rise of the social sciences was (displayed in Table 1.1). In a span of just 20 years, then, a whole battery of social sciences would come to establish an institutional presence in the United States.

☐ Sociology's Family: Siblings

While all the social sciences were born from a similar impulse to understand the emerging social worlds spawned by industrialization and urban growth, there was considerable disagreement over where to go from that common starting point. So how did sociology come to differ from other social sciences? We would point to two fundamental distinctions:

TABLE 1.1 DATES OF THE FOUNDING OF MAJOR SOCIAL SCIENCE PROFESSIONAL ASSOCIATIONS

American Economics Association: 1885
American Psychological Association: 1892
American Anthropological Association: 1902
American Political Science Association: 1903
American Sociological Association: 1905

1. Our concepts and theories cover a wider range of topics than other disciplines—we are promiscuous in what we study.
2. Our explanations of how the external world shapes behaviors of individuals and social outcomes are broader than those of other disciplines and encompass different units of analysis. Sociologists move *from individuals to groups to institutions to global society*. Sociology is the social science discipline that is most concerned about how different units of analysis link up to and mutually influence one another.

Of course, the danger in working with such a broad spectrum of topics is that it can be hard to define the parameters of sociology. As professional sociologists we are often asked, what exactly *is* sociology? Sometimes we struggle to give a short, simple answer. Unlike other social scientists, sociologists don't define ourselves according to a specific institution or area of life. We don't claim one piece of the external world as our sole area of expertise. For the most part, other social scientists do precisely this: Political scientists are primarily concerned with topics that involve governments and the policies they produce. Economists are mainly concerned with individuals' economic behavior (microeconomics) and the performance of the national or global economy (macroeconomics). Psychologists are interested in understanding the workings of the mind and the dynamics of the psyche. And anthropologists claim expertise in the practices of diverse cultures and how they vary across time and place.

Sociology cannot easily be pigeonholed in this way. Sociologists can and do move into all the areas that are the "home turf" of the other social sciences. But we do so just as systematically and rigorously as other social scientists. As our name indicates, we claim scientific expertise over those parts of life we call the "social" and in topics with "social" significance. But the "social" is a bit fuzzier of an area than those studied by our counterparts. That is, most people know exactly what a political scientist means when he or she studies "government"—or what an economist does when researching the "economy." But sociologists often get perplexed looks when we say we study the "social world." It took one of our grandmothers 20 years to stop telling the women she lunches with that her granddaughter was a professor of "socialism" or "social work." For her, this was a concrete way to make sense of the social and to translate it into something meaningful (albeit a bit scary, as

How we see a community or social setting is shaped by what vantage point we use. Viewed from space, social life doesn't appear very different, but the closer we get the greater the differences we can see.

she was a staunch Republican). So while sociologists' refusal to break up the world into small, narrow slices and proclaim expertise over them does cause confusion, most of us would have it no other way.

To make sociology even messier (but, in some ways, more exciting), there is enormous flexibility in how sociologists approach our topics of study. We have considerable leeway to decide what to analyze in our research. As we outlined earlier, sociology consists of the many contexts shaping our lives—from the small to the large, from the local to the global. This means that we focus on many different levels of analysis when examining a given topic; we can choose to highlight one or more surrounding contexts. And we have more freedom to make these choices than most of our social scientific siblings.

Another way to say this is that sociology works with different **units of analysis**. These are the pieces of a topic that a researcher bites off when she or he studies it. They are akin to the camera lens settings you use when taking a picture—say of a family. A narrow lens might zoom in on only the individual members of the family. This would allow a sociologist to capture the interpersonal dynamics of family members with great detail and nuance, but not the larger context in which the photo was taken. An alternative is to pull back a bit and try to capture the environment the family is posing in—perhaps revealing the neighborhood around them or the surrounding natural environment. Or even further, use a wide-angle lens to place each family member in the organizations they are part of, from the places they work to the schools they attend, to the clubs they participate in, to the friendship networks they value. Or even more dramatically, replace the camera with a camcorder to draw into view all the ways in which families can change over time. And all of these devices can be used to study different types of families and to compare them historically or in different societies.

Sociologists have all of these techniques at our disposal. And unlike our social scientific siblings, we use them all. In doing so, we offer multifaceted perspectives on similar social phenomenon. Continuing with our example of how sociologists study the family, like psychologists many sociologists are interested in the emotional life of families. In fact, a classic

What units of analysis do sociologists work with, and how do these differ from those of other disciplines?

sociological study addresses this: Nancy Chodorow's best-selling 1978 book *The Reproduction of Mothering*. Yet unlike the classic psychological studies of family life, which tend to isolate the family unit to study patterns of interaction and their psychological effects, Chodorow places family life and the dynamics between family members in a larger context. She asks, why is it that women are the ones to parent offspring? How does women's exclusion from the world of work shape the kind of parenting they do? Does it lead them to treat boys and girls differently? And does that lead boys and girls to develop different senses of self and emotional needs? All of these questions then push Chodorow to yet another unit of analysis: What happens to family life when these traditional patterns of caretaking break down? Historically, as more women work outside the home, do they parent differently? And do families then have to change the emotional ties that bind them? In effect, Chodorow's sociological approach uses multiple lenses to zoom in and zoom out on her topic—and thus to gain different perspectives on the complexities of contemporary family life (Chodorow 1978).

Units of analysis are important not only because they affect what aspects of our topics we can see—they also shape the explanations sociologists provide. Precisely because sociologists work on different levels, with different units of analysis, they typically address a wider range of connections than other social sciences. Consider again the difference between sociology and psychology. Psychology is centered on the study of the mind, the psyche, and the physical brain. Sociologists have much to learn from psychological findings, some of which we've already mentioned in this chapter. At the same time, sociologists part company with psychologists in insisting that individuals must also always be located in larger social contexts. For sociologists,

Why are some occupations typically "female" and others "male"? What kinds of changes have to take place for that to change?

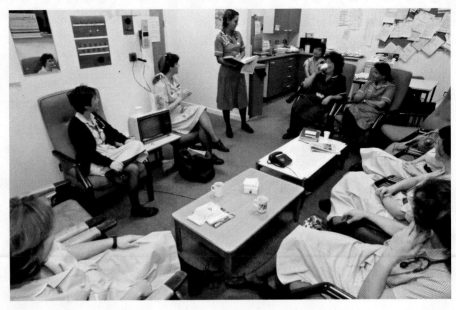

it is not enough to explain individual behavior by simply understanding the intricacies of the psyche. Going back to the family example, most individuals are embedded in families (of some sort), which are themselves embedded in communities, which are themselves embedded in cultural, economic, and political environments. To explain individual action, these other contexts must also come into view.

A similar gap separates sociology from economics. Economists pride themselves on building and testing models of economic behavior using clear and simple assumptions about human nature (e.g., that everything being equal, we will always act in ways that we think will enhance our self-interest and financial well-being). Their ideas and mathematical models of human behavior are often elegant and lead to clear predictions that can be tested by researchers. Sociologists, by contrast, tend to believe that for all of their impressive advances, economists sometimes miss important outcomes because they don't consider a wide enough range of factors and forces affecting human behavior. Sociologists argue that there are many things motivating individuals—altruism as well as self-interest, reputations and status as well as money. And in a different context, the same person might behave differently. So while sociological theories tend to be messier and more difficult to test than economic theories, they can also produce a wider range of possible explanations that, when successful, can produce genuinely new understandings.

What are some of the spin-off fields that originally started in sociology?

All of this sibling rivalry aside, most social scientists today end up drawing on the ideas and insights of other fields and disciplines. After more than a century of building their own disciplines and professional associations, there is now increasingly a move to blur the boundaries. **Interdisciplinary research**, as it is known, is an increasingly central part of learning about any topic in the social sciences. Few students and scholars in the social sciences would be foolish enough not to draw on ideas in the neighboring social sciences. And sociology is perhaps the most likely to do so—it is the most interdisciplinary of all the traditional social science disciplines. Depending on the question at hand, sociologists will need to know something about the research and theories developed by economists, political scientists, psychologists, or anthropologists. We also often draw on the work of historians—a discipline that is in the humanities but is closely related to the social sciences. Although our main interest in this book is introducing you to sociological insights and approaches, and indeed it is impossible to start thinking interdisciplinarily until you have at least some grasp of disciplinary knowledge, we would certainly *not* want to leave the impression that sociology by itself has all the answers to all the questions that social scientists raise. It does not.

☐ Sociology's Children

One interesting side note on the relationship between sociology and the other social sciences is the way in which sociology has mothered a number of new areas of study into existence. In most universities today, there is a large group of spin-off majors and programs that have developed out of one of the social sciences, more often than not sociology. This list includes such fields as criminology, gender studies, African American Studies, Latino/a studies, organizational or management studies, industrial relations or labor studies, demography, and others. There was once a time when much of the research and scholarship on these topics was done within the discipline of sociology. But for various reasons, these subfields would eventually split off from sociology to became independent fields of study and develop their own knowledge bases and professional associations. Indeed, it is remarkable just how many spin-off fields originally started (at least in part) in sociology. Explore the Infographic on page 22.

Looking at this list of these other fields of study, it is clear that sociology has long served as an important *incubator* for new arenas of investigation. Even today, there are exciting new areas of study in sociology that may eventually grow into disciplines of their own. In this sense, learning the basics of sociology is an essential foundation for any one of these newer fields. At its core, sociology will remains a foundational discipline for many of the interdisciplinary social sciences.

Sociology in America

Infographics *visually highlight complex data, information, and concepts. These graphic representations target particularly difficult or complex concepts that would be unwieldy to present in text form.*

Sociology has come a long way. Unlike long standing academic fields such as physics, history, or philosophy, which were established centuries ago, sociology emerged relatively recently. This is particularly true of sociology in America. In fact, the first sociology department in America wasn't established until 1892 at the University of Chicago, and it was not until around the 1940s that a large number of American universities had a department of sociology. Up until then, if and when sociology was taught, it was ... ics, histo

*Each Infographic comes to life in MySocLab with a **Social Explorer** activity that expands on the topic and allows students to actively explore the data, compare change over time, and see what's happening in their own communities.*

Sourc
Sociol

Explore the **Data** on Sociology in America in **MySocLab** and then …

■ Think About It

What is a possible explanation for the decline in sociology students from the mid-1970s to the mid-1980s, and then the subsequent increase?

■ Inspire Your Sociological Imagination

After reviewing the list of areas in sociology, what new areas do you see emerging in the twenty-first century?

Today, there are **816** sociology departments in the United States.

And compared with 1930 when only 40 people received PhDs in Sociology, in 2010 that number increased to 638 people.

Bachelors degrees in sociology

(y-axis: 5,000 / 10,000 / 15,000 / 20,000 / 25,000 / 30,000 / 35,000)
(x-axis: 1970 1980 1990 2000 2010)

Masters degrees in sociology

(y-axis: 300 / 600 / 900 / 1,200 / 1,500 / 1,800 / 2,100)
(x-axis: 1970 1980 1990 2000 2010)

Think About It and Inspire Your Sociological Imagination prompts accompany the Infographics to immediately get students connecting to the data and concepts illustrated.

Doctorates in sociology

(y-axis: 100 / 200 / 300 / 400 / 500 / 600 / 700)
(x-axis: 1970 1980 1990 2000 2010)

Sociology is a dynamic field. As the world changes what sociologists study changes. One of the powerful aspects of the sociological imagination is that it can be applied to a diverse set of issues and problems.

Membership in 14 of the 51 sections of the American Sociological Association

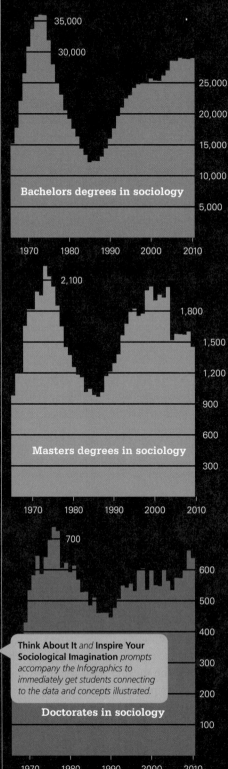

Rank in 2011	Section	2002	2011
	No. of members:	889	1,228
1	Culture		
4	Race, Gender and Class	787	999
6	Political Sociology	602	884
7	Collective Behavior/ Social Movements	606	874
8	Economic	505	872
10	Education	622	862
13	Teaching and Learning	460	804
14	Comparative and Historical	547	708
15	Community and Urban	556	696
17	Religion	496	672
20	International Migration	349	630
21	Aging	490	612
24	Sexualities	296	507
28	Children and Youth	345	447

4 How Can This Book Help You Develop
a Sociological Imagination?

LOOKING AHEAD

👁 **Watch** the **Big Question Video** in **MySocLab**

Our goal for this book is to provide enough background on the key areas and findings of sociological research to provide our readers with the foundation for developing your own sociological imagination. By understanding how individuals' lives are embedded in particular social contexts that are not always of their own choosing, we hope that you will learn to appreciate how personal issues that individuals face often can also be understood as larger social problems facing society.

This book is organized into five sections, each containing four chapters. The first section discusses foundational issues to the discipline, such as research methods, social interaction, and social systems. The second section of the book provides the "building blocks" for applying sociology to understand the individual and society. Topics covered include culture, politics and power, organizations and markets, and cities and communities. The next section covers processes of social inequality, with chapters on class, race and ethnicity, gender and sexuality, and immigration. Next are chapters exploring four main social institutions that individuals face in their lives—the family, religion, education, and the criminal justice system. We conclude with a section on different dimensions of large-scale social change, including social movements, environmental change, health and population change, and globalization.

The authors of each of the chapters in this book are writing about the topics that they do research in and teach courses on. We believe that a collective approach to presenting the discipline of sociology provides a better way of unearthing and exciting our readers' sociological imaginations. In the course of thinking about (and teaching) the topics we are writing about, we have developed deep appreciation for the complexities, but also the excitement, of our respective topics.

In order to create a unified text, we've taken a number of steps to make it easier for our readers to move from chapter to chapter. Each chapter opens with a puzzle or story that highlights one or more of the key sociological problems that will be tackled in the chapter. Following this, each chapter identifies a set of big questions that have defined the research and teaching puzzles of the field. These questions organize what follows as the authors explore how sociological thinking about each question has developed. At all points, some basic facts and data are helpful to have in hand, but at the same time we want our readers to learn to think sociologically through learning how to ask hard questions and where to look for answers.

In short, we want to stress that this book—and indeed sociology as a discipline—truly is a *project:* something we are col... ...omething for which the... ...ettled answers. The pro... ...e hard questions be-cau... ...uence individuals and gro... ...y endlessly interesting and a... ...iology... very much worth acquiring.

What does it mean to describe this book and sociology as a whole as a *project*?

> **Applying Your Sociological Imagination**
> *videos conclude each chapter, illustrating key concepts with real-world examples. Each Applying Your Sociological Imagination video is accompanied by an activity that allows students to upload their own videos or submit a short essay illustrating how these concepts apply to their own lives.*

👁 **Watch** the **Video** Applying Your Sociological Imagination in MySocLab

Each chapter concludes with a section called **The Big Questions Revisited.**

 Study and **Review** in **MySocLab**　　 **Watch** the **Video** Inspiring Your Sociological Imagination in **MySocLab**

MySocLab features a number of self-study and review activities for students, including interactive flashcards, quizzes, and a personalized study plan.

How Can a Sociological Imagination Help You Better Understand Your World? *(p. 6)*

 Watch the **Big Question Video** in **MySocLab** to review the key concepts for this section.

This section introduced the concept of the sociological imagination and explored how it helps us learn to ask hard questions.

THE SOCIOLOGICAL IMAGINATION (p. 6)

Looking through a Sociological Lens (p. 6)

Here, students can see the Big Questions along with short summaries of the main points and a clearly articulated learning pathway through MySocLab.

- **How can a sociological imagination help us to cha... stereotypes?**

Engaging our Sociological Imaginations: Learning to Ask Good Questions (p. 7)

From Personal Puzzles to Sociological Questions (p. 8)

- **What types of questions are sociologists particularly well equipped to explore?**

The Endless Reach of the Sociological Imagination (p. 11)

 Read the **Document** *Invitation to Sociology* by Peter L. Berger in **MySocLab**. In this reading, Berger invites readers to discover their passion while they observe the world around them.

KEY TERMS

social network *(p. 4)*

society *(p. 4)*

sociology *(p. 4)*

globalization *(p. 4)*

sociological imagination *(p. 6)*

stereotype *(p. 7)*

discrimination *(p. 7)*

social theory *(p. 8)*

research method *(p. 8)*

2 Why Do Social Contexts Matter? *(p. 12)*

 Watch the **Big Question Video** in **MySocLab** to review the key concepts for this section.

Sociology is fundamentally concerned with how we are influenced by society. All of us are situated in an array of social contexts. This section explored how these influence us and our behavior.

SOCIAL CONTEXTS: FROM INDIVIDUALS TO SOCIETY (p. 12)

Families and Communities as Context (p. 13)

- **How do our families and communities shape our social development?**

 Explore A Sociological Perspective in **MySocLab**

Organizations and Institutions (p. 13)

- **How do the organizations and institutions we are a part of help us form our identities?**

Social and Economic Contexts (p. 15)

Sociology as the Study of Social Contexts (p. 15)

- **What is the distinction between social interaction and social structure?**

KEY TERMS

social context *(p. 12)*

social interaction *(p. 15)*

norm *(p. 15)*

social structure *(p. 16)*

social hierarchy *(p. 16)*

institution *(p. 16)*

role *(p. 16)*

Where Did Sociology Come From, and How Is It Different from the Other Social Sciences? *(p. 17)*

 Watch the **Big Question Video** in **MySocLab** to review the key concepts for this section.

This section examined the context in which sociology began to develop and explored the question of how sociology fits into, and relates to, the other social sciences.

THE SOCIOLOGY OF THE SOCIAL SCIENCES (p. 17)

Sociology and the Industrial Revolution (p. 17)

- **What was the historical context in which sociology began to develop?**

Sociology's Family: Siblings (p. 19)

- **What units of analysis do sociologists work with, and how do these differ from those of other disciplines?**

Sociology's Children (p. 21)

- **What are some of the spin-off fields that originally started in sociology?**

 Explore the **Data** on Sociology in America in **MySocLab**

Social Explorer activities engage students with data visualization, comparisons of change over time, and localizing data to their own communities.

KEY TERMS

social science *(p. 17)*

industrialization *(p. 18)*

urbanization *(p. 18)*

urban area *(p. 18)*

union *(p. 19)*

social movement *(p. 19)*

unit of analysis *(p. 20)*

interdisciplinary research *(p. 21)*

How Can This Book Help You Develop a Sociological Imagination? *(p. 23)*

 Watch the **Big Question Video** in **MySocLab** to review the key concepts for this section.

Our goal for this book is to provide enough background on the key areas and findings of sociological research in foundation for you to develop your own sociological imagination.

LOOKING AHEAD (p. 23)

- **What does it mean to describe this book and sociology as a whole as a *project*?**

 Watch the **Video** Applying Your Sociological Imagination in **MySocLab** to see these concepts at work in the real world

The instructor's resource program is tagged to the Big Questions so you can organize, lecture, and assess students' understanding of each of the major points of sociological inquiry.

5
CULTURE, MEDIA, and COMMUNICATION

((· Listen to the **Chapter Audio** in **MySocLab**

by ERIC KLINENBERG
with DAVID WACHSMUTH

More people live alone now than at any other time in history. In prosperous American cities— Atlanta, Denver, Seattle, San Francisco, and Minneapolis—40 percent or more of all households contain a single occupant. In Manhattan and in Washington, nearly one in two households is occupied by a single person. In Paris, the city of lovers, more than half of all households contain single people, and in Stockholm, Sweden, the rate tops 60 percent. The decision to live alone is increasingly common in diverse cultures whenever it is economically feasible.

The mere thought of living alone once sparked anxiety, dread, and visions of loneliness. But those images are dated. Now the most privileged people on earth use their resources to separate from one another, to buy privacy and personal space.

How has this happened? At first glance, living alone by choice seems to contradict entrenched cultural values—so long defined by groups and by the nuclear family. But after interviewing more than 300 "singletons" (my term for people who live alone) during nearly a decade of research, it appears that living alone fits well with modern values (Klinenberg 2012). It promotes freedom, personal control, and self-realization—all prized aspects of contemporary life. It is less feared, too, than it once might have been, for the crucial reason that living alone no longer suggests an isolated or less-social life.

Our species has been able to embark on this experiment in solo living because global societies have become so interdependent. Dynamic markets, flourishing cities, and open communications systems make modern autonomy more appealing; they give us

MY SOCIOLOGICAL IMAGINATION
Eric Klinenberg

I grew up in the center of Chicago, and my interest in the sociology of culture and cities grew out of my experiences there. I lived in a bohemian but rapidly gentrifying neighborhood called Old Town, a place that was long famous for its vibrant street life and for its blues clubs, jazz bars, cafés, and counterculture scenes. Chicago is a segregated city, and Old Town is wedged between two of the city's most affluent areas, the Gold Coast and Lincoln Park, and Cabrini Green, a housing project (recently demolished) where most of the residents were African American and poor. I was always puzzled by this arrangement, and trying to understand it as a child was the beginning of my sociology career.

My research examines cities, culture, climate, and communications. My first book, *Heat Wave: A Social Autopsy of Disaster in Chicago*, explores the two questions, Why did so many people die during a short heat spell in 1995? And why was this disastrous event so easy to deny, overlook, and forget? My second book, *Fighting for Air: The Battle to Control America's Media*, examines how media consolidation has affected newspapers, radio stations, television news, and the Internet and tracks the emergence of the global media reform movement. My latest book, *Going Solo: The Extraordinary Rise and Surprising Appeal of Living Alone*, analyzes the incredible social experiment in solo living that began in the 1950s and is now ubiquitous in developed nations throughout the world.

Despite the stereotype that living alone is an isolating experience, more and more Americans are choosing to live alone.

👁 **Watch** the **Video** in **MySocLab**
Inspiring Your Sociological Imagination

the capacity to live alone but to engage with others when and how we want and on our own terms. In fact, living alone can make it easier to be social because single people have more free time, absent family obligations, to engage in social and cultural activities.

Compared with their married counterparts, single people are more likely to spend time with friends and neighbors, go to restaurants, and attend art classes and lectures. Surveys, some by market research companies that study behavior for clients developing products and services, also indicate that married people with children are more likely than single people to hunker down at home. Those in large suburban homes often splinter into private rooms to be alone. The image of a modern family in a room together, each plugged into a separate reality—be it a smartphone, computer, video game, or TV show—has become a cultural cliché. New communications technologies make living alone a social experience, so being home alone does not feel involuntary or like solitary confinement. The person alone at home can digitally navigate through a world of people, information, and ideas. Internet use does not seem to cut people off from real friendships and connections.

Yet some pundits have predicted that rates of living alone would plummet because of the challenging economy: Young people would move into their parents' basements; middle-aged adults would put off divorce or separation for financial reasons; the elderly would move in with their children rather than hold on to places of their own. Thus far, however, there's little evidence that this has happened. True, more young adults have moved in with their parents because they cannot find good jobs, but the proportion of those between 20 and 29 who live alone decreased only slightly, from 11.97 percent in 2007 to 10.94 percent in 2011. In the general population, living alone has become more common in both absolute and proportional terms. The latest census report estimates that more than 32 million Americans live alone today, up from 27.2 million in 2000 and 31 million in 2010.

All signs suggest that living alone will become even more common in the future, at every stage of adulthood and in every place where people can afford a place of their own. Modern culture has shifted in ways that have made this dramatic change in the way we live possible. In this chapter, we will explore the sociology of culture and look more carefully at how these changes in culture and communication are changing the way we live our lives. One important part of the sociology of culture involves studying people's daily routines and practices. Another involves examining the values, social norms, and collective beliefs that make some behaviors acceptable and others suspect. Fortunately, the search for this kind of information is as rewarding as its discovery, which explains why the sociology of culture is one of the fastest-growing parts of the field today.

Modern culture has shifted in ways that have made this dramatic change in the way we live possible.

The United States isn't the only place where more people are choosing to live alone. Here, Dai Haifei, 24, reads a book in his egg-shaped cabin in Beijing, China.

THE BIG QUESTIONS

👁 **Watch** the **Big Question Videos** in **MySocLab**

1 What is culture?
When sociologists talk about culture, they refer to systems of collective meaning making as well as the ways people use those systems in their lives.

2 How does culture shape our collective identity?
Cultural practices both reflect and define group identities, whether the group is a small subculture, a nation, or a global community.

3 How do our cultural practices relate to class and status?
People's cultural habits help define and reproduce the boundaries between high status and low status, upper class and lower class.

4 Who produces culture, and why?
The cultural field is the place for creativity and meaning making. But it is also a battlefield: Who controls the media and popular culture, and what messages they communicate, are central to how social life is organized and how power operates.

5 What is the relationship between media and democracy?
The media are arguably the most important form of cultural production in our society. The news is vital to democracy, and new ways of participating in the media are changing how democracy works.

1 | What Is Culture?

THE MANY MEANINGS OF CULTURE

Watch the Big Question Video in MySocLab

The latest song by Beyoncé, a performance of the opera, our assumptions about monogamy, a series of posts on Twitter, a headline in the newspaper, the reason one person sleeps in and another wakes up early: These are all examples of culture. People use the word *culture* to refer to all sorts of things, from art to traditions to individual learned behavior. In everyday language, culture is often a synonym for art or artistic activities, as indicated by the expression "getting some culture," or a synonym for refined taste, as when we call a person "cultured." These are certainly two of the ways that sociologists use the word, but there are a number of others. In fact, as one writer puts it, "culture is one of the two or three most complicated words in the English language" (Williams 1976:87).

The modern Western history of the concept of culture begins with the rise of world travel in the eighteenth and nineteenth centuries, when merchants from Europe came into contact with non-Europeans for the first time. These merchants were struck not only by the physical differences between themselves and the non-Europeans but also by the differences in how they behaved. This included everything from how they dressed to the way their families were organized. In an attempt to make sense of these differences, scientists in the nineteenth century connected the physical differences with the behavioral differences, arguing that people's biology—and particularly their race—determined how their societies were organized.

Toward the end of the nineteenth century, anthropologists began to criticize this idea and instead argued that it was not race that was responsible for these differences but something else—something that was not hereditary but rather learned; something that was not natural and biological but rather socially produced. That something was culture. These days, the argument that the differences between groups of people are more than just biological, and that we learn how to behave, seems obvious. But at the time, it was an important discovery.

From this early research came three basic conclusions about culture, which continue to influence cultural sociology today. First, culture is a characteristic not of individuals but of groups. Second, culture is a way of understanding differences between groups and similarities within groups. Last, culture is an aspect of social life that is different from nature or biology. Indeed, what makes culture a social phenomenon is precisely that it is not natural. While it's difficult in practice to draw a line between nature and culture, sociologists now recognize that certain biological things about humans are relatively constant throughout history (for example, everyone gets hungry), while cultural things are not (for example, the kind of food we eat and how we eat it).

In the early twentieth century, sociologists and anthropologists generally used these insights to define culture as the entire way of life of a people. If you were transported back to ancient Rome, what kinds of things would you need to fit in? You would certainly need language and information about art, customs, and traditions. But you would also need all sorts of material objects, including clothing, tools, and a house. This was all considered part of a society's culture. Today, when sociologists talk about **culture**, however, they are usually referring to one of two things: either a shared system of beliefs and knowledge (which is often called a system of meaning) shared among a group and transmitted to individuals through social interactions; or a set of tools for social action—a "tool kit" of assumptions and behaviors for daily life. In other words, culture is a system and culture is a practice (Sewell 2005).

Culture as a System: The Balinese Cockfight

Every society is full of **symbols** that communicate an idea while being distinct from the idea itself. Some are straightforward: For example, in contemporary American society, a red heart implies love and a green traffic light tells you that you are allowed to drive. Other symbols are less obvious: When a car commercial shows a car driving off-road at high speeds, it is likely that the advertiser is trying to make you think about freedom and excitement and associate those ideas with the car. A national flag might have a number of different meanings for different people. Symbols, whether simple or complex, are things that communicate implicit meaning about an idea. Taken together, a group's symbols can be considered its culture. Explore *A Sociological Perspective* on page 116 and consider how culture and context are related.

The anthropologist Clifford Geertz demonstrated the idea that culture is a system of collective meaning by analyzing a Balinese cockfight in 1950s Indonesia (Geertz 1972). Cockfights—boxing matches between roosters—were outlawed by the national government but were still important events in local communities. Multiple pairs of birds would fight over the course of an afternoon, and hundreds of residents would watch, cheer, and place bets. Geertz studied the cockfight the way a student of literature might study a novel, as an object full of symbols needing to be interpreted. For example, Geertz found that participants in the cockfights often gambled far more money than seemed to be rational from an economic perspective. He concluded that the betting wasn't just about winning or losing money; it was a way of indicating and reworking

status hierarchies (those who bet aggressively and were successful were simultaneously securing and displaying high status in the eyes of other participants). The cockfights allowed the Balinese to collectively interpret their own status hierarchies: "a story they tell themselves about themselves" (Geertz 1972:26).

Symbols always exist in specific social contexts—a green traffic light would be mysterious to someone raised in a society without cars, for example, while you would probably find the rituals of a Balinese cockfight equally mysterious. For this reason, studying symbols helps us understand things about society that are not often discussed, such as distinctions of honor, inequality, and competition. For instance, if Geertz had asked them directly, the Balinese cockfighters would not have told him that betting was more a status issue than a financial one. That was something that he could only perceive through careful observation of a place where he had moved and a group that he had gotten to know well. This research method, based on lengthy and intimate observation of a group, is called **ethnography**.

How could we use Geertz's insights to interpret the collective symbols of the contemporary United States? In the place of a cockfight, we could study the Super Bowl—the most-watched cultural event in the country, which features familiar rituals and symbols such as betting on the outcome, Super Bowl parties with friends and family, an elaborate half-time show, and blockbuster television ads. These rituals demonstrate common **values**—or judgments about what is intrinsically important or meaningful—such as patriotism, competitiveness, and consumerism. And the uproar that followed Justin Timberlake exposing Janet Jackson's breast during their half-time performance in 2004 demonstrates

What are some collective symbols of contemporary U.S. culture?

The collective rituals we display in our cultural events, such as this cockfight in modern Indonesia, can demonstrate shared values. What cultural events could reveal shared American values?

A SOCIOLOGICAL PERSPECTIVE

What is the meaning of this?

We've all experienced moments when we see something happening, perhaps when visiting a country other than our own, and have been confused by what exactly we are witnessing. For many sociologists, "What is the meaning of this?" is at the heart of understanding culture. To understand culture is to uncover the meaning of things.

In order to uncover culture, Clifford Geertz argued the need for "thick descriptions," or detailed accounts of the context that allow us to understand the meaning behind behaviors. As he put it, sometimes a wink may mean one thing (flirting with someone), and sometimes it may mean another (sharing a secret with someone) – it depends on the cultural context. When we are trying to not only act in but also explain the world, it is important to have a good grasp of the cultural context.

How could the similar looking gestures in these photos potentially be confused by a person unfamiliar with sporting events or Nazi Germany?

Consider similar behaviors such as children raising their hands in class or a person hailing a taxi. What cues in these and other gestures you've encountered help differentiate the cultural context of each?

 Explore A Sociological Perspective in **MySocLab** and then …

■ Think About It

The same symbol can mean very different things in different cultural contexts. What is another common behavior or gesture that people from different cultural backgrounds would interpret differently?

■ Inspire Your Sociological Imagination

Some hand gestures can elicit strong reactions; a raised middle finger and the "V" peace sign are two examples. What gives some hand gestures their importance or cultural power? Can you think of examples of gestures that have switched from a positive to a negative meaning, or vice versa?

values that are *not* commonly associated with the event. But collective symbols don't have to be massive spectacles to be meaningful. Nowadays we might focus on different cultural events, such as popular videos on YouTube, which would uncover a different America. From music videos to people filming their cats to back-and-forth video debates about politics or technology, sites such as YouTube display our new collective symbols by allowing people to share and interpret culture together (Burgess and Green 2009).

Culture as Practice: Habitus and Tool Kit

For Geertz, culture was out there in the world, expressed through the collective meaning given to objects and events. But how does such collective meaning help to shape our social behavior? Is culture just a set of values and ideas, or does it actually influence how we live our lives? In other words, how is culture actually practiced?

How is culture actually practiced?

The answer is that culture influences the kinds of decisions we make in our lives, whether or not we are aware of it.

Some sociologists see culture as guiding our behavior by establishing goals for us. The values we develop in the course of our lives may lead us to want to earn a lot of money, make a positive difference in the world, raise a family, travel, or countless other possibilities. But in recent decades, this approach has become much less common. Instead, now sociologists usually study culture's effect not on the goals or *ends* of our behavior but rather on the *means* of our behavior: in other words, less the "why" and more the "how" of social life.

The French sociologist Pierre Bourdieu argued that we all develop certain sets of assumptions about the world and our place in it: our tastes, preferences, and skills. We develop these habits—what Bourdieu called **habitus**—in the course of growing up and socializing with others, and they become so routine that we don't even realize we are following them (Bourdieu 1992). The kind of habitus we develop depends upon our upbringing. Poor Americans are much less likely to have bank accounts than middle-class and rich Americans, and a large part of the explanation for this fact is their different habituses. If you are born into a poor family, not only will you have less money than someone born into a rich family, but you'll have a different education and assumptions about how to handle money, and these differences will become harder and harder to change as you grow older. If you didn't observe your parents and peers using bank accounts, you won't take for granted that you should have your own account the way that a middle-class or rich child would.

Bourdieu's concept of habitus helps explain how our future choices and opinions are always guided by our past experiences. Someone raised in a wealthy family on the Upper West Side of Manhattan will have no trouble fitting in at a fancy dinner party but probably quite a bit of trouble fitting in on a farm, while someone raised on a farm will have the opposite experience. But people are exposed to all sorts of different cultural systems and forms of meaning, after all. So how is it that you choose to act one way at one time and a different way at another? One way to answer this question is to think of culture as a **tool kit**—a set of symbolic skills or devices that we learn through the cultural environment we live in and apply to practical situations in our own lives (Swidler 1986). If a friend introduces you to someone, how do you behave? If you're single and interested in flirting, you'll draw on one set of cultural tools you've developed; if you're just trying to be polite, you'll draw on a different set of tools. Just as a car mechanic has a box of tools at her disposal for fixing a variety of problems, people have a kind of tool kit of behaviors and opinions that they apply to different situations they find themselves in. Some people will have better tools for certain situations, and some people will have better tools for others. What's more, even though people immersed in the same cultural environments will tend to have similar cultural tools in their tool kit, they probably will have quite different levels of expertise and familiarity with the tools. So two people who hang out in similar social circles might have the same basic set of conversational tools in their cultural tool kits, but the one who keeps to himself will be less comfortable using them than the one who frequently chats with people she doesn't know very well.

One researcher studying love in contemporary America found that the two most important cultural tools are love as a voluntary choice and love as a commitment (Swidler 2003). Most Americans have both of these tools available to them, but their personal backgrounds will affect which one they tend to rely on and which one they are more competent with. Your own past experiences with love might make you leery of thinking of it in terms of commitment, so this will change how you navigate future romantic encounters. Or you may not have had much experience with commitment, such that when you try to use that cultural tool you don't do a good job of it. From this perspective, culture does not just establish differences in how we interpret the world and give it meaning but rather influences what kinds of strategies and actions are practically available to us.

Culture and Communication

Both culture as a system and culture as practice describe forms of *communication,* which is the sharing of meaningful information between people. One important way this occurs is through language. **Language** refers to any comprehensive system of words or symbols representing concepts, and it does not necessarily need to be spoken, as the hundreds of different sign languages in use around the world suggest. Culture and language are closely related. The ancient Greeks called the supposedly uncultured peoples they encountered "barbarians," which literally means people who babble—who have no language.

Researchers have disagreed over the years as to the importance of language for culture. At a basic level, language is a **cultural universal**, a cultural trait common to all humans: As far as we know, all human groups throughout history have used language to communicate with each other. Some linguists have even argued that language is the fundamental building block of thought—that if you don't have a word for something, you literally can't think it. The implication of this view is that a group's language is directly responsible for many of its cultural symbols and practices. A simple example is the distinction between two different words for "you" in French: an informal *tu* and a more formal *vous*. English used to have a similar distinction (*thou* versus *you*), but it died out over time. As a result, English speakers would possibly place less emphasis on formality in their communication with each other and hence in their group culture.

But just because people speak the same language does not mean they share the same culture. Canadians and Americans both speak English, but of course there are many cultural differences between (and within) the two countries. Now most linguists and cultural sociologists believe that language *influences* culture without completely determining it. So while English no longer has an informal *you* and a formal *you*, this doesn't mean that all our conversations are informal. Instead, we have developed different ways of communicating those concepts, such as the frequent use in the South of *ma'am* and *sir* when speaking to an elder.

Communication can occur between individuals, or it can occur at large within society—what is normally called **mass communication**. In recent history, mass communication has occurred primarily through the mass media: television, radio, and newspapers. Prior to the emergence of the mass media, meaning was still communicated on a large scale, just not quite as large or as quickly; the Balinese cockfight could be considered a form of mass communication at a smaller scale, for example, as could a minister giving a sermon to a large congregation.

In recent years the Internet has emerged as the main medium for mass communication. People increasingly access traditional media sources online via newspaper websites or video sources such as Hulu and YouTube. In so doing, they also transform formerly passive media consumption into something they can participate in by writing comments, reposting stories, and creating their own mashups. Old media and new media now blur together (Jenkins 2006). But the Internet has also created a whole new set of communication possibilities only loosely tied to previous forms of mass communication, most notably through social networks and instant messaging.

Social media have altered the way children, adults, and (increasingly) the elderly engage with each other, both online and in person and at distances near and far. They have changed the ways corporations as well as anticorporate activists operate, the ways that charitable organizations raise funds (especially after a catastrophe), the ways that political officials campaign and govern, and the ways that social movements organize. They have affected the ways we get, and sometimes even make, news and entertainment. Cultural sociologists are curious about how and to what extent social media have transformed everyday life for people at different ages and in different places, as well as about how the rising use of social media will affect our interest in other kinds of media, from newspapers to telephones and radios to books.

The social theorist Manuel Castells argues that we are participating in a new form of Internet-centered communication that he calls mass self-communication because it can potentially reach a global audience but its content is self-generated and self-directed (Castells 2009:58). In other words, the Internet offers both the large scale and ever-present nature of the mass media and the individualized content of interpersonal communication. Facebook, for example, has exploded in size such that it rivals the scope of the largest of the traditional media. As Figure 5.1 shows, there were 145 million active Facebook users by the end of 2008, 350 million by the end of 2009, and fully 800 million users by the end of 2011. That's more than 10 percent of

In what ways is culture a form of communication?

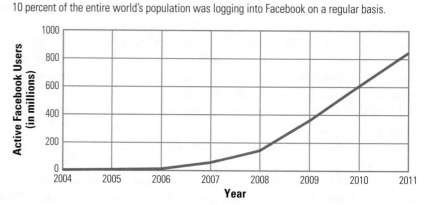

FIGURE 5.1 THE FACEBOOK EXPLOSION By the end of 2011, more than 10 percent of the entire world's population was logging into Facebook on a regular basis.

Source: Fromer (2012).

the entire world's population logging into Facebook on a regular basis.

How are the Internet and mass self-communication changing cultural systems and practices? If the constant flow of communications, information, and entertainment online makes it difficult to focus, does this also mean that our work and our relationships will suffer? Will our accumulation of Facebook friends be offset by a loss in deep friendship, or does connecting through social media make us more likely to spend time with others offline? Will our ideas become more superficial because we'll lack the attention span necessary to develop them? Will we lose interest in certain cultural genres—traditional news reporting, literary novels, nonfiction books—in favor of others—news briefs, pulp fiction, video games—that either require less of our minds or deliver more immediate rewards?

It's hard to know for sure: When it comes to information and communication, the last few decades have probably been the most rapid period of transformation in history. Access to technology may be creating new divisions of haves and have-nots in the form of the social, economic, and cultural gap between those with effective access to information technology and those without such access, known as the **digital divide**. This is the divide between those who are connected and those who are not; between those with high-speed access and those in the slow lane; between those with the education and media literacy to navigate around the more innovative and independent sites and those who mainly visit the big commercial sites (Klinenberg 2007); between "digital natives" born into the age of the Internet and older "digital immigrants" who have to try to keep up with the changes (Palfrey and Gasser 2008). As computers and the Internet become more important to everyday life around the world, understanding the causes and effects of the digital divide (Norris 2001) will be one of the most important tasks for sociologists of culture and communication.

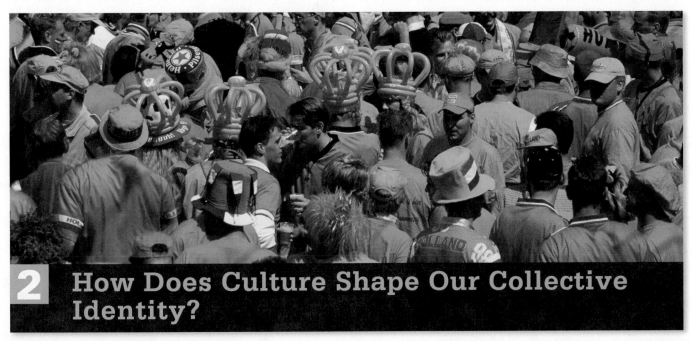

2   How Does Culture Shape Our Collective Identity?

CULTURE AND GROUP IDENTITY

👁 **Watch the Big Question Video in MySocLab**

We all think of ourselves as belonging to numerous different groups. Some of these groups are relatively easy to define—for example, nationality or religion—but others are less clear. Are football fans a group? What about university students? If so, how can you tell? More fundamentally, what makes up group identity, and how do sociologists study it? It turns out that culture is central to group identity—both in defining a group and in maintaining it. Some scholars suggest that we should only use the word *culture* to refer to differences and similarities that form the basis for groups coming together or clashing with each other (Appadurai 1996:13).

In the absence of clear ways to define where one group ends and another begins, we need to take our cues from shared behaviors. One way of thinking about identity in cultural terms is through the concept of **group style**, or the set of norms and practices that distinguishes one group from another (Eliasoph and Lichterman 2003). Different groups have different **norms**—shared assumptions about correct behavior—and because most people belong to many groups (for example, your school, your national identity, and your gender); we learn to adopt the right style for the right occasion. Adopting the right style is not always a simple matter, though—think of how difficult it would be for you to fit in if you were transported to a different time or place. Group style is thus a way for people to communicate belonging or not belonging. According to this account of identity formation, culture is a practice of communication.

Mainstream Culture, Subcultures, and Countercultures

Some groups deliberately set themselves off from **mainstream culture**—the most widely shared systems of meaning and cultural tool kits in a society. In the United States, well-known examples include hippies in the 1960s and online gamers in the 2000s. Historically, these groups were often considered to be deviant. But contemporary sociologists refer to such groups as **subcultures**, or relatively small groups of people whose affiliation is based on shared beliefs, preferences, and practices that exist under the mainstream (literally *sub*cultures) and distinguish them from the mainstream. Other examples include rock climbers, hunters, ballroom dancers, and chess players. The American sociologist Claude Fischer (1975) claimed that subcultures are most likely to emerge in cities, where—unlike in small towns and traditional villages—the large, concentrated population allows many such groups to flourish. Some subcultures may have a clearly articulated sense of common purpose or definition, while others may be only loosely connected by mutual interests.

While subcultures tend to exist in harmony with mainstream culture—there's nothing socially threatening about rock climbers—cultural-studies scholars in the United Kingdom argued that some subcultures express differences in political and economic power and that setting yourself apart from the cultural mainstream is often an act of "resistance through rituals" (Hall and Jefferson 1975). This type of subculture is usually called a **counterculture**—a group whose ideas, attitudes, and behaviors are in direct conflict with mainstream culture and who actively contest the dominant cultural practices in the societies of which they are a part.

What distinguishes a subculture from the mainstream?

In the 1960s, hippies were a counterculture, as are contemporary militias and the recent Tea Party and Occupy Wall Street movements. Sociologists consider culture an arena of struggle within which different mainstream cultures, subcultures, and countercultures are unequally ranked and often stand in opposition to another, each fighting for supremacy in determining what counts as culture and seeking to reap the rewards that come from it (Clarke et al. 1975:11).

Read the **Document** *The Code of the Streets* in **MySocLab**.

United States: Hegemony, Culture Wars, or Multiculturalism?

Subcultures and countercultures only make sense when there is a dominant mainstream culture that they can challenge. But is there a single mainstream culture in the United States in the twenty-first century?

The early-twentieth-century Italian revolutionary Antonio Gramsci argued that the dominant classes in a society maintain their rule by encouraging certain moral and cultural understandings that are favorable to them. When elites gain legitimacy and power from widely shared yet taken-for-granted beliefs about what is right or wrong, proper or improper, valuable or not, this is called **hegemony**. For example, it's common sense these days that people should work in order to earn enough money to survive and that people who choose not to work should only be entitled to the bare minimum of financial support, but such common sense ultimately serves the interests of wealthy business owners who need to find hard workers for their businesses. Gramsci argued that movements seeking to radically transform a society needed not just to win political power but to overthrow cultural hegemony—to fight common sense with good sense. Culture, in other words, is not just entertainment; it's a war.

These days, such **culture wars** in the United States usually refer to arguments over the proper role of family and

Countercultures such as punks use their appearance and behaviors to deliberately set themselves off from mainstream culture. What are other examples of contemporary "resistance through rituals"?

religious values in certain questions of state policy: abortion rights, immigration rights, and gay rights are three of the most important. The sociologist James Davison Hunter argued in the early 1990s that people tended to line up on the same sides on many of these issues—positions he labeled "progressive" and "orthodox"—and that being progressive or orthodox didn't necessarily correspond to social class or political affiliation. The main battle lines of American electoral politics, he concluded, were shifting from economic questions to moral questions (Hunter 1991). The journalist Thomas Frank made a compatible argument about the defection of white working-class voters from the Democratic Party. On the basis of an increasing turn away from economic issues and toward moral issues, these voters have come to identify with the Republicans and to see the Democrats as a party of the elite, even though Republican economic policies are clearly the more elite-driven of the two parties (Frank 2004).

At the same time, the idea of culture wars suggests that there are two dominant cultures squaring off against each other: a liberal culture and a conservative culture. This is at odds with another important way to describe the contemporary group-identity landscape of the United States: multiculturalism. **Multiculturalism** refers to beliefs or policies

How is the concept of culture wars at odds with the multicultural landscape of the United States?

promoting the equal accommodation of different ethnic or cultural groups within a society. Immigrant societies such as the United States have to reckon with a considerable number of different cultural backgrounds and systems of meaning, which make a simple liberal-versus-conservative understanding of culture an insufficient one.

Historically, the standard metaphor used to describe the model of cultural accommodation in the United States is the *melting pot*. Immigrants come from all sorts of diverse cultural backgrounds but are gradually assimilated into American society until they become, at some point, genuinely American, at a minimum by learning to speak English. The melting pot ideal is now generally recognized by sociologists as problematic because it privileges a specific (white, English-speaking, middle- and upper-class) notion of what it means to be American—a notion that is hard to take seriously when 40 percent of Americans are nonwhite and 30 percent do not speak English in their home (see Figure 5.2). The melting pot is thus an example of **ethnocentrism**: an inability to understand or accept cultural practices different from one's own. Perhaps reflecting these realities, the melting pot idea has declined somewhat in mainstream discourse since the twentieth century, although it still thrives in right-wing political discourse,

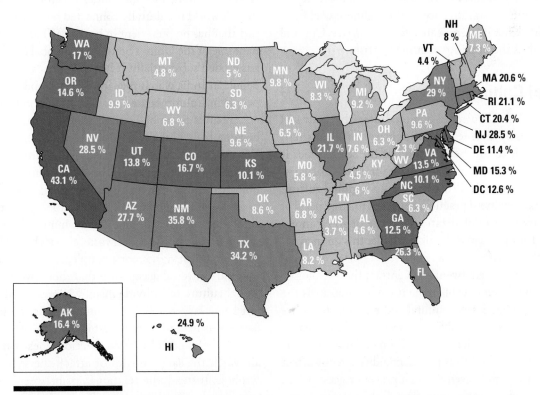

FIGURE 5.2 THE MULTILINGUAL UNITED STATES Although English is our dominant national language, America has always had a history of multilingualism, and with every new wave of immigration the linguistic diversity of the United States continues to grow. As the map shows, the percentage of Americans who do not speak English at home varies widely, from only 2.3 percent in West Virginia to 43.1 percent in California.

Source: U.S. Census Bureau (2012).

Immigrants come to the United States from all sorts of national, ethnic, cultural, and linguistic backgrounds. Why is it important for sociologists studying immigration to practice cultural relativism?

particularly with respect to immigration and English-language-use policy.

The problem with ethnocentrism is that it leads us to make incorrect assumptions about others on the basis of our own experience. If Clifford Geertz had observed the Balinese cockfight from an ethnocentric point of view, he simply would have concluded that many Balinese made risky and irresponsible bets. Or imagine if you went to a Chinese restaurant and concluded that the owners must not have heard about forks and knives because they brought you chopsticks. Although we have all been raised in specific cultural contexts that will influence our thinking in unacknowledged ways—and so we can never escape ethnocentrism entirely—these kinds of assumptions make it difficult to understand other cultures with any kind of depth. We will misinterpret shared meanings or fail to grasp what is important in a given situation. For this reason sociologists do their best to practice **cultural relativism**—evaluating cultural meanings and practices in their own social contexts. For example, Geertz didn't try to discover the cultural significance of the Balinese cockfight in general but rather its significance *for the Balinese*. Cultural relativism is thus the opposite of ethnocentrism.

☐ Global Culture

The existence of subcultures demonstrates that cultural practices can help define group identity for very small groups. But what about the other end of the scale? Does it make sense to talk about group identity for a group as large as the entire human race? What would such a **global culture** that incorporates cultural practices common to large parts of the world look like? Globalization and the ongoing interconnection of people across the planet make this an increasingly plausible idea, if not yet a reality.

Writing in the early twentieth century, the sociologist Max Weber attempted to explain the rise of capitalism as the consequence of a large-scale cultural and religious transformation. He observed that Calvinism (a variant of Protestantism) preached that an individual's salvation or damnation was predestined by God, and thus people couldn't directly affect their chances to go to heaven through prayer or good deeds, as Catholics believed. At the same time, Calvinists were anxious to look for signs of whether God had chosen them for salvation, and they came to believe that practicing hard work and thrift was such a sign. Weber argued that this **Protestant ethic**, when applied to an emerging money economy such as eighteenth-century America, encouraged savings and investment instead of luxury and thus had the unexpected consequence of launching the capitalist cycle of investment, production, and reinvestment. When capitalism subsequently spread around the world, in other words, it was not just an economic system that spread but a cultural one as well (Weber [1905] 2002).

In Weber's time, the cultural values associated with the Protestant ethic had only spread as far as Western Europe and North America for the good reason that culture did not travel very well, and only under certain circumstances. But today's world is culturally connected on a planetary scale in a way that has no precedent in history. What's more, the dominant role of the United States in the global cultural landscape has eroded substantially. It has been the case for decades that people in India watch the latest Hollywood movies, but now people in California are watching Bollywood movies, too.

Thanks to globalization, certain cultural systems have become truly global. Some of these are obvious: Microsoft Windows, for instance, is used by hundreds of millions of people worldwide and provides the basis for a common technological vocabulary that transcends language. Other aspects of global culture are more abstract: Concepts such as citizenship, economic development, and human rights are widely assumed to apply to everyone everywhere (Meyer et al. 1997). Human rights, for example, could not have achieved the near-universal acceptance that they have except within a global culture of individualism, where the individual—and not some larger social grouping such as the family or the nation—is held to be the most important (Elliot 2007).

Global cultural interconnection doesn't mean that we all watch the same movies or attach the same meaning to symbols. Instead, the relationships between place and culture have become more complex. Some cultural events and products are now widespread and *homogenous* like never before: McDonald's has restaurants in over 120 countries. But other aspects of culture have become more diverse and *heterogeneous:* A number of indigenous languages that were dying out have seen revivals in recent decades in part in reaction to globalization (Van Der Bly 2007). Therefore, we should think about global culture not as a single thing but as a set of *flows:* some ideas, people, and commodities circulate smoothly, and others do not (Appadurai 1996).

☐ National Cultures

Even in the era of globalization, though, the most important group identity in the modern world is surely the nation. The entire world is divided into nation-states, and most people are a citizen or subject of a single one of them. So it is not surprising that **national culture**, the set of shared cultural practices and beliefs within a given nation-state, is an important principle for sociology. Are there differences between cultural norms, assumptions, and identities between different nations? If so, what are they, what produces and reproduces them, and what effects do they have? These are the questions that sociologists try to answer about national cultures.

What produces and reproduces global and national cultures, and what effects do they have?

Today it seems obvious that the world should be divided into nations and that people should think of themselves in these terms: I'm American and you're Canadian, she's British and he's Chinese. But it wasn't always so. The rise of **nationalism**—the fact that people think of themselves as inherently members of a nation—was a large-scale cultural transformation, perhaps even a sign of a new global culture. Nations are *imagined communities:* Their members share an assumption of commonality with each other, even though they come from diverse class and ethnic backgrounds, and most will never meet (Anderson 1991). In a country like the United Kingdom, with a strong national government and a common language, this is a plausible enough assumption. But what about Indonesia, composed of 13,000 islands and home to over 700 languages? With the notable exception of some separatist regions at the periphery, Indonesians generally also imagine themselves to be a single national community. And importantly, they view their community as limited, as one among many. A national community is not like a religious community, whose practitioners may hope to convert the entire world to their faith. Indonesians don't want to make all Italians Indonesians.

National communities came about with the origination of *print capitalism*—the mass production of books and then newspapers written in local languages for simultaneous mass consumption by an increasingly literate public (Anderson 1991). When French people read French newspapers and German people read German newspapers, they not only learn what's happening in their respective countries; they

also confirm their membership in two different shared national cultures. Even today, when newspaper readership is on the decline, other forms of shared media consumption follow the same pattern. A study of the geography of Twitter, for example, found that people's networks are generally national and unilingual—although in theory your experience of Twitter could be a truly global one, in practice it is likely to reinforce your sense of belonging to a certain national imagined community (Takhteyev, Gruzd, and Wellman 2012).

In contemporary life, cultural sociologists generally take nations for granted the same way we all do, and many of them study the differences between national cultures: What makes national cultures different from one another, and what are the implications of the differences? Americans are generally thought to be more individualistic than people in other countries, for example, but they are far less likely to live alone than are residents of apparently less individualistic nations, such as Sweden, Norway, Finland, and Denmark (Klinenberg 2012). Why might this be? It can't be because of genetics or different types of human nature: There isn't anything fundamentally different about people in different countries. It turns out that a combination of different factors—including economic prosperity, the rising status of women, the communications revolution, mass urbanization, and the longevity revolution—all influence whether people want to and are able to live alone, and these factors vary widely across national contexts. Explore the Infographic on page 124 to learn more about the new culture of living alone.

Indeed, many important social, political, economic, and cultural institutions are organized along national lines, and these have systematic effects on the way people live their lives and the kinds of attitudes and worldviews they develop. (The effects are not always uniform; social security policies vary substantially between countries, for example, and heavily impact the elderly while having a smaller impact on others.) These different worldviews can in turn have a big impact on other features of national life. In Japan, CEOs are paid on average 16 times more than workers; in the United States, it is 319 times more. Researchers have struggled to explain this enormous and persistent difference between the two countries on the basis of economic considerations alone, suggesting that there are likely cultural factors at work.

One important area of research is early childhood, because it is when we are children that many of our cultural assumptions are formed. One study of preschools in Japan, China, and the United States revealed the very different roles that preschools play in forming cultural identities in

The Culture of Living Alone

Percentage of households that are people living alone

Seattle 42%

Portland 34%

San Francisco 40%

Las Vegas 28%

Santa Monica 48%
Los Angeles 30%

San Diego 30%

Phoenix 28%

Santa Fe 41%

Minneapolis 43%

Denver 40%

Fort Worth 28%   Dallas 35%

Houston 32%

St. Louis 45%

Knoxville 51%

New Orleans 36%

Chicago 35%   Detroit 38%   Cleveland 40%

New York 31% (Manhattan 46%)

Washington 48%

Atlanta 45%

Tampa 37%

Miami 36%
Miami Beach 49%

Map is shaded by county.

Labels show one-person household percentages for cities.

38%
35
32
29
26
23
20

In 1950 the number of people living alone in the U.S. was about 4 million. Today that number has skyrocketed to 33 million, or **28 percent of American households**. What does this trend say about America? For a long time, ours has been a culture organized around the classic idea of the nuclear family and a belief in living and doing things together. But does the choice to live alone mean that Americans are disconnected from each other and no longer care about community life? The truth is that people living alone are not isolated, but actually very well connected. In fact, as compared with married people, people who live alone are more likely to spend time friends and neighbors and they're even more likely to volunteer with civic organizations. And most of all they are more likely to live in cities, where high population densities, and the concentration of restaurants, coffee shops and social groups, provides this new group of people with the capacity to live alone but not *be* alone.

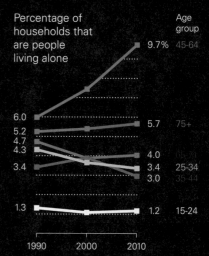

Percentage of households that are people living alone

	Age group
9.7%	45-64
6.0	
5.7	75+
5.2	
4.7	
4.3	
4.0	
3.4	25-34
3.4	
3.0	35-44
1.3	
1.2	15-24

1990   2000   2010

Sources: Based on data from Susan Weber and Andrew Beveridge, Queens College, CUNY; U.S. Census Bureau.

 Explore the **Data** on the Culture of Living Alone in **MySocLab** and then . . .

■ Think About It

In 1950, living alone was most prevalent in rural areas around the Northwest. Today, it is concentrated in big cities. Why this shift in the location of going solo? And how have people who live alone changed the culture of cities?

■ Inspire Your Sociological Imagination

Women are more likely than men to live alone, but men are more likely to be socially isolated. Why is this? And what are some of the challenges related to the rise of living alone and social isolation - for individuals, families, cities, and nations?

these three countries (Tobin, Wu, and Davidson 1989). By recording classroom activities and then discussing the videos with teachers and parents, the researchers found that U.S. preschools put heavy emphasis on creativity and respect for the children as individuals. In China the emphasis was on instilling order and discipline in the children, an understandable objective in the context of China's single-child families where "little emperors" are often seen as spoiled by their parents and grandparents. In Japan, meanwhile, educators left children to their own devices to a much greater degree than in the other two cases, forcing them to learn to get along respectfully with others.

These might seem like stereotypes, but that's exactly the point. If there are durable differences in cultural norms between different countries, we would expect to find evidence of them in institutions such as preschool. As the authors of this study indicate, preschool both *reflects* national culture—because teachers and parents are influenced by certain ideas and try to pass them along—and helps *reproduce* it—because children inherit these same ideas.

Preschools follow very different educational approaches in different countries. Why is preschool an important place to study national cultural differences?

3 How Do Our Cultural Practices Relate to Class and Status?

CLASS, STATUS, AND CULTURE

Watch the Big Question Video in MySocLab

How do you know whether someone is wealthy or powerful? You can't see their bank account or know who is in their phone address book. The chances are that you know because of cultural signs: the way someone dresses, how they speak, the sports they play, the music they like, the kinds of things they like to do, in short, **taste**—their cultural preferences.

Although we normally think about social class in mainly economic terms, taste—and culture more broadly—plays a crucial role in setting and maintaining class distinctions. In one famous study, the French sociologist Pierre Bourdieu even argued that taste is fundamentally the distaste for the taste of others. In culture wars, as in all others, the stakes can be high.

☐ Cultural Capital

Contrary to popular assumption that it is the land of opportunity, the United States is an intensely class-bound society, second in the developed world only to the United Kingdom. Someone who is born into the working class is very likely to stay working class for her entire life, and the same is true for someone born into the upper class. One way of understanding why that is the case is to think about the kinds of resources people can bring to bear in their lives. One kind of resource is money and other economic assets; another is social connections and networks of friends and acquaintances. Bourdieu referred to these as *economic capital* and *social capital,* respectively. He also suggested that there is a third type of resource important for determining class position: In addition to the money you have and the people you know, your success in life is also influenced by your **cultural capital**. This is your education, your attitudes, and your preferences, which collectively confer upon you a higher or lower status in the eyes of others. (Bourdieu 1984).

Cultural capital is serious business. In the summer of 2011, the character The Situation from *Jersey Shore*—a very popular but low-status reality TV show—prominently wore clothing from Abercrombie and Fitch. The company, worried about having its higher-status brand tarnished by association with *Jersey Shore* (and also probably looking for some easy publicity) offered to pay The Situation to *stop* wearing its clothing—the very opposite of a standard marketing arrangement!

We use our cultural capital all the time in interactions with others and often don't even realize we are doing so. Bourdieu did not consider public or over-the-top displays of status symbols to be an important form of cultural capital; instead, he emphasized the various ways that people display taste in everyday life. Discussing why you enjoyed the Spanish director Pedro Almodóvar's latest film, for example, signals to others that you have good taste in movies. Taste also implies distaste; if the person you are talking to doesn't know who Almodóvar is, you are likely to make negative judgments about

What is cultural capital, and in what ways have American elites become cultural omnivores?

his own tastes and status. Even if you don't *consciously* judge other people on their tastes, the chances are that tastes will influence the kinds of people you want to spend time with or avoid. Tastes, therefore, help maintain status boundaries between different groups (Holt 1998).

Cultural capital requires scarcity: Cultural experiences that everyone can share cannot serve as the basis for status distinctions. Before the Swedish home-products company IKEA began to sell its inexpensive furniture, the aesthetic it applied (minimalist Scandinavian modernism) was considered a sign of high status. But because the middle class can afford IKEA furniture and shops there extensively, this aesthetic is no longer an embodiment of significant cultural capital. The issue is not money but difficulty: In order to provide a basis for signaling distinction, high-status cultural consumption must not be easy to participate in, and if it becomes easy it will stop being high status.

Does this notion of cultural capital apply to contemporary life in the United States? The United States has a more pervasive mass culture than many other countries, and recent research has suggested that American elites are becoming less snobbish and increasingly behaving as **cultural omnivores**, or cultural elites who demonstrate their high status through a broad range of cultural consumption, including low-status culture. American elites today are more likely than average to consume not only high culture but popular culture as well. It is a sign of distinction to have wide-ranging tastes (Peterson and Kern 1996). At the same time, we shouldn't overstate the inclusive nature of elite tastes. While, for instance, cultural elites show a fondness for country music (a low-status genre more associated with

Cultural capital is only valuable if it is rare or hard to obtain. Now that the middle class can easily buy modernist furniture at Ikea, that kind of furniture is no longer an important status symbol.

the working class), the type of country music elites generally enjoy is not the commercial country of Garth Brooks or Tim McGraw but rather more alternative country acts such as Wilco or Blue Mountain (Holt 1997).

Symbolic Boundaries

The kinds of distinctions that people make between themselves and others on the basis of taste are just one kind of **symbolic boundary**. Two other important symbolic boundaries are *socioeconomic status*—the amount of money you make and the kind of job you have—and *morality*—the moral considerations that guide the way you live (or appear to live) your life. Sometimes these three types of symbolic boundaries overlap in people's thinking about status and class, and sometimes they don't.

For instance, in debates about the scope and generosity of public assistance in the United States, politicians and commentators often draw the distinction between the "deserving poor" and the "undeserving poor." The former are thought to be hardworking people who nevertheless have struggled to get ahead, while the latter are lazy "welfare queens" or drug addicts. Leaving aside the fact that evidence of this distinction is slim, it is nevertheless a case where moral boundaries are being drawn independently of socioeconomic ones. A similar moral distinction is often drawn between hardworking business leaders and corporate fat cats. Some sociologists have argued that moral boundaries in the United States are more important for indicating status than they are in other countries and that cultural boundaries are less important (Lamont 1992).

When we use discuss symbolic boundaries, we often use terms such as "out of place" or "knowing your place." In many cases, this is just a metaphor—there isn't literally a geographical place you are out of. But sometimes there is: Symbolic boundaries often take geographical form. A person dressed a certain way or with a certain skin color can appear perfectly normal in one neighborhood and strange (or threatening) in another. The symbolic boundaries associated with cultural practices have spatial boundaries as well. Graffiti artists in 1970s New York City developed a highly structured artistic community with informal but well-maintained norms of conduct and apprenticeships for beginners. But they made their art in public places in violation both of the law and of middle-class norms of public space use (significantly, most graffiti artists were people of color and were not middle class). In other words, their artwork was both symbolically and spatially beyond set boundaries.

There were two main responses to the graffiti movement: One was an attempt—in particular by local politicians and media—to portray graffiti as deviant and criminal; the other was an enthusiastic embrace of graffiti by trendy art

galleries in some New York neighborhoods. Even though they disagreed about its merits, graffiti's admirers and detractors both agreed about it being out of place and were eager to move it off the streets (an inappropriate place for art) and into the galleries (an appropriate place for art). Sometimes "out of place" is both a metaphor and literally true (Cresswell 1996).

How Culture Reproduces Class

An important topic for sociologists concerned with power and inequality is the process that causes class boundaries and distinctions to be maintained over time, known as **class reproduction**. There are lots of reasons why some people are rich and others poor, but how do those boundaries get maintained in the short term and the long term? Bourdieu's theory of taste attempts to explain short-term class reproduction. In countless everyday interactions, we remind ourselves and others about our relative statuses and thus ensure that our status differences stay prominent. But what explains class and status reproduction over the long term? Why are middle-class children likely to grow up into middle-class adults and working-class children likely to grow up into working-class adults?

One obvious answer is money: Wealthier families will have an easier time affording private schools, SAT preparation courses, college tuition, and personal tutors, for example, and they will also likely leave sizeable inheritances to their children. But money only explains part of the story: Sociologists have shown that people make meaningful choices about how to live that are limited but not solely determined by their economic circumstances. The question of how and why we make the choices we do is what culture explains.

The ethnographer Paul Willis (1977) followed a set of boys from working-class homes in a British industrial town in the 1970s. They frequently behaved badly in school, were rebellious, and didn't seem to care much about their futures. A standard opinion at the time was that such cases were simply people failing to make the right choices to get ahead in life. But Willis found it was quite the opposite: The boys' apparently unproductive behavior in school was in fact them adapting to their class circumstances. The same attitudes that got them in trouble with their teachers turned out to serve them very well in factory work a few years later, where standing up to authority and not working hard on command help workers gain collective leverage against their bosses. The boys were learning how to be working-class men.

A more recent study compared middle-class and working-class families in the United States to see how different class positions affect parents' approaches to childrearing and what the implications of the differences are for children's futures. During the study, it became clear that there were two

How do symbolic boundaries relate to culture?

quite different approaches. Middle-class parents followed an approach of *concerted cultivation*, actively fostering their child's talents and intervening on their behalf, thereby instilling a sense of entitlement. Working-class parents, by contrast, followed an approach of *accomplishment of natural growth*, caring for their children but leaving them to fend for themselves socially, thereby instilling a sense of constraint (Lareau 2003). The middle-class children's sense of

What explains class and status reproduction over the long term?

entitlement will make it more likely that they push to succeed socioeconomically when they are older, while the reverse is true of the working-class children's sense of constraint, making it more likely that as they get older the children will stay in the class they were born into.

The implication of both of these studies is that class is reproduced not only through the money you have but through the culture you practice.

4 Who Produces Culture, and Why?

THE CONDITIONS OF CULTURAL PRODUCTION

👁 Watch the **Big Question** Video in **MySocLab**

In 1845, Karl Marx and Friedrich Engels argued that the people who have the most wealth and power in a society generally also have the greatest ability to produce and distribute their own ideas and culture (Marx and Engels [1845] 1972). In nineteenth-century Europe, these people were capitalists, such as factory owners and bankers, who valued their rights to private property and their freedom to run their businesses as they saw fit. By using their influence with newspaper owners and intellectuals, they were able to make liberty and freedom the dominant ideas of the age.

Marx and Engels's argument allows us to see cultural production as a historical phenomenon. Ideas and fashions don't just change randomly over time; they respond to other changes in a society's political and economic circumstances. At the same time, in the nineteenth century it was much more difficult to spread ideas than it is today. Printing presses were expensive, and much of the population was illiterate. Today, with the Internet and social media, is it still the case that powerful people and classes have control over the production of culture? Sociologists of culture need to pay careful attention to the *conditions of cultural production:* Who controls the production of ideas in society, and to what ends?

☐ The Public Sphere

A basic premise of public life in a democracy such as the United States is that everyone is allowed to participate. In theory, everyone over 18 can vote, can run for public office, and can try to convince other people of their point of view. In practice, public participation is massively unequal—for example, former felons are stripped of their right to vote in many states, and it is very hard to attract an audience for your ideas or your art if you don't have a fair amount of money—but as an ideal, this vision of equal participation in public life is a powerful one.

The German sociologist Jurgen Habermas calls this ideal the **public sphere**, and it is the most influential sociological account of how ideas are produced and exchanged in modern society (Habermas 1962). According to Habermas, the highest form of public life in capitalist society is private citizens assembled in a public body to confer about matters of general interest. In this ideal public sphere, citizens set aside their own interests, as well as their wealth and status, and meet as equals to collectively debate and generate ideas about how to govern collectively.

In eighteenth-century Europe, when the public sphere began to emerge, it was centered in a range of institutions such as newspapers, pubs, social clubs, and coffee shops—in short, any location where people could gather and discuss the news of the day. The public sphere stood apart from the state and offered citizens a way to criticize and influence the government, which was a novel idea in an age of absolute monarchies. In modern welfare states such as the United States, the public sphere is where different social groups organize to become political actors and compete for influence. Activists such as the Tea Party or Occupy Wall Street movements, and lobby groups such as the National Rifle Association or the AARP, are examples of the kinds of groups that are prominent in today's public sphere. An important way they compete is by trying to shape public opinion through the production of ideas, for example in newspapers, on television, and with advertising.

Some sociologists have criticized Habermas's theory of the public sphere for ignoring the power differences that inevitably prevent all citizens from participating equally in public life. For example, the Tea Party movement has received many millions of dollars in funding from a small number of wealthy conservatives, while Occupy Wall Street has raised much smaller amounts of money, generally from small donations. As a result, the Tea Party has been able to spend more money on advertising and promotion, on bankrolling their preferred political candidates, and on other activities that give them influence in the public sphere. In general, sociologists argue that the same things that give some people power over others in private life—such as race, gender, class, and education—will give some people more influence in the public sphere, regardless of Habermas's ideal of equal participation (Fraser 1992). Furthermore, they argue that there has never been one overarching public sphere, as Habermas suggested. Instead, subordinated social groups—or subcultures—have frequently constituted their own **counterpublics**, alternative public spheres through which they produce and circulate their own values, beliefs, and ideas. Factory and

union culture in the first half of the twentieth century, the network of black churches that formed the backbone of the civil rights movement, and the bars and clubs where the gay liberation movement began are all examples of American counterpublics over the years.

Fragmented publics do not necessarily need to be subordinate, either: The concept can apply to any subculture. One researcher describes the users of social networking sites such as Facebook as constituting a **networked public**, or online public sphere. Networked publics attract participation from teenagers in particular because of things they offer that face-to-face public settings cannot. Social networking allows for persistence (you can browse through your friends' profiles and message histories years after initial friend requests and conversations), searchability (you can seek out other people with similar interests and connect with existing friends regardless of geographical proximity), replicability (it is hard to distinguish the "original" from the "copy" when copy-and-paste is ubiquitous), and invisible audiences (much of our activity on social networks is potentially being observed by people we don't know, and perhaps at totally different times), and these features make networked publics distinct public spheres (Boyd 2008). Regardless of whether there is one public sphere or many, the concept encourages us to think about how ideas and culture are produced and how people participate in that production.

The Culture Industry versus Cultural Democracy

Who controls popular culture today, and who benefits from it? Is it the corporations that produce it at a profit, or the public who consumes it, shares it, and enjoys it? If record labels, movie studios, and advertising agencies heavily push the latest songs and movies on us, when we enjoy them are we dupes or are we exercising cultural free will? Sociologists have been largely split on these questions between two perspectives: one that sees popular culture as an industry, and one that sees popular culture as a democratic arena—a cultural public sphere.

Writing after the Second World War, the German sociologist and philosopher Theodor Adorno argued that the popular culture that dominates the public sphere encourages a passive, conservative public. He was referring to popular music, movies, and other types of mass culture, all of which he labeled the **culture industry** (Horkheimer and Adorno [1947] 2002). His chief complaint was that popular culture encourages audiences to passively consume what they are watching, reading, or listening to rather than participating

How does the concept of the public sphere explain how culture is produced in society?

or engaging creatively with the work. The kind of culture that the culture industry produces is standardized, commoditized, and does not challenge the status quo; at the end of the day, it is advertising rather than art.

Other sociologists have argued that Adorno's critique of popular culture (along with others like it) was too pessimistic. They instead believe that popular culture provides an arena through which we all debate the meaning of the good life and the conditions for attaining it—an explicitly cultural version of Habermas's public sphere. One response, for example, to Adorno's claim that most people passively receive the culture that is offered to them is that popular culture is user driven. Cultural producers want to attract an audience, so they tailor their art to reflect popular preferences (Gans 1999). Movie studios wouldn't keep releasing the same kind of movies if people didn't want to watch them, and when people vote with their time and money by choosing not to watch a certain kind of movie, studios will probably stop making that kind of movie. According to this perspective, popular culture is an element of *cultural democracy*. In the cultural marketplace, lots of different tastes—including those of subcultures that elites disapprove of—are accommodated. Different cultural styles exist "because they satisfy the needs and wishes of some people, even if they dissatisfy those of other people" (Gans 1999:91).

The debate between the culture industry and cultural democracy perspectives on cultural production generally concerns the kinds of art and media produced by large corporations. The culture industry perspective argues that people passively accept what they are given by corporate media, and the cultural democracy perspective argues that corporate media gives people what they legitimately want. But there is another possibility, which is that people don't just passively accept corporate culture but actually intentionally disrupt and subvert it in reaction to the common view that corporations have too much influence in social life. Naomi Klein calls this *culture jamming* (Klein 2000). Most of us can't avoid constant exposure to corporate media on television and the Internet, but also on signs and billboards in public spaces. Culture jamming relies on this constant exposure in order to mock it, perhaps by directly modifying billboards with graffiti. Culture jammers reject the idea that marketing has to be passively accepted as a one-way information flow.

Culture jamming takes corporate imagery everyone is familiar with and subverts it to show anti-corporate or countercultural messages. Is this form of cultural protest effective?

☐ The Medium Is the Message

Debates over whether popular culture is democratic, conservative, or something else often focus not only on the content of popular culture but just as often on its form. If

Is popular culture an industry or a cultural democracy?

the same content is broadcast on cable TV and on Twitter, will it communicate the same thing? The answer from communications theory is that it won't. As Marshall McLuhan famously declared, the medium is the message (McLuhan 1964). By this, McLuhan meant that different media encourage different ways of communicating, of organizing power, and of centralizing or decentralizing social activity.

Compare listening to a news bulletin on the radio with reading the same news on a website. There are some obvious differences: For example, when you hear the news on the radio, you hear only what the announcer says, while on a website you have the opportunity to follow hyperlinks and look up unfamiliar things on Wikipedia. In this respect, the web offers a richer experience than the radio. But there are some other differences that may not be as obvious. On the radio you can't follow hyperlinks, but you also have a harder time skimming the material the way you can on a website. Radio dominates one of your senses—hearing—and prompts you to devote most of your attention to receiving and processing the information you are hearing. A website, by contrast, provides you with a more ambiguous sensory experience. There might be sound and video on the webpage, but there might be just text. You might be listening to music in the background, or you might have an instant messaging window open simultaneously. Reading news on a website requires more of your direct engagement than listening to the radio does. Different forms of communication can thus provide very different experiences even when communicating the exact same content.

Does communication change with the form or medium?

For this reason, sociologists say that media are biased (Innis 1951). Bias here doesn't refer to political bias—the way, for example, that many people believe Fox News has a right-wing slant—but rather to the different types of engagement that different forms of communication encourage. Some scholars further argue that different media actually change our notions of truth and our values (Postman 1985). As a result, sociologists of culture and the media need to pay careful attention to changing patterns of media consumption and engagement. If we read fewer books and more webpages, the implications may be much broader than just how we get our news and entertainment.

Cultural production in the United States is increasingly occurring online. But an arguably greater transition was from the age of typography to the *age of television* (Postman 1985). From the sixteenth century until midway through the twentieth century, public discourse in the West was based in writing, a medium biased towards careful and considered thought. Personal communication largely occurred via letters, which took a long time to write and be delivered, encouraging people to thoughtfully consider what they wanted to say. Similarly, large-scale communication occurred through books and pamphlets, which also encouraged thoughtfulness. According to some communications scholars, meanwhile, the age of television has been an age of irrelevance, impotence, and incoherence in public discourse. How much of what we see on the news has any actual relevance for our lives in the sense that it will cause us to make different decisions? Endless reporting of distant natural disasters, for example, is irrelevant to our daily lives, and this helps promote a loop of impotence because we become used to passively receiving information without expecting to be able to act on it in any meaningful way. What's more, the information we receive through television tends to arrive in a series of short, disconnected sound bites, which make it difficult for us to put them in any coherent context. Ultimately, the bias of television as a medium is toward stimulation and entertainment, possibly at the expense of understanding.

Do we still live in the age of television? Things have changed since the 1980s, when these trends were first identified. Ronald Reagan was president, the Internet only existed in a few laboratories, and no one had cell phones. Our media consumption habits have changed as well. On the one hand, Americans watch more television than ever before—American households had the TV turned on 8.5 hours per day on average in 2011, compared to only 6.5 hours per day in 1980 (Nielsen 2011:16). And, in fact, 40 percent of American households have the TV turned on during all waking hours—regardless of if anyone is watching or not (Gitlin 2007:18). On the other hand, we spend a lot of time on the Internet, where media consumption isn't necessarily as passive as it is with television. Have things gotten better or worse? Is this still the age of television?

Evidence suggests that many of the trends from the age of television have actually intensified. Long-form fiction reading has substantially declined, for example; the percentage of American adults who have read a novel, play, or the like in the last year shrunk from 57 to 47 percent between 1982 and 2002 (Gitlin 2007:213). And although we watch more television than ever before, we spend far less of that time watching the news: In 1980, 23 percent of Americans watched the evening news on average each night, compared to only 7.5 percent in 2010 (see Figure 5.3; Pew Research Center 2012). At the same time, it is possible that the entertainment we watch on television is of higher quality than it used to be, with the increasing popularity of high-brow TV shows on channels such as HBO and the increasing sophistication of more mainstream fare on the large networks

FIGURE 5.3 IS THIS STILL THE AGE OF TELEVISION? Although Americans watch more television than ever before—in fact, 40 percent of American households have the TV turned on during all waking hours—there have been dramatic changes in what role television plays in our lives.

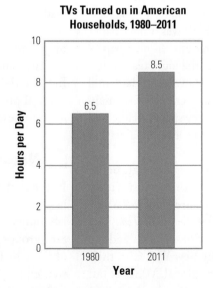

TVs Turned on in American Households, 1980–2011

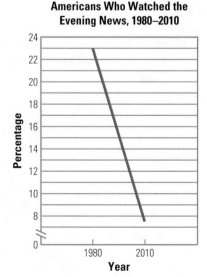

Americans Who Watched the Evening News, 1980–2010

Source: Nielsen (2011).

(Johnson 2005). But arguably the most important trend is an increase in cultural multitasking—when you watch TV, how often are you also checking Facebook, browsing the Internet, or instant messaging with a friend? The contemporary media environment is a "torrent": a nonstop flow of information that we rarely if ever disengage from. The torrent doesn't so much command our active attention as it forms a sensory background for our lives (Gitlin 2007). As we all live our lives in an increasingly online and interconnected fashion, just how cultural production continues to change in the years ahead will be a crucial question for both sociologists and the public at large.

5 What Is the Relationship between Media and Democracy?

MEDIA AND DEMOCRACY: A CHANGING LANDSCAPE

👁 Watch the **Big Question** Video in **MySocLab**

Before he helped to found the Chicago School of sociology and launch the modern social science of the city, Robert Park was a newspaper journalist. The connection between newspapers and the city is actually a strong one. As the journalist Walter Lippmann once argued, "There is, I believe, a fundamental reason why the American press is strong enough to remain free. That reason is that the American newspapers, large and small, and without exception, belong to a town, a city, at most to a region" (Blethen 2002).

Lippmann's observation about newspapers all being based in cities is not true anymore. The three most widely read newspapers in the United States are the *Wall Street Journal, USA Today,* and the *New York Times. USA Today* is a national newspaper, and while the *Wall Street Journal* and the *New York Times* are nominally based in New York City, their readership is largely national or even global. What about the other half of Lippmann's argument? Is the American press still "strong enough to remain free"? With newspaper readership in free fall, does this even matter? Should we be asking instead about whether blogs are strong enough to remain free? What is the relationship between media and democracy, and how has it changed since Robert Park's time? Because the media are arguably the most important form of cultural production in our society, these are important and urgent questions for cultural sociologists.

☐ Newspaper Citizens

In the first half of the twentieth century, Park and his colleagues at the University of Chicago treated the city as a laboratory to study social relations. One of the most important groups of people they studied was immigrants. Many of these had only recently left their home countries and still wanted to keep track of goings-on at home. In the days before television, radio, and the Internet, newspapers provided the only practical means of doing so. Park observed that foreign-language newspapers were an important institution in Chicago, and reading, which was generally an elite practice in the countries where immigrants had previously lived, became not only common but a necessity in the U.S. city (Park 1923:274).

Foreign-language newspapers didn't just provide a link to home countries. They also addressed the experience of the new groups to which immigrants—whether German Americans, Russian Americans, or Chinese Americans—belonged. Immigrants were changed through the process of immigration, and the newspapers provided a new set of common themes, stories, characters, and even a vocabulary for making sense of the new world. The new American metropolises of the early twentieth century were enormous, chaotic, and sometimes mysterious. Police departments and courts, department stores and restaurants, hotels and boarding houses, train stations, stock exchanges, concert halls and saloons: No one could possibly experience it all, but newspapers would delve into these worlds, allowing readers to sample tastes of the city life they might not experience firsthand. News was aimed at the common reader, with stories of love and romance targeted to women, and sports and politics targeted to men.

Some newspaper publishers, such as William Randolph Hearst, saw the news as a form of entertainment. Others, such as Joseph Pulitzer, saw the news as information. But they commonly saw newspapers as vehicles of social integration. Benedict Anderson emphasized the role of newspapers in creating national imagined communities, but Hearst and Pulitzer's papers also created urban imagined communities. According to the historian Richard Hofstadter, newspapers created "a mental world" for migrants moving from the countryside to the city. For these migrants, the urban environment could be both cruel and fascinating, both mysterious and enticing, and newspapers were one of the main guides they used to interpret it. Newspapers thus helped close the social distance between readers and emphasize their common circumstances (Hofstadter 1960:188). The notorious showman and scam artist P. T. Barnum put it more directly: "He who is without a newspaper is cut off from his species" (Barnum [1880] 1990).

City newspapers helped to make people citizens, but citizens of what? What community did newspapers help make people feel a part of? In a small village, people could keep up with the goings-on of their neighbors directly through word of mouth, but in large cities, Park argued, newspapers helped perform this role by reporting on events of local importance (Park 1923:277–78). According to Park, and most media scholars who have followed, if we are to have a politics built on public opinion and informed debate,

the newspaper must tell us about ourselves, informing us who we are by letting our experiences and ideas surface on its pages.

☐ Making the News

If the news is vital to democracy, then it matters a great deal how the news operates. **Journalism** is above all a form of communication: It is the production and dissemination of information of general public interest. But sociologists of the media are in broad agreement that the news does a lot more than just pass along facts to the public. By deciding what to cover and how to cover it, journalists don't simply report on the news, they actually help to create and change it (Schudson 2003:11).

How do journalists make the news?

How does the news have this kind of power, and is it a good thing? There are plenty of arguments about the power of the media. Common left-wing critiques suggest that the mass media support corporate power, militarism, and the interests of the wealthiest. Common right-wing critiques suggest that the media make culture liberal and spread feminism, environmentalism, and the acceptance of homosexuality. Political insiders on all sides believe the media exerts agenda-setting power that can change the course of political events and determine careers.

The problem is that it is difficult to prove that the media actually have this influence. One famous incident of apparent media influence was during the Vietnam War. Up until 1968, TV news coverage was favorable to the war, sanitizing violence and especially U.S. casualties. That changed in 1968, most famously with CBS news anchor Walter Cronkite's February editorial calling for negotiations with the Viet Cong, and the popular narrative is that media criticism of the war prompted a turning point in public opinion. But when the coverage became more critical, polls found a temporary increase in support for the war as people rallied to support the president and the campaign.

Because the media are so visible and audible, they are presumed to be an important force in society. But if the public doesn't passively receive whatever the media tell it, how do the media have their influence? According to media scholar Michael Schudson, the media act as a cultural system: They set the context for making events in the world intelligible. They do this by helping construct a community and a public conversation. Regardless of your opinions on a given issue, when you hear about it in the news you are more likely to treat it as an event of importance. This is why public relations experts say, "There's no such thing as bad press." The news amplifies issues and makes them publicly legitimate.

☐ Media Bias: Domination or Framing?

Are the media biased? There is no doubt that certain topics get very little coverage in the news. Abortion is hotly debated, as are tax breaks for businesses. But the desirability of capitalism is very rarely mentioned. There are different explanations for why this is the case.

Edward Herman and Noam Chomsky have developed a "propaganda model" of the media: The role of the media, they argue, is to inform, entertain, and ingrain citizens with national values and to suppress dangerous oppositional perspectives. In the case of state-run media in nondemocratic countries, this propaganda role is obvious, but Herman and Chomsky claim that the private-sector media in countries such as the United States operate in the same way. They give five reasons why this is the case: first, the concentration of media ownership in a small number of wealthy hands; second, the fact that advertising is the primary source of revenue for the media; third, the media reliance on government officials, corporate leaders, and public relations as sources for reporting; fourth, the power of governments and big business to discipline and threaten media that is too critical; and finally, the ubiquity of anticommunist sentiment to be aroused (Herman and Chomsky made their arguments in the context of the Cold War, and Chomsky has subsequently suggested that the war on terror is the contemporary equivalent).

The result of these five factors, according to Herman and Chomsky, is that the media will give sustained attention to stories that are useful to powerful institutions and very little attention to stories that are not. For example, there were similar periods of state violence in Cambodia and Indonesia during the 1970s, but the media largely ignored the episode in Indonesia (a U.S. ally) while relentlessly covering that in Cambodia (a U.S. enemy). Their argument can be seen as a modern version of Marx and Engels's belief that the ruling ideas of an age are the ideas of the ruling class. Herman and Chomsky give provide a model to explain how, in the contemporary United States, ideas useful to ruling elites are promoted and other ideas are silenced (Herman and Chomsky 1988).

Herman and Chomsky's propaganda model is an example of a media domination argument: They hold that the media tell (or try to tell) the public what to believe, and the message they communicate is a biased one. Today, sociologists of the media more commonly argue that the news is slanted because of media **framing**. Reporters cover a diversity of topics, but they tend to do so through certain existing storylines and narratives. Schudson gives the example of the coverage of race in local news. Local news consistently shows a higher percentage of blacks as perpetrators of crime

Why do certain topics get very little news coverage?

and as recipients of public assistance than is in fact the case. Is this bias? Are reporters trying to push a certain ideological line? Schudson argues that they generally are not, but that their coverage fits and helps confirm the frame of African Americans as prone to criminality and poverty. "Media frames, largely unspoken and unacknowledged, organize the world both for journalists who report it and, in some important degree, for us who rely on their reports" (Gitlin 1980:7).

The explanation for how framing operates has as much to do with institutional factors as personal ones. On the one hand, journalists themselves tend to be economically conservative, upper middle class, and socially liberal. Minorities and the poor are underrepresented in the newsroom. This means that journalists tend to cover stories in ways that make sense to the white upper middle class, for example by assuming the virtue of individualism and political moderation. On the other hand, there are institutional factors that impact how the news gets made. The media are generally for-profit enterprises, and they want to tell exciting stories to sell newspapers or attract viewers. This means that the news tends to focus on visible events, action and conflict, and personal drama. For the same reason, the media tend to focus on bad news; as the saying goes, "if it bleeds it leads."

☐ Corporate Media Concentration

One of the premises of the free press in a democracy is that citizens will be exposed to a variety of perspectives and sources of information in order to participate meaningfully in public life. But just six corporations own most of the media in the country. How much choice do U.S. media consumers actually have? Three trends in the U.S. media landscape suggest that the relationship between media and democracy is only likely to grow more troubled (McChesney 1999; Klinenberg 2007).

The first is consolidation: Fewer and fewer corporations own more and more of the media outlets in a given market. Consolidation limits consumer choice—in an extreme case, the corporation Clear Channel once owned all the commercial radio stations in the city of Minot, North Dakota. This is a monopoly and is still comparatively rare, but oligopolies (markets controlled by a handful of firms) are now the norm in the media. Consolidation also makes it difficult for new entrants to break into the market, increasing the likelihood that the media market will stay dominated by the same players.

A second trend is conglomeration, which describes a firm controlling multiple types of media functions. For example, the Walt Disney Company, one of the big six U.S. media corporations, owns ABC, ESPN, hundreds of radio stations, and various print media operations. When Disney has a new movie to release, it can rely on its subsidiaries to promote the movie on its stations and television programs and to ensure that the coverage is positive. This is called *synergy,* and Disney is the master of synergy.

The final trend is hypercommercialism. It has long been standard for movies to feature some sort of product placement—advertising where shots or mentions of a product are integrated into the movie itself as opposed to a separate ad. But product placement has soared to new heights in recent years and shows no sign of abating. The 2010 romantic comedy Valentine's Day, for instance, featured product placements for 60 different products—one every 125 seconds! This is an example of hypercommercialism, and it is a defining feature of today's corporate media—blurred lines between advertising and editorial content in newspapers; the ubiquity of outdoor advertising; the spread of media companies into retail businesses, such as the ESPN Store; and sponsored programming, such as the corporate naming of nearly all professional sports venues.

According to communications scholar Robert McChesney, these three trends have put enormous commercial pressure on journalism. Within the bounds of profitability and corporate acceptability, the media produces a wide range of content; outside of these bounds, nothing.

☐ Media, Democracy, and the Internet

Writing one hundred years ago, the journalist Walter Lippmann was skeptical of the media's ability to provide the public with the information necessary for a democracy. He argued that "news and truth are not the same thing." Democracy requires truth, but the news can only describe and discuss events from day to day. Lippmann believed that democracy required a collective intelligence, which could only be had with extensive social organization, and that here the press could only play a small part, although a necessary one (Lippmann 1922:358).

The notion that the press is vital to democracy is an old one. Thomas Jefferson, for instance, famously said that "Were it left to me to decide whether we should have a government without

How much choice do U.S. media consumers actually have?

newspapers, or newspapers without a government, I should not hesitate a moment to prefer the latter." Many First Amendment scholars believe that the media are necessary to provide a forum for debate (to help constitute the public sphere, in other words), give a voice to public opinion, serve as citizens' eyes and ears in politics, and serve as a public watchdog over government and business (Graber 2003).

But the relationship between the media and democracy looks different in the age of corporate media consolidation and the Internet. Corporate consolidation inevitably means that media are less responsive to the local communities that they serve, and the quality of democratic politics and cultural life suffers as a result (Klinenberg 2007:26). Less local staffing, less local news gathering, and less interaction with the local community means less ability to play the democratic role Park and Lippmann thought was necessary.

At the same time, people are fighting back, and they're increasingly doing so online. Citizen journalism has exploded in the last decade, in large part because barriers to entry are so low. In the mid-1990s, a group called Radio Mutiny set up an unsanctioned pirate radio station in West Philadelphia as a challenge to corporate media, but doing so took nine months of hard work to build the transmitter (Klinenberg 2007). Setting up a blog, by contrast, takes only a minute or so. The Internet has lowered the bar for entering into the public sphere, allowing the people formerly known as the audience to assert their own voices, if not nearly as forcefully as the conglomerates such as Clear Channel, Disney, and even Google.

The most spectacular incidence of Internet activism and democracy of recent years is the 2011 Arab Spring uprising in the Middle East, and particularly the mass Tahrir Square demonstrations in Egypt that overthrew the

Increasingly, corporate marketers believe the best advertising is the kind you don't even realize is an ad. Do product placement and other forms of hypercommercialism threaten the integrity of the media?

Massive protests swept through the Middle East in 2011, reaching their peak with millions of people gathering in Tahrir Square in Cairo, Egypt to overthrow the Mubarak Regime. Many have argued that social media played an important role in allowing these protests to be organized and spread. What other ways might social media be changing the way democracy is practiced around the world?

Mubarak regime. Across the region, people protested against their governments, most visibly by gathering in large numbers in public squares. Within a few months, four national governments were forced from power, and a number more only narrowly avoided that fate. Here social networks, and in particular Twitter, were often held to be crucial to activists' organizing efforts, by allowing people to coordinate their protests and get up-to-the-minute information on what was happening elsewhere. At the same time, governments in Egypt and other parts of the Middle East also used social media in their attempts to repress the civilian uprising.

Despite the ongoing development of grassroots and citizen-led media activism, it would be a mistake to view the Internet as the remedy for the troubles of the contemporary media landscape. Although it empowers people to easily post and share content with each other, setting up a blog is of course no guarantee that anyone will read it. There is evidence that readership online follows roughly the same pattern as readership offline—a large majority of people get their news from a tiny number of sites, while a large majority of sites get virtually no traffic at all (Hindman 2008). Moreover, the Internet has not necessarily made it any easier to monitor the activities of the powerful—a key traditional role of journalism. And corporations are increasingly finding ways to subvert the apparently democratic nature of social media by hiring people to post and monitor content. Finally, the actual efficacy of online activism, for example in the Arab Spring, has yet to be proven. There is no doubt that activists are using Twitter as a key tool for communication and mobilization, but we don't yet know if this actually makes a difference to the outcomes. It is more realistic to say that the Internet has created both new opportunities and new dangers for the free media and for democracy.

In what ways has the Internet created new opportunities and new dangers for the free media and for democracy?

CONCLUSION CULTURE ONLINE AND OFFLINE

It is the nature of culture that it changes dramatically over time and across locations. The collective meaning and shared rituals of the Balinese cockfight from 50 years ago would probably be scarcely recognizable to contemporary Indonesians. And no doubt the culture of early twenty-first-century America will seem equally strange to Americans in 50 or 100 years. What would be shocking is if culture stayed the same.

But even compared to a baseline of ongoing cultural change, it is fair to say that a dramatic cultural transformation has been occurring in recent decades in the United States and throughout the world with the rise of the Internet and global cultural flows. Many of the most pressing questions for cultural sociologists in coming years, therefore, will likely be concerned with the cultural implications of the Internet and other new forms of interconnectivity.

We shouldn't make the mistake, though, of assuming that the increasing prominence of the Internet in society means that all of our important cultural questions will be online ones. The persistence of offline forms of social life—street life, public performances, print media, poorer communities that do not have easy access to the necessary technology, and more—in an online world will be an increasingly urgent focus of research and public policy. Will the digital divide get wider or narrower in years to come, and what will be the implications for cultural production, communications, and democracy?

 Watch the **Video** in **MySocLab**
Applying Your Sociological Imagination

Study and **Review** in MySocLab   **Watch** the **Video** Inspiring Your Sociological Imagination in MySocLab

---

What Is Culture? *(p. 114)*

 Watch the **Big Question Video** in MySocLab to review the key concepts for this section.

This section explored how sociologists talk about culture and the systems of collective meaning we make as a group.

THE MANY MEANINGS OF CULTURE (p. 114)

Culture as a System: The Balinese Cockfight (p. 115)

- **What are some collective symbols of contemporary U.S. culture?**

 Explore A Sociological Perspective: What is the meaning of this? in **MySocLab**

Culture as a Practice: Habitus and Tool Kit (p. 117)

- **How is culture actually practiced?**

Culture and Communication (p. 117)

- **In what ways is culture a form of communication?**

KEY TERMS

culture *(p. 114)*

symbol *(p. 115)*

ethnography *(p. 115)*

value *(p. 115)*

habitus *(p. 117)*

tool kit *(p. 117)*

language *(p. 117)*

cultural universal *(p. 118)*

mass communication *(p. 118)*

digital divide *(p. 119)*

How Does Culture Shape Our Collective Identity? *(p. 119)*

 Watch the **Big Question Video** in MySocLab to review the key concepts for this section.

This section explored how cultural practices both reflect and define group identities, whether the group is a small subculture, a nation, or a global community.

CULTURE AND GROUP IDENTITY (p. 119)

Mainstream Culture, Subcultures, and Countercultures (p. 120)

- **What distinguishes a subculture from the mainstream?**

 Read the **Document** *The Code of the Streets* by Elijah Anderson in **MySocLab**. This reading examines the subculture of the inner city poor and how their norms and values contradict those of the dominant society.

United States: Hegemony, Cultures Wars, or Multiculturalism? (p. 120)

- **How is the concept of culture wars at odds with the multicultural landscape of the United States?**

KEY TERMS

group style *(p. 119)*

norm *(p. 120)*

mainstream culture *(p. 120)*

subculture *(p. 120)*

counterculture *(p. 120)*

hegemony *(p. 120)*

culture war *(p. 120)*

multiculturalism *(p. 121)*

ethnocentrism *(p. 121)*

cultural relativism *(p. 122)*

global culture *(p. 122)*

Protestant ethic *(p. 122)*

national culture *(p. 123)*

nationalism *(p. 123)*

Global Culture (p. 122)

National Cultures (p. 123)

- **What produces and reproduces global and national cultures, and what effects do they have?**

 Explore the **Data** on The Culture of Living Alone in **MySocLab**

3 How Do Our Cultural Practices Relate to Class and Status? *(p. 125)*

 **Watch** the **Big Question Video** in **MySocLab** to review the key concepts for this section.

In this section, we discussed how people's cultural habits help define and reproduce the boundaries between high status and low status, upper class and lower class.

CLASS, STATUS, AND CULTURE (p. 125)

Cultural Capital (p. 126)

- **What is cultural capital, and in what ways have American elites become cultural omnivores?**

Symbolic Boundaries (p. 127)

- **How do symbolic boundaries relate to culture?**

How Culture Reproduces Class (p. 127)

- **What explains class and status reproduction over the long term?**

4 Who Produces Culture, and Why? *(p. 128)*

 Watch the **Big Question Video** in **MySocLab** to review the key concepts for this section.

The cultural field is the place for creativity and meaning making. But it is also a battlefield. In this section, we explored who controls the media and popular culture, and what messages they communicate.

THE CONDITIONS OF CULTURAL PRODUCTION (p. 128)

The Public Sphere (p. 128)

- **How does the concept of the public sphere explain how culture is produced in society?**

The Culture Industry versus Cultural Democracy (p. 129)

- **Is popular culture an industry or a cultural democracy?**

The Medium Is the Message (p. 130)

- **Does communication change with the form or medium?**

5

What Is the Relationship between Media and Democracy? *(p. 132)*

 Watch the **Big Question Video** in **MySocLab** to review the key concepts for this section.

The media are arguably the most important form of cultural production in our society. This section examined the media's relationship to democracy and the new ways in which it is changing how democracy works.

MEDIA AND DEMOCRACY: A CHANGING LANDSCAPE (p. 132)

Newspaper Citizens (p. 132)

Making the News (p. 133)

- **How do journalists make the news?**

Media Bias: Domination or Framing? (p. 134)

- **Why do certain topics get very little news coverage?**

Corporate Media Concentration (p. 134)

- **How much choice do U.S. media consumers actually have?**

Media, Democracy, and the Internet (p. 135)

- **In what ways has the Internet created new opportunities and new dangers for the free media and for democracy?**

 Watch the **Video** Applying Your Sociological Imagination in **MySocLab** to see these concepts at work in the real world

10
RACE and ETHNICITY

((• Listen to the Chapter Audio in MySocLab

by ANN MORNING, with NANDI DILL, RACHEL GARVER, and JOHN HALUSHKA

What exactly is race? Does biology play a role in it? What about culture? Is it something that people invented, or has it always been part of the human experience? The study of race and ethnicity has long been central to American sociology and has also featured prominently in other fields, like anthropology, psychology, and biology. Yet in spite of this longstanding scholarly attention, we have yet to come up with widely agreed-upon definitions of *race* and *ethnicity*.

About 10 years ago, I traveled around the northeastern United States to interview anthropology and biology professors about how they understood the concept of race. What I found surprised me because it ran counter to what many of my graduate school professors had told me—that social and natural scientists today all agree that race is a human invention without any basis in biological characteristics. When I actually spoke with anthropologists and biologists, though, it immediately became clear that their views on race varied a great deal and hardly reflected the consensus that my graduate school advisors presumed.

One of the discoveries that intrigued me the most was the way they used *me*—or more specifically, my physical appearance—to back up their views. In several instances, the professor I was interviewing would say something about *my* race in order to support his or her definition of the term in general. What struck me most, though, was that even with the same "data" at

MY SOCIOLOGICAL IMAGINATION
Ann Morning

My sociological imagination developed from my experiences growing up with people from many different cultural backgrounds. I was raised in Harlem, the famous African American neighborhood in New York City. But even though my home community was very ethnically homogeneous at the time (it isn't anymore), I was exposed every day to people from all over the globe because I studied at the United Nations International School. The contrast between those two worlds really got me curious about how social environments shape our thinking. As a sociologist today, my research focuses precisely on how people from different social backgrounds think differently about some of the things that seem most natural or objective to us, like racial identities or scientific knowledge. My research connecting these areas was recently published in my first book, *The Nature of Race: How Scientists Think and Teach about Human Difference* (2011).

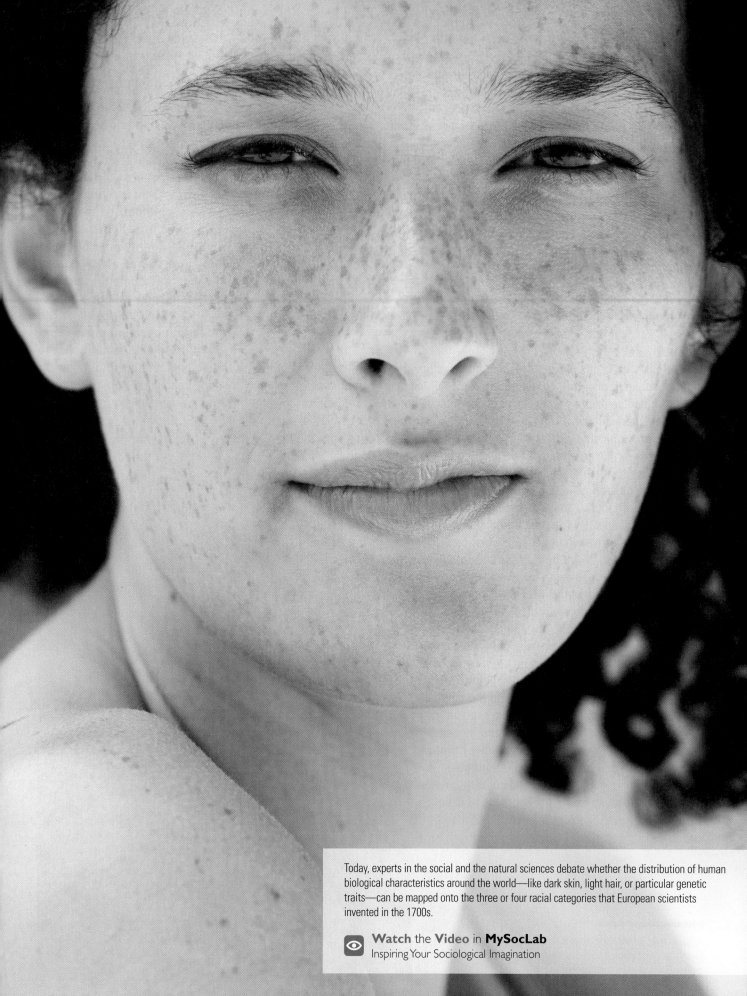

Today, experts in the social and the natural sciences debate whether the distribution of human biological characteristics around the world—like dark skin, light hair, or particular genetic traits—can be mapped onto the three or four racial categories that European scientists invented in the 1700s.

Watch the **Video** in **MySocLab**
Inspiring Your Sociological Imagination

hand—namely, me and my physical features—these academics came up with wildly different interpretations of race.

In one of my very first interviews, a cultural anthropologist at a large urban public university asked me how I identified myself in racial terms. It's a question I'm used to because with my African, European, Asian, and American Indian ancestry, people are often curious about my background. The anthropologist's reaction was to use me as evidence that race does not really have any biological underpinning. "You're a perfect walking example of why [race] doesn't work," he concluded. "I just wonder, looking at you," he went on, "how anybody could maintain that there are these hard and fast races...."

A few weeks later, a biology professor at a state university explained to me how race might come up in a lecture on genetics. Skin color, he suggested, "could be used as an example of quantitative genetics ... the general thought is that by and large, although there are some environmental influences, there are four sets of genes which determine skin color." Peering over his glasses at me, he mused, "I take a look at you, and you might have—don't be offended—you have, if there are four ... that means there are eight genes, and I would say you have three or four black genes and four or five white genes ... Just on skin color." In contrast to the cultural anthropologist who felt that my appearance disproved the existence of races, this biologist thought I was a textbook example of how race is rooted in DNA.

Finally, one rainy afternoon a physical anthropologist at an Ivy League university gave me a tour of his large laboratory, pointing out various human skeletons and the traits he argued reflected their racial heritage. Soon our talk turned to the uncertainty involved in determining race from skeletal remains. "Environments have changed enormously," the anthropologist explained. "There's been more intermixing." Then he turned to me and said, "I mean, if you give me your skull and so forth, and I look at your nasal aperture, I'm not going to have a clue that you have any black ancestry." But then he

corrected himself: "Now I might, given your teeth, because they're large."

As these anecdotes suggest, contemporary scientists' ideas about race—and what it has to do with biology, society, or anything else—span a wide spectrum. The cultural anthropologist thought it was impossible to identify clear-cut races (and thus that they do not exist); the biologist thought that race could easily be traced back to an individual's genetic profile; and the physical anthropologist allowed that identifying a person's race is not always easy but that ultimately our bodies display telltale signs of our racial heritage. For me, these encounters sum up a fundamental characteristic of today's scientific perspectives on human difference: thoughtful and highly trained specialists, working with the same data, have yet to reach a consensus on the basic question of what race is.

> **Thoughtful and highly trained specialists, working with the same data, have yet to reach a consensus on the basic question of what race is.**

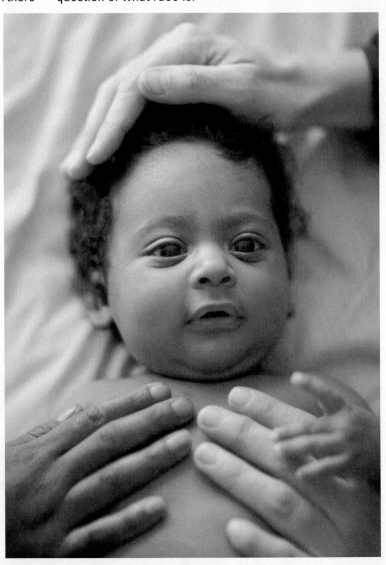

What exactly is race? Sociologists make clear distinctions between race and ethnicity and use the two terms to describe different kinds of categories and identities.

THE BIG QUESTIONS

👁 Watch the Big Question Videos in MySocLab

1 **What is the difference between race and ethnicity?** More often than not, the words *race* and *ethnicity* get used interchangeably, as if they mean the same thing. And indeed they have more than a passing resemblance. But sociologists make clear distinctions between race and ethnicity and use the two terms to describe different kinds of categories and identities.

Is race real? If there's one thing academics agree on, it is that race is real. Where they part ways is on the question of whether race is anchored in deep-seated physical differences between individuals or whether it is an invention that is not determined by human biology but which nonetheless is "real" because it has an unmistakable impact on daily life.  **2**

3 **What is racist and what isn't?** In classroom discussions of race and ethnicity, students often preface their comments with phrases like, "I don't know if I should say this, but …" or "I'm not sure what the right term for this group is, but …" Concern about the "political correctness" of our ideas, speech, and behavior is a prominent feature of both public and private conversations on race today. Sociologists have thought a lot about prejudice and discrimination, providing ample food for thought on racism in the contemporary United States.

Do race and ethnicity matter anymore? In the wake of President Obama's historic election, many people have wondered whether it is fair to say that the United States has entered a "postracial" era. Sociological research suggests that while it may not be too soon to talk about a "postethnic" era, race is still closely linked to socioeconomic inequality.  **4**

5 **How are race and ethnicity changing in the twenty-first century?** At the start of the twenty-first century, the face of America is very different from what it was 200 years ago. Immigrants come from a wider range of countries than ever before; people are more likely to marry partners from a different racial background; and changing attitudes have led more and more people to identify themselves as multiracial. These and other demographic changes will certainly have an impact on the nation's racial and ethnic makeup, on its patterns of socioeconomic inequality, and on its inhabitants' attitudes and beliefs about race and ethnicity.

1   What Is the Difference between Race and Ethnicity?

UNDERSTANDING RACE AND ETHNICITY

👁 Watch the Big Question Video in **MySocLab**

The introduction to this chapter described disagreement among social and natural scientists about the best way to define race. When we focus only on sociologists, however, we find that they share fairly precise understandings of both race and ethnicity.

The sociological distinction between the two terms runs counter to everyday practice, where *race* and *ethnicity* are often used as synonyms for each other. People from all walks of life—journalists, teachers, doctors, advertisers, and politicians—routinely use the two terms interchangeably. Even dictionaries lump together the two words. As part of its definition for race, the *Oxford English Dictionary* (2011) describes it as "[a] group of several tribes or peoples, regarded as forming a distinct ethnic set," or alternatively as "any of the major groupings of mankind, having in common distinct physical features or having a similar ethnic background." Similarly, one of its definitions for the adjective *ethnic* is "pertaining to race."

Why do we tend to treat race and ethnicity as the same thing? Sometimes the term *ethnicity* is seen as a polite replacement for *race*—a way to avoid using a term that is associated with racism, racial inequality, and racial discrimination. Another, less well-known factor may have to do with the federal government's designation of Hispanics (also referred to as "Latinos") as an "ethnic group," when Americans in general increasingly seem to view them as simply another racial group, akin to blacks, whites, and Asians.

How do contemporary sociologists define race and ethnicity?

But the confusion between race and ethnicity is also due simply to the fact that, at their core, the two concepts share a great deal in common. Both are systems for classifying human beings into groups based on shared ancestry. The crucial distinction between them lies in the different kinds of characteristics that are used to assign people to ethnic or to racial groups.

Sociological Definitions of Race and Ethnicity

Max Weber (1864–1920), one of sociology's founding figures, was also one of the first sociologists to define ethnicity and race. Weber described ethnic groups as "those human groups that entertain a subjective belief in their common descent," spelling out that "it does not matter whether or not an objective blood relationship exists" (Weber 1978). The most striking aspect of Weber's definition is that the key ingredient for ethnic membership is *belief* in shared descent. The subjective dimension of ethnicity would go on to become a central fixture of later sociologists' thinking.

Weber did not portray race as equally subjective, however. Instead, like most scholars of his era, he felt that races stemmed from "common inherited and inheritable traits that actually derive from common descent." This is an essentialist view of race (called **essentialism**); that is, it presumes that an individual's

Barack Obama, pictured here as a young man with his maternal grandparents, is often considered to be the United States' first black president. Given his multiracial family tree, however, there is no logical or scientific reason to classify Obama as "black" rather than "white."

racial identity depends on fundamental and innate characteristics that are deep-seated, inherited, and unchangeable. These traits are thought to be part of a person's "essence," their very being. Whereas Weber observed that many different characteristics or experiences could serve to indicate who belonged to which ethnic group—including physical resemblance, historical memories, and common cultural practices—he believed that it is physical makeup alone that determines an individual's race. In a nutshell, ethnicity is based on people's cultural practices, and race on their biological traits.

While contemporary sociologists share Weber's view of ethnicity, most reject his definition of race. Instead, sociologists today believe that racial identification is as subjective a process as ethnic classification. The major difference between race and ethnicity lies in the basis on which group boundaries are drawn. In other words, we look for different clues or signs when we think about a person's ethnicity as compared to their race.

Why then do contemporary sociologists reject Weber's description of race as based solely on inherited physical traits? The difference in viewpoints is subtle but meaningful. In a sense, today's sociologists have taken to heart Weber's message about the subjectivity of group definitions and have come to believe that even our perceptions of biological similarity are subjective. So our racial classifications are based not on some objective measure of physical resemblances (as Weber claimed) but rather on our beliefs and socially influenced perceptions of which kinds of people are biologically similar and which are different.

A useful illustration comes from the United States's **one-drop rule**, a custom that became enshrined in many state laws around the turn of the nineteenth century. According to this longstanding method of identifying a person's race, someone with one black grandparent and three white grandparents is a black person because their "drop of black blood" means they somehow have more in common with blacks than with whites. This is the same reasoning that leads us to label President Obama as black even though his mother was white. Clearly, there is no natural biological rule that makes him more black than white. Instead, there are social rules—cultural customs—that determine how we classify people by race and even how we "see" race.

Now we have all the ingredients we need to lay out definitions of race and ethnicity. In this chapter, we define **ethnicity** as a system for classifying people who are believed to share common descent, based on perceived cultural similarities. We define **race** as a system for classifying people who are believed to share common descent, based on perceived innate physical similarities. Framing the two concepts in this way makes clear how much they have in common, but it also highlights the fundamental difference between them.

Key Distinctions between Race and Ethnicity

Contemporary sociologists have written extensively on the similarities and differences between the concepts of race and ethnicity (Cornell and Hartmann 2004; Cornell and Hartmann 2007).

Which Matters More: Race or Ethnicity? One of the first things that researchers point out is that in any given place, the notions of race and ethnicity may not be equally important for people (Cornell and Hartmann 2007). In the United States, race has historically mattered much more than ethnicity. For most of the nation's history, being white was a necessary requirement in order to enjoy the full benefits of citizenship. Not only did whiteness protect one from enslavement in the antebellum period (1789–1860), but even after the Civil War, it opened access to the voting booth, to better jobs, to schools and hospitals, and to more affluent neighborhoods. Until 1952, only white immigrants could become U.S. citizens, and it was not until 1967 that nonwhites were allowed to marry whites throughout the nation. Although ethnic groups such as Irish, Italian, and Jewish Americans have faced considerable discrimination, their exclusion was not written into U.S. law to the same extent as race-based barriers. Not surprisingly then, racial differentials in key socioeconomic outcomes—like income, wealth, and educational attainment—are much wider today than

Which matters more, race or ethnicity?

Recognized ethnic groups are often, but not always, descendants of immigrants. These Hopi people constitute a distinct ethnic group in the United States, even though their ancestors were indigenous to the area, not recent arrivals.

comparable gaps between ethnic groups. In other words, being white rather than black makes a bigger difference than being Swedish rather than Polish, or Jamaican rather than Haitian—and that has been true throughout the nation's history.

Distinguishing Racial and Ethnic Labels So far we have talked about race and ethnicity in the abstract, without specifying just which groups are ethnic and which are racial. Any list or taxonomy, however, depends entirely on time and place. In my research on censuses conducted around the world (Morning 2008), I discovered that the official racial and ethnic categories used by different countries to classify their populations vary widely. In Guatemala, ethnic groups on the census include "Garifuna" and "Ladino" people; in Bulgaria, the main categories are "Bulgarian," "Turkish," and "Gypsies." The New Zealand census classifies people as "New Zealand European," "Maori," "Samoan," "Tongan," "Chinese," and "Indian" (among others), while Sri Lanka recognizes ethnic groups like "Sinhalese," "Sri Lanka Tamil," "Indian Tamil," "Sri Lanka Moor," "Burgher," "Malay," "Sri Lanka Chetty," and "Bharatha."

Despite such immense local variation, there is a rule of thumb we can use to distinguish racial labels from ethnic ones. Race is anchored in color terms—like "black" and "white"—that denote vast, continental groupings that include millions if not billions of people. "Black" might refer to people from sub-Saharan Africa or the Caribbean, "white" to natives of Europe. Even if they are not frequently used today, color terms like "red," "yellow," and "brown" refer to similarly large-scale groups: indigenous (or native) Americans, Asians, and Hispanics.

In contrast, ethnic groups tend to be much smaller in size and associated with local, national, or regional geography rather than with continents. It is not surprising then that different countries recognize startlingly different sets of ethnicities; they are concerned with groups that differentiate themselves within national borders. Sometimes these ethnic groups are considered native to the area, like Hopi or Navajo people in the United States; other times they are recognized to be descended from immigrants, like Korean Americans, German Americans, and Cuban Americans. Often though the historical distinction between native and migrant is murky. When the United States annexed large swaths of Mexican territory in the nineteenth century, many people went overnight from being residents of Mexico to becoming residents of the United States. Were these Mexican Americans then an immigrant or a native ethnic group?

Power Relations: Race as a Tool of Domination The concept of race gained much of its power and reach from Europeans' imperial encounters with Africans, Asians, indigenous Americans, and others beginning in the fifteenth century. Prior to that, Western medieval societies were divided by religion (i.e., Christians versus non-Christians), and going back even further, the ancient Greeks distinguished between themselves and "barbaric" peoples. But a color-coded hierarchy of race as we understand it today did not yet exist in the Western imagination. Instead, it was not until European explorers, armies, clergy, and settlers sought to dominate peoples across the globe that the race idea formed. Europeans came to believe that the differences they observed in appearance and behavior between themselves and others could be explained by intrinsic, racial characteristics. Equally importantly, they were persuaded that races fell along a hierarchy in which they occupied the top rung, so European domination and colonization of others was only natural. Beliefs about racial difference then grew out of a context of conquest, exploitation, and enslavement and were further cultivated to justify power inequalities.

With this colonial era as a backdrop, many scholars have argued that race—as opposed to ethnicity—has several features that reflect its historical use as a tool of domination. One has already been mentioned: races tend to be conceived as forming a hierarchy, with superior races on top and inferior ones on the bottom. Ethnic groups, in contrast, are not generally viewed this way. The distinction between Jamaican American and Trinidadian American, for example, is not widely associated with superior versus inferior value judgments. (Members of these groups, however, may be quick to point out their own ethnicity's relative merits.)

Another key difference is that racial categories tend to be imposed on individuals or groups by others, while ethnic labels

How did race come to be used as a tool of domination?

are more likely to be chosen for themselves by the individuals or groups concerned. This contrast can be described as external versus internal classification. Racial terms like "black," "American Indian," "Asian," and even "white" have historically originated with European-dominated states that enacted policies toward these groups that treated them as homogeneous masses, even if the individuals so categorized did not identify at all with those labels. The "Hispanic" category is an excellent case in point. Although the U.S. government considers Hispanics to be an ethnic and not a racial group, they have effectively been "racialized" into being considered by many to be a race comparable to whites, blacks, and so forth. Yet the very notion of a Hispanic race—or even a Hispanic ethnicity—is a very recent one, stemming from the federal government's attempts in the 1970s to develop a set of official racial classifications (Graham 2002). Before then it was not obvious that people from Central America like Mexicans and Guatemalans had much to do with people from the Caribbean like Cubans and Dominicans, let alone with people from South America like Peruvians and Argentines. So although they did not choose or invent the label for themselves, people with origins in any of these places now find themselves in a society in which, regardless of how they prefer to identify themselves, they are labeled by the government, other institutions, and other people as Hispanic.

Due in part to the United States's long history of classifying its inhabitants by race, individuals usually cannot choose their race (although they can fill out whatever they like on forms). A person who is considered by others to be black will probably not be taken seriously if she insists that she is white or prefers to think of herself as white. In contrast, ethnic terms are free from regulation by the U.S. government—that is, there is no official list of ethnic groups—and individuals have much more leeway in choosing the ethnic identity they prefer for themselves. Americans who ancestors arrived from many different European countries can choose which ethnic group(s) they identify with (Waters 1990). For example, a person with German, Irish, and French ancestry might prefer to describe himself simply as "Irish American" without facing others' insistence that he identify as German, French, or something else. Moreover, his reason for doing so—for example, because he inherited an Irish last name, or spent time in Ireland, or grew up in an Irish American neighborhood—would probably not be questioned.

2 **Is Race Real?**

THE SOCIAL CONSTRUCTION OF RACE

👁 **Watch** the **Big Question Video** in **MySocLab**

Sociologists often describe race as a **social construct**, or a social phenomenon that was invented by human beings and is shaped by the social forces present in the time and place of its creation. The idea of *invention* often leads people to assume that something that is socially constructed is not real. But since when are inventions not real? Thomas Edison invented the light bulb, but it is real. Steve Jobs invented the iPad, and it's real. The Beatles invented the real song "I Want to Hold Your Hand." Similarly, the belief that human beings come in four or five colors or flavors called "races" is invented—and it's real. Or to put it differently, races are real—but they are not biological. They are real social groupings that have real effects on people's lives, much like religious groups. No one would say religion is not "real"; it has exercised an enormous influence on human affairs since time immemorial. People have lived and died for their religious beliefs and identities. But we don't usually think of religious groups as being determined by individuals' biological characteristics. Instead, we understand that a complex array of social processes go into making a person a member of a particular religious group. The same is true of race.

Race and Society

The definition of race as socially constructed means several things. First is the idea that race is a classification system that is invented, created by human beings, and therefore man-made rather than natural. Second is the perspective that it is *socially* created—not the work of a single individual but rather the product of masses of people who form a society. In that sense, race is a lot like language: no single person invented English, or Spanish, or Korean, but languages are real social phenomena that millions of unnamed people have shaped. Third, the social foundation of race implies that as societies change, so do their ideas about race. Many sociologists, historians, and anthropologists investigate just how societal factors—such as economic conditions and organization, shifts in cultural values, or political upheavals—influence beliefs about race.

One puzzle that has fascinated researchers is how Americans' ideas about who is white have changed over time. Many people whom we consider to be white today would not have been classified as such a century ago. Americans of Irish, Italian, Jewish, and other European ancestries were routinely excluded from the white category. Consider for example the nineteenth-century Ohio newspaper that complained of Germans "driving 'white people' out of the labor market" (Jacobson 1998: 47). Or a century earlier, Benjamin Franklin's complaint that "[t]he number of purely white people in the world is proportionally very small," for

> ...the Spaniards, Italians, French, Russians, and Swedes are generally of what we call a swarthy complexion; as are the Germans also, the Saxons only excepted, who, with the English, make the principal body of white people on the face of the earth. (quoted in Jacobson 1998: 40)

In Franklin's view, only the English and some Germans could be counted as white, unlike Swedes, Italians, and Russians. The historian Matthew Frye Jacobson, who uncovered these long-ago examples of racial categorization, argues that the massive wave of European immigration to land in the United States over the period of roughly 1880 to 1920 had a major impact on who was considered white. If whiteness had seemed self-evident at the founding of the Republic, when the European-origin population was largely of English

descent (though with Irish, Scottish, Dutch, and French members as well), its boundaries were much less clear when immigrants began arriving from places like Poland, Italy, Greece, Hungary, and Russia in the late nineteenth century. As a result, politicians, scientists, and everyday people started to view the newcomers as members of separate races, distinct from—and inferior to—"true" whites, who were of northwestern European origin.

So why do we consider Polish Americans and Greek Americans today to be white? Or, in the memorable phrase of one anthropologist, "How did Jews become white folks?" (Sacks 1994). Paradoxically, it is because prejudice against these "nonwhite" Europeans became so great that Congress passed a law—the 1924 Immigration Act—that sharply limited the numbers of people who were allowed to emigrate to the United States from Southern and Eastern Europe. The sharp downturn in European immigration that followed meant that over the following generations, fewer and fewer Americans of European descent were immigrants who spoke foreign languages and practiced unfamiliar customs, while more and more were native-born, English-speaking U.S. citizens who embraced American cultural forms, from music and dress to sports and food. In other words, southern and eastern Europeans underwent cultural **assimilation**, a process by which immigrants come to be incorporated into their new society by taking on the cultural tastes and practices of the new society. For example, the first-generation Pole had a second-generation Polish American son, who might simply have a third-generation American daughter. And part of the process of becoming American for these immigrant groups was being quietly folded into the white population. At the end of this section, we'll explore whether other groups may become white in the future.

Changing American definitions of who counts as white lend support to the **constructivist** view of race—that is, the argument that racial categories are social creations, not biological facts. If race were simply a matter of our physical makeup, the boundaries of the white category would not have shifted so dramatically over the last 200 years; people's bodily characteristics have not changed over that time. What changed instead were Americans' beliefs about who belonged to what race, so they went about constructing and reconstructing race categories.

Race and Biology

The hardest thing for most people to accept about the constructivist perspective on race is that it seems to contradict what they see with their very own eyes. How can anybody claim that race is not a biological fact, when we can easily "see" race? Every day we come across people whom we can

How have Americans' ideas about who is white changed over time?

Racial categories are not simply straightforward reflections of human physical diversity; they have everything to do with the beliefs that are prevalent in the societies that use them. In the U.S., people from countries like India are considered to be part of the same 'Asian' race as people from countries like China, despite their surface physical differences. But in Canada, they are classified as members of separate races.

immediately identify in racial terms, for example as white or Asian.

The simple answer is this: We can easily spot surface physical differences between people. But the ways in which we then assign people to racial groups is purely a matter of socialization—that is, of having been trained (consciously or not) to pick out particular bodily characteristics and then associate them with particular groups.

Consider a very simple example. Pretend you are in a laboratory with a researcher who puts three colored blocks in front of you—red, yellow, and blue—and asks you to divide them into two groups. You might decide that red and yellow go together, while blue remains its own category, or perhaps you might choose to group red and blue together, leaving yellow on its own. There is no obvious similarity here, no clear-cut grouping of which two colors go together. But if every time you make a choice, the researcher corrects you by putting the yellow and blue blocks together and leaving the red apart, you will learn very quickly that the colors yellow and blue fit together. From that point forward, you will easily be able to classify yellow and blue—but not red—as part of the same group, even when you're asked to sort toy cars or beach balls instead of blocks. Matching items to groups based on color will become an automatic reaction you don't even have to think about; after a while, it will seem natural that yellow and blue go together, but not red.

Is race determined by biology?

Race works the same way. We grow up learning to look for certain pieces of information about a person's body (notably their skin color, hair color, hair texture, and eye color and shape) while disregarding other things, like height, weight, ear shape, and hand size, to come up with an idea of which race they belong to. And today at least, we're usually right: The race we think the person belongs to is in fact the race with which he or she identifies. But that does not mean that our racial classification of others, and their racial identification of themselves, are based on some innate racial characteristics they possess and that we simply observe. Instead, it's more like a situation in which, instead of blocks, we have yellow-colored, blue-colored, and red-colored people, and we've all been trained to think of the yellow and blue people as being in a different racial category than the red ones. In other words, both the observers and the observed share exactly the same mental rules of who belongs to what race. But that does not mean there is anything natural or necessary

about blues and yellows being matched together, or about reds being held apart.

Human beings vary in their surface (and other) biological traits as we move around the world. And we are very good at spotting physical differences between the members of our species. We can generally see physical differences between Norwegians and Italians, Italians and Nigerians, Nigerians and Ethiopians, Ethiopians and Indians, and Indians and Koreans. We can even see physical differences between siblings! But we don't generally consider those differences to indicate that a brother and sister are members of different races. Similarly, we may or may not consider the physical differences we notice between different groups around the world to reflect racial differences. For example, we can see surface differences between Norwegians and Nigerians and Koreans, and indeed we usually consider them to be members of different races. In these examples, racial difference maps onto observable physical difference. But in other cases, like the comparisons of Norwegians to Italians, or Nigerians to Ethiopians, or Indians to Koreans, we see physical differences between them but classify them as members of the same racial group. Despite their distinctive surface characteristics, in the United States today Norwegians and Italians are considered to be racially white, Nigerians and Ethiopians black, and Indians and Koreans, Asian. It is not biology that dictates that Indians and Koreans are members of the same race while Ethiopians are not, but rather socially created and widespread rules for grouping people.

In the last few decades, some scientists have started to argue that even if surface physical features are not a reliable indicator of race, genetic characteristics—that is, patterns in our DNA—reveal the existence of human racial groups. This assumption underpins criminal forensic experts' analysis of DNA evidence (extracted from crime-scene specimens like blood or saliva) to try to guess the perpetrator's race. It is also behind the new pastime of genetic genealogy, where companies analyze their clients' DNA to estimate the racial

In Brazil, race labels are meant to give more specific details about people's appearance in terms of facial traits, skin color, eye color, hair color and hair texture. This focus on physical appearance means that a person's race depends on how they look as much as if not more so than on their ancestry. As a result, even full siblings can be considered to be of different in races in Brazil. Would you say that the members of this family in Brasilia all belong to the same race?

makeup of their family tree. But just as in the case of sorting blue and red blocks, racial analysis of DNA starts with man-made rules for assigning individuals to racial groups. Before looking at a customer's—or a suspect's—DNA sample, scientists have to decide which characteristics of the DNA will be indicative of which kind of racial ancestry. And to do that, they have to come up with a list of which race(s) they believe are out there, and then sample individuals from those assumed races to find out what kinds of genetic characteristics they typically have. In the United States, genetic genealogy firms generally try to identify European, African, or East Asian ancestry. In the United Kingdom, where much of this forensic technology was developed, the categories of interest are "Caucasians, Afro-Caribbeans, and Asians from the Indian subcontinent" (Evett et al. 1996: 398). In both cases, scientists divide humankind into racial categories that are familiar given their society's histories. But the technology could be used with any kind of geography-based grouping—even a simple division of human beings into "red" and "blue" races. Once two or more categories have been created, and individuals selected to provide representative DNA for each of those categories, then it is simply a matter of working through a statistical algorithm for assessing how similar the particular customer's (or suspect's) gene variants are to those typically found within the "red" or "blue" sample. Crucially, the genetic genealogy companies' estimates can never be disproved or properly assessed: If you are informed that your ancestry is 30 percent African, 40 percent Asian, and 30 percent European, what independent and reliable data can you use to verify this statement?

For many people, the constructivist view of race is hard to truly grasp because it flies in the face of what we think we see and know. Its basic premise is that even though we may *think* race is grounded in human biology, it isn't really—it just claims to be.

Race and Place

The sociological view that race is socially constructed is grounded in a comparative (or cross-national) perspective. Depending on location, the race concept has emerged in different forms, at different times, or perhaps not at all. (By

Why is race understood differently around the world?

"race concept" or "race thinking," I mean people's beliefs about race including their notions of what it is, which groups are races, and who belongs to which race.) Because Western scholars have focused less on societies outside Europe and North America, the study of race thinking elsewhere is still in its infancy. But the research that has been done in this area offers some fascinating insights on important questions about race around the globe.

One question that researchers ask is how we can explain the noticeable variations in the way people around the world think about race. One study of West Africa found that local racial groupings like black, white, and red had little to do with individuals' surface physical appearance but instead were based on whether individuals were believed to have noble ancestry (which in this context meant Arab heritage) (Hall 2011). Similarly, Brazilians do not link physical appearance to racial group the same way Americans do; in Brazil, dozens of racial labels exist to classify people based on very specific combinations of skin color, hair color, hair texture, facial features, and so forth. As a result, full siblings can be of different races in Brazil, a situation that is unthinkable by American standards. Finally, scholars have noted that while contemporary Americans attribute racial differences to genes, people elsewhere (and at different times) have thought of racial difference as residing in the blood, or the mind, or the soul (Nelkin and Lindee 1995). What causes the race concept to take on such different forms?

To date, researchers have concentrated on two types of explanation for such variations in race thinking. The first is that as the Western race concept spread across the globe in the wake of imperial conquest, it blended with local traditional beliefs and prejudices to create many new versions of race (Dikötter 2008). For example, South Koreans' ideas of race today likely reflect a mixture of ideas brought by U.S. military personnel stationed there since the mid-twentieth century, historical Korean and Japanese color preferences, Confucian beliefs about groups' proper places, and longstanding images of Korea as being a nation based on shared blood (Kim 2008).

The second approach for explaining local variants of race tends to focus on demographic, economic, and political factors. Why, for example, have Americans traditionally classified people with white and black ancestry as black, while Australians thought that mixture between whites and Aboriginal peoples would result in white, and not native, descendants? A key difference lies in the economic roles that European settlers expected African Americans and Aboriginal Australians to play. Because black slaves in the United States were a source of free labor, it was in white Americans' best interest to increase their numbers, and the one-drop rule of treating mixed-race people as black was one way to add to the black population. In contrast, for white Australians Aboriginal people represented a source of free land, but to successfully occupy that land, they had to empty it of Aborigines. For the European settler community in Australia then, it was preferable to erase the Aboriginal population by absorbing it into the white one—or by removing it and concentrating it on undesirable lands (Wolfe 2001).

But why then did Brazilians develop a belief in the potential "whitening" of the descendants of black slaves rather than do the same thing as Americans and treat everyone with black ancestry as black in order to increase the slave population? Here demography (the characteristics of human populations) seems to have played a decisive role. Portuguese colonists made up a much smaller share of the Brazilian population than English settlers did in North America, and so they worried about being outnumbered by the people they enslaved. One solution to their problem was to fuel divisions within the African-descent population that would lessen the likelihood of slave rebellions, and color was a key tool for doing so. In other words, the Brazilian system for using many different race labels to describe people, rather than lumping them into a single "black" category as in the United States, was originally a way to create and emphasize distinctions between people whose solidarity might otherwise jeopardize Portugal's colonial venture in South America. Again, there is nothing natural or inevitable about the way human beings have created racial categories; the conventions and classifications we come up with are reflections of the social, economic, and political worlds we live in.

3 What Is Racist and What Isn't?

CONTEMPORARY RACISM

Watch the **Big Question Video** in **MySocLab**

Americans use the word *racist* to describe an astonishingly long list of things. In addition to labeling people as racist, we also talk about ideas, speeches, sermons, movies, songs, books, policies, laws, and political parties as being racist. Whether something

or someone is racist is often the subject of heated debate. Is the April 2010 Arizona law making unauthorized immigration a crime racist? Are sports mascots and team names representing American Indians racist? These controversies stem in part from the lack of an explicit, widely shared notion of what racism is.

What Is Racism?

For sociologists, the term **racism** includes two phenomena: *prejudice* and *discrimination*. **Prejudices** are negative beliefs or attitudes held about entire groups. They are broadly applied and are based on subjective and often inaccurate information. Prejudices involve prejudgments of individuals based on **stereotypes**, which are simplified generalizations about a group. These blanket images are hard to change because, as psychologists have shown, we tend to look for and remember information that seems to confirm our stereotypes while ignoring or dismissing information that does not support them. Explore *A Sociological Perspective* on page 273 to see how we often confuse race with ethnicity by drawing heavily on stereotypes when we dress up in costumes on Halloween.

Discrimination differs from prejudice in that it involves actions rather than beliefs. It includes any behavior that harms individuals or puts them at a disadvantage on the basis of their group membership. Discrimination maintains and reinforces social hierarchy by keeping subordinate groups from advancing. This can vary in degrees of severity. The mildest form of racial discrimination is the use of negative words or phrases in reference to a particular group. While names or phrases may be hurtful or even work toward perpetuating stereotypes, they do not impact people's life chances. A more extreme type of discrimination involves placing limits on people's opportunities based on their racial group. This involves preventing specific racial groups from equally accessing schools, employment, housing, and other institutions that are part of membership and participation in society. At its most extreme, discrimination can be carried out as acts of violence against an individual or members of a racial group. In the era following the Civil War, lynching was an act of racial discrimination used to intimidate, punish, and terrorize primarily blacks in the South. Many other societies, such as South Africa, Rwanda, and Bosnia, have also experienced violent forms of racially and ethnically charged discrimination, including **genocide**, which is the deliberate and systematic killing of a category of people.

Acts of racial or ethnic discrimination can be classified as individual or as institutional and structural. **Individual discrimination** is an intentional action carried out by an individual or small group that is meant to harm members of a certain group. An employer refusing to hire blacks, a landlord who does not rent apartments to Mexican Americans, or a group of teenagers who paint swastikas on a Jewish synagogue are all examples of individual-level discrimination. In these cases, individuals or small groups take purposeful actions to negatively affect members of specific racial or ethnic groups.

People are not the only actors who may discriminate, however. Sociologists maintain that institutions can also be discriminatory. **Institutional (or structural) discrimination** occurs when the actions or policies of organizations or social institutions exclude, disadvantage, or harm members of particular groups. Jim Crow—a system of laws and social norms that governed interactions between blacks and whites in the American South in the early twentieth century—represented an institutionalized system of discrimination. Schools, housing, transportation, and public facilities all formally engaged in discriminatory practices by keeping blacks and whites separate and in grossly unequal facilities. South Africa's system of apartheid is another example of this institutional form of discrimination where whites were able to secure their social position by excluding nonwhites from the majority of institutions.

An important difference between individual and institutional discrimination is that while individuals who discriminate do so intentionally, institutions' discriminatory policies may or may not arise from the intention to put certain groups at a disadvantage. An example of intentional institutional discrimination would be the United States' 1790 naturalization law, which explicitly stipulated that only white immigrants could become citizens. An example of unintentional discrimination could be the federal sentencing guidelines that penalize individuals in possession of crack cocaine more heavily than those possessing powder cocaine. Although the guidelines do not explicitly refer to race—and so do not appear to be intentionally discriminatory—the fact that powder cocaine is used disproportionately by whites and crack by blacks means that African Americans are more likely than whites to face the heavier penalties dictated by the sentencing guidelines. As this example suggests, however, it is not easy to determine whether institutional discrimination is intentional or not. Even though the guidelines do not overtly base criminal sentences on race, they may well have been adopted because they were likely to have a disproportionately harsh impact on African American offenders. Either way, sociologists consider institutions to be discriminatory if the ultimate impact of their actions is to exacerbate inequality, regardless of whether or not that was the intention.

> **Read** the **Document** *Names, Logos, Mascots, and Flags: The Contradictory Uses of Sport Symbols* in **MySocLab**.

Why Does Racism Occur?

Some of the earliest research on prejudice and discrimination was conducted by psychologists, who saw racism as an expression of particular personality disorders. Yet psychological approaches to prejudice have been criticized for overlooking the context that gives shape to the beliefs and behaviors that underlie racism. They also treat racism as if it

What is the difference between prejudice and discrimination?

A SOCIOLOGICAL PERSPECTIVE

Who are you going to be for Halloween?

Halloween costumes sometimes reinforce popular notions about race and ethnicity that a sociological perspective challenges, such as the belief that race is something we can readily see. Using recognizable symbols, they suggest that racial and ethnic groups can be differentiated by visual cues. What results are exaggerated misrepresentations drawn heavily from stereotypes that may be humorous to some and offensive to others.

These types of costumes also confuse race and ethnicity. For example, retail stores often label costumes as "Asian" or "Arabian" which are both broad geographic categories typical of racial groupings. However, the individual features of the costumes, such as attire and headpieces, represent cultural markers often associated with smaller, more narrowly-defined ethnic groups. Presented this way, race and ethnicity are shown to be interchangeable.

How could wearing this costume impact a child's perception and understanding of Native American culture?

Cute or harmful? Do even innocent representations of cultural stereotypes reinforce prejudice?

⊙→ **Explore** A Sociological Perspective in **MySocLab** and then . . .

▪ Think About It

How would you create a Halloween costume to represent the racial and ethnic group(s) to which you identify? Is it possible to make this costume without the use of stereotypes? Would it be recognizable in the absence of stereotypes?

▪ Inspire Your Sociological Imagination

What characteristics do racial and ethnic costumes tend to have in common, regardless of the specific groups they are meant to portray? And how do gender stereotypes influence the design of these costumes?

273

were an abnormal condition, when in fact, historically, large numbers of Americans have held prejudices and acted in a discriminatory fashion. Accordingly, sociologists have developed normative theories, which pay attention to the role of social rules and guides to behavior that vary across social contexts. Normative theories of prejudice consider the type of situations where norms are in place that could encourage or give rise to prejudicial beliefs or discriminatory acts. Through socialization, people learn the norms that operate in an environment or society at large. Research has shown that even very young children absorb racial prejudices and act upon them—for example, when choosing play partners (Van Ausdale and Feagin 2001). In short, people learn to think and act in a racist fashion—they are socialized into racism.

The challenge remains, however, to explain why racism comes to permeate a given society in the first place. Sociologists have responded by highlighting the connection between racism and power. Whether we think of the origins of racial thinking in contexts of imperialism and slavery, or more contemporary manifestations like the official racial segregation of schools until the 1950s, it is evident that racist exclusions and handicaps both reflect and perpetuate imbalances in the amount of power that different groups hold. Race-based hierarchies do not occur by chance but rather are the product of human efforts to acquire and preserve social privileges. In other words, we can ascribe racism to groups' sustained efforts, conscious and unconscious, to shore up their own status in society.

Does Racism Still Exist in the United States?

Researchers have used a wide variety of methods to gauge racial prejudice and discrimination in the post–civil rights era.

Prejudice Surveys today show relatively low public support in the United States for Jim Crow–era measures like racial segregation in public facilities or transportation. For example, in 1942, 68 percent of whites polled in a national survey were in favor of separate schools for black and white students, but in 1995, only 5 percent supported such an arrangement. Similarly, in 1958, 96 percent of whites surveyed opposed racial intermarriage, but by 1997, that figure had dropped to a third (33 percent). And while only 37 percent of whites in 1958 said they would be willing to vote for a black presidential candidate, in 1997, 95 percent said they would (Schuman et al. 1997).

Such surveys are not a sure-fire indicator of public prejudices, however. The optimistic interpretation of survey findings is that whites have become less prejudiced toward blacks over time. The pessimistic interpretation is that whites have simply become less likely to admit to racial prejudice, but their true sentiments have not changed much over time.

Accordingly, some scholars have turned to analyses of everyday talk for a better measure of how Americans truly think about race. Through long, in-depth interviews, they have found ample evidence that whites in particular often try to avoid openly discussing race and that they frequently use "color-blind" rhetoric that downplays the possibility of racism still playing a role in American life (Bonilla-Silva 2002; Frankenberg 1993). These studies pay attention to the strategies individuals use to resolve the tensions and complexities within present-day racial beliefs, like the conflict between prejudice and the idea that our nation is an egalitarian one.

Evidence that racial prejudice persists has also been taken from mass media portrayals of racial groups. These portrayals are often based on stereotypes in which minority groups are presented in roles that are defined by negative or demeaning characteristics. Studies of newspapers, television programming, and movies as well as the Internet use a research method called content analysis that looks for patterns in presence and meaning in order to study how racial groups appear in the media. Research has found that since the 1970s and 1980s, media representation of racial groups has become more diverse and positive, with minority groups taking on more prominent roles.

Discrimination Racial discrimination is not easy to measure in an era in which such behavior is widely frowned upon and, in some instances, legally prohibited. In many social settings it has become a form of deviance, a phenomenon that sociologists often try to study using indirect, unobtrusive, or anonymous measures. Surveys and interviews on the other hand pose the same problems for discrimination research as they do for the investigation of prejudice. For example, employers are not likely to admit to interviewers that they practice racial discrimination—and they may not even be aware of it. To adequately explore discrimination, social scientists often try to observe behavior through two principal strategies: experiments and ethnographies.

How can people be socialized into racism?

Does racial prejudice and discrimination still exist in the U.S. today?

Deryl Dedmon, 19, was sentenced to two concurrent life sentences for murdering a black man, 47-year-old James Craig Anderson, by running him over with his pickup truck in June 2011. What do you think this case says about the existence of racism in the contemporary United States?

One experimental study of discrimination garnered so much public attention that presidential candidate Howard Dean cited it during his 2004 campaign. Sociologist Devah Pager (2003) tested the influence of a criminal record on the resumes of black and white job applicants. With the help of two black and two white college students pretending to apply for entry-level jobs at 350 different companies, Pager demonstrated that the negative effects of a criminal record are 40 percent greater for black job applicants than white job applicants. Considering the disproportionate number of black men who have been incarcerated, this bias disadvantages a large segment of the black applicant pool. The study was also remarkable for showing that white applicants *with a criminal record* were more likely to be considered for a job than black applicants without one. Pager (2007:91) concluded, "Being black in America today is just about the same as having a felony conviction in terms of one's chances of finding a job."

Another widely noted experiment involved creating fictitious résumés of both high and low quality, and then randomly assigning some résumés either a stereotypically white name (like "Emily" or "Greg") or a stereotypically black one (like "Lakisha" or "Jamal"). The researchers sent out these fake résumés in response to over 1,300 sales, administrative support, clerical, and customer service job listings found in the *Boston Globe* or *Chicago Tribune* Sunday newspapers. Their results showed that when controlling for applicant quality and neighborhood, résumés with "white names" received 50 percent more follow-up phone calls than résumés with "black names." Moreover, an increase in the quality of the applicant did not reduce this difference. In fact, the study showed that the disadvantage of a "black name" increased as the quality of the résumé increased (Bertrand and Mullainathan 2004). Like the Pager study, this experiment makes a strong case that racial discrimination plays a significant role in employment in the United States today.

A different approach to investigating racial discrimination is to observe it ethnographically. Deirdre Royster's

(2003) study of 25 black and 25 white working-class men with comparable levels of intelligence, education, and dispositions toward work debunked the idea that the job market is a meritocratic and fair arena where the most qualified candidates are the first to be hired. In contrast, Royster found that employment was determined by social networks that led to personal referrals and recommendations among the white blue-collar community. Not only were black blue-collar workers disadvantaged by the absence of connections to owners, managers, or supervisors that were integral for white workers in finding employment, but the white blue-collar community erroneously perceived blacks as having an advantage through affirmative action policies and practices. This myth of "reverse racism" meant that white workers were often unwilling to make recommendations or referrals for black workers. Although the advent of affirmative action policies has been used to claim reverse discrimination, sociological research maintains that discrimination against racial minorities, specifically black applicants, remains a significant explanation for racial stratification in employment.

4　Do Race and Ethnicity Matter Anymore?

THE IMPACT OF RACE AND ETHNICITY TODAY

👁 Watch the **Big Question Video** in **MySocLab**

T he empirical evidence of ongoing prejudice and discrimination that social scientists have documented contradicts an image that many have of the United States. The passage of the Civil Rights Act of 1964 and the Voting Rights Act of 1965 – both of which legally prohibited discrimination – is often thought of as the culmination of the civil rights movement, marking the end of the long and arduous struggle to secure civil and political rights of African Americans and other minority groups. Many Americans point to the passage of these laws as the moment when race became insignificant in the United States. No longer were racial minorities legally prohibited from pursuing their academic, political, or economic aspirations. How could skin color be a barrier to success any longer?

How do sociologists explain racial gaps in socioeconomic status?

Sociologists have taken this question seriously. In addition to developing experimental, survey, and ethnographic measures of contemporary racism, they have conducted sophisticated statistical analyses that compare the socioeconomic status of different racial groups. According to almost any measure they have explored, a clear racial hierarchy emerges, with whites (and sometimes Asians) on top, and Hispanics, blacks, and American Indians on the bottom.

▯ Racial Disparities in Socioeconomic Status

To begin to answer the question of whether race and ethnicity matter in the contemporary United States, we need a statistical snapshot of how different groups live today. What the numbers reveal is that ethnicity no longer seems to have much of an impact on key life outcomes like who individuals marry, what kind of job they have, or where they live. In contrast, however, race continues to make a big difference on all these dimensions and more.

Income and Wealth　Nonwhite families have experienced substantial gains in household income since World War II. Despite these gains, sociologists and economists have documented persistent gaps in family income between white and nonwhite households for the last 40 years (see Figure 10.1). Although the income gap between white and minority families narrowed following the civil rights movement, this narrowing leveled off in the 1970s and has not changed much since. For example, the average black household in 2010 had a median income of $32,068. This is just 60 percent of the median white household of $54,620, an income disparity that has not changed significantly since the 1970s (U.S. Census Bureau 2011; Brown et al. 2003; Marger 2003; see Table 10.1). When we compare Hispanic families to white families during the same period, we see that the income gap between these groups has actually increased. In 1972 the median family income of nonwhite Hispanic households was 74 percent of white households, a ratio that has shrunk to 69 percent in 2010 (U.S. Census Bureau 2011).

In addition to income gaps, black and Latino families are more likely than white families to fall below the poverty line.

In 2009 a quarter of all black and Latino families were living in poverty, compared to just 10 percent of white families (see Table 10.1). The disproportionate number of black and Latino families that fall below the poverty line largely accounts for the different income patterns between white and minority families. However this general trend should not obscure the fact that there is a stable base of middle- and working-class minority families that earn incomes comparable to white families. In fact, if we compare college-educated blacks to college-educated whites, the racial gap in income is substantially diminished, although it does not entirely disappear (Marger 2003:279; Conley 1999).

Although there remains a substantial income gap among whites, blacks, and Latinos, it is important to note that whites are not at the top of the income hierarchy in the United States. As Table 10.1 illustrates, Asian Americans have the highest median household income among racial and ethnic groups in the United States. However, we should be cautious with our interpretation of these data. Because these data are not separated by country of origin or specific Asian ethnicity, they may cover up the fact that Asian families tend to fall at both ends of the income spectrum. For example, some Asian groups, such as Vietnamese and Cambodian Americans, are at the bottom of the income hierarchy, while other Asian groups, such as Chinese, Filipino, and Japanese Americans, are at the top of the income hierarchy (Marger 2003:367). These household income figures may also be misleading because they do not take into account the number of people in a household whose income contributes to the total. In other words, Asians' higher median household income may simply be the result of their households containing more working members than do white households.

In addition to the racial gap in household income, sociologists have also identified a racial gap in household wealth. Wealth refers to "the accumulated sum of assets (house, cars, savings and checking accounts, stocks and mutual funds, retirement accounts, etc.) minus the sum of debt (mortgages,

FIGURE 10.1 REAL MEDIAN HOUSEHOLD INCOME BY RACE AND HISPANIC ORIGIN: 1967–2010

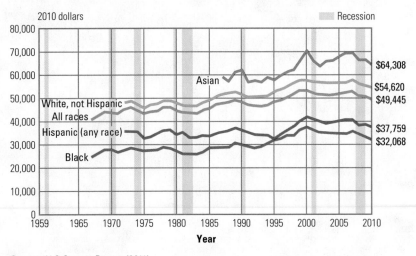

Source: U.S Census Bureau (2011).

auto loans, credit card debt, etc.)" (Kochlar, Fry, and Taylor 2011:4). While black Americans have made gains in income, education, and occupation since the civil rights movement, the black-white wealth gap endures and is central to current patterns of racial inequality (Conley 1999). The accumulation of wealth depends heavily on intergenerational transfers between parents and children (e.g., gifts, informal loans, and inheritances). Because black families have experienced multiple generations of exclusion from home ownership and other forms of asset accumulation, they have been unable to build up a base of assets to pass on from generation to generation (Massey and Denton 1993; Oliver and Shapiro 1997; Brown et al. 2003). Black families that are able to purchase a home are more likely than any other racial group to live in a segregated neighborhood, which diminishes property value and home equity, and they are more likely to receive unfavorable terms on their home mortgage than comparable whites (Brown et al. 2003:14). As a result the net worth of black families persistently lags behind the net worth of white families. Explore the Infographic *Race and Inequality* on page 278 to learn more about the changing demographic patterns and persistent trends in socioeconomic inequality in the United States.

TABLE 10.1 INCOME, POVERTY, AND UNEMPLOYMENT

Race/Ethnicity	Median Household Income in 2010	Percent of White Income	Percent of Families in Poverty in 2009	Unemployment Rate in 2012
White	$54,620	100%	9.9%	7.4%
Black	$32,068	59%	27.4%	13.6%
Hispanic	$37,759	69%	26.6%	10.5%
Asian	$64,308	118%	12.1%	6.7%

Source: U.S. Census Bureau (2011); U.S Bureau of Labor Statistics (2012).

Race and Inequality

Over the past 100 years the United States has experienced dramatic shifts in its racial composition. **In 1910, 89 percent of the U.S. population consisted of non-Hispanic whites, and the Census Bureau predicts that figure will drop to just 46 percent by the year 2050, making the U.S. a "majority-minority" nation for the first time in its history.** Despite these changing demographic trends, patterns of socioeconomic inequality remain a persistent feature of race relations in the United States. The most striking indicator of inequality is the racial gap in wealth. The recent economic recession took a far greater toll on the wealth of minority families, exacerbating these already existing inequalities.

Becoming a Majority-Minority Nation

Percentage of population that is white (non-Hispanic)

90%
80%
70%
60%
50%

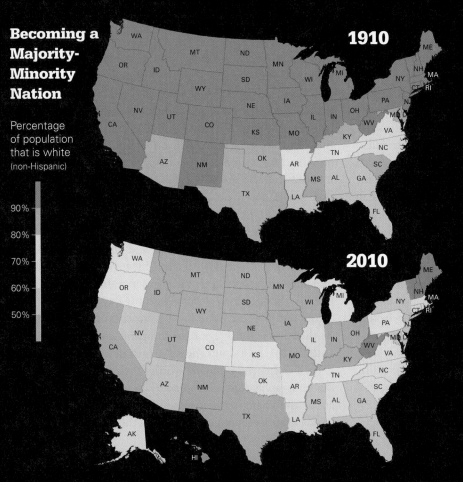

1910

2010

Sources: Based on data from U.S. Census Bureau (2012); Pew Research Center (2011).

 Explore the **Data** on Race and Inequality in MySocLab and then...

◼ Think About It
How might trends in fertility, mortality, and/or migration contribute to the decrease in the share of the white population, and to the relative increase in the Hispanic and Asian populations?

◼ Inspire Your Sociological Imagination
What might be some of the effects of America becoming a majority-minority nation?

Whites
2005: $134,992

2009: $113,149

The Wealth Gap

Despite changing demographic trends, the racial gap in wealth remains a persistent feature of socioeconomic inequality in the United States, reflecting generations of discrimination and disadvantage faced by minority families. The racial wealth gap is the largest it has been in the past 25 years, reflecting the uneven impact of the Great Recession.

Hispanics
2005: $18,359

2009: $6,325

Blacks
2005: $12,124

2009: $5,677

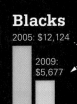

Down 16%

Down 66%

Down 53%

Median net worth of households, 2005–2009

Employment and Unemployment Since the passage of the Civil Rights Act of 1964, which legally ended discrimination in the labor market, African Americans have been able to move into middle- and upper-middle-class occupations from which they had previously been excluded (Landry and Marsh 2011). Many of these middle-class occupations are concentrated in the government sector, such as primary and secondary education, social work, and public administration. This is largely because antidiscrimination laws were more easily enforced in public bureaucracies than in the private sector (Brown et al. 2003). A smaller proportion of African Americans were also able to move into upper-middle-class occupations such as law, medicine, and executive and managerial positions. Despite these gains, blacks remain underrepresented in professional and managerial positions and overrepresented in the lower-wage service sector (Conley 1999:11). Moreover, sociologists have noted that upper-middle-class blacks still only earn about 85 percent of the income of whites in similar professions (Landry and Marsh 2011:385).

Despite the upward mobility of middle-class blacks since the civil rights movement, African Americans continue to lag behind whites in a key dimension of inequality: unemployment. In 2012 the unemployment rate for blacks was 13.6 percent, nearly twice the rate for whites (7.4 percent) (U.S. Bureau of Labor Statistics 2012; see Table 10.1). The black-white unemployment gap has been a durable feature of racial inequality since the 1960s. In fact, the unemployment rate for blacks has been consistently double that of whites in the 50 years since the civil rights movement (Conley 1999).

Education African Americans have experienced substantial gains in educational attainment over the last three decades. Between 1980 and 2010 blacks' rates of high school completion have risen by nearly two-thirds and rates of college completion have more than doubled, while rates of high school drop-out have shrunk by nearly half (see Figure 10.2a). Hispanics have experienced similar patterns of educational attainment since 1980. Between 1980 and 2010, rates of high school completion have risen by over 40 percent for Latinos while rates of college completion have doubled, and rates of high school drop-out in 2010 are half of what they were in 1980. However, many of the educational gains made by blacks and Hispanics during this period were paralleled by gains among whites. Thus, although blacks and Latinos have made a great deal of progress over the last three decades, gaps in educational attainment between whites, blacks, and Hispanics remain. At the same time, rates of educational attainment among Asians have remained high and stable since the 1980s. Asian Americans have the highest rates of educational attainment in the country. Rates of college completion

The unemployment rate for African Americans has been consistently double that of whites in the 50 years since the civil rights movement.

What patterns of educational attainment have minority groups experienced over the last 30 years?

among Asians are nearly triple those of blacks and quadruple those of Hispanics (see Figure 10.2b). Sociologists point out that the high levels of educational attainment among Asians are largely tied to the fact that Asian immigrants tend to come from middle- and upper-middle-class families, in contrast to the poor and working-class backgrounds of many Latino immigrant groups (Steinberg [1989] 2001).

Residential Segregation Despite the fact that the Civil Rights Act of 1968 outlawed discrimination in housing markets, African Americans continue to be the most residentially segregated group in the United States (Massey and Denton 1993; Sharkey 2008). In addition to being spatially isolated, black families are also more likely to live in low-income neighborhoods over successive generations than

FIGURE 10.2 GAINS IN EDUCATIONAL ATTAINMENT

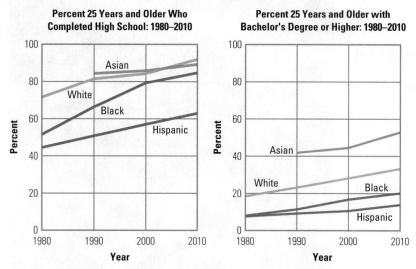

Source: National Center for Educational Statistics (2011a); National Center for Educational Statistics (2011b).

any other racial group. Over half of all black families live in the poorest neighborhoods in the United States and have done so over multiple generations since the 1970s (Sharkey 2008:933). Black children who grew up in poor neighborhoods in the 1970s were more likely than any other group of children to remain in those poor neighborhoods as adults.

Sociologists have documented how growing up in poor, isolated neighborhoods—or **ghettos**—severely truncates the life chances of black families. Residents of ghetto neighborhoods are more likely to attend low-quality schools and be exposed to crime and violence, and are less likely to have access to economic opportunities and employment networks (Sharkey 2008). Sociologists have also shown that residents of segregated inner-city neighborhoods have less political influence than residents of more racially diverse suburban neighborhoods (Massey and Denton 1993).

Why do disparities in health exist among racial groups?

Criminal Justice Supervision On any given day in America, over 2 million adults are serving time behind bars, accounting for a quarter of all prison and jail inmates worldwide (Liptak 2008). However, incarceration is not evenly distributed in the population. African American men account for 40 percent of the prison population—while accounting for only 12 percent of the general population (Pager 2007:3). In 2010 black men were seven times more likely to be incarcerated than white men and about twice as likely as Hispanic men (U.S. Bureau of Justice Statistics 2011; see Figure 10.3).

The incarcerated population is heavily concentrated among young African American men without a college degree. Among black men who finish high school, but do not attend college, nearly one in three will serve time in prison.

For those who drop out of high school, 60 percent will be incarcerated at some point in their lives (Western 2006). Sociologist Bruce Western calls this cohort of young, disadvantaged men the "mass imprisonment generation." For this generation of young black men, incarceration has become a common life event, more likely than college attendance or military service. Sociologists estimate that a third of adult black men have a felony conviction on their record. When misdemeanor convictions and arrests are taken into account, about half of all black men have a criminal record (Pager 2007:157).

Health and Healthcare Coverage Racial inequality is not just reflected in socioeconomic indicators like income, wealth, and education; racial and ethnic groups also show disparities in a variety of indicators related to health. For example, coronary heart disease is the leading cause of death in the United States, but African Americans are much more likely to die from this condition than any other racial group (Centers for Disease Control and Prevention 2011; see Table 10.2). African Americans also have the highest rate of infant mortality in the United States, a rate that is more than double that of whites, Asians, and Hispanics. One of the most striking disparities in mortality is in the area of homicide. For example, in 2007 the homicide rate for black males was over 10 times the rate for white and Asian males and about 4 times the rate for Latinos and Native Americans. Moreover, blacks have by far the highest rates of HIV infection among any racial or ethnic group in the United States.

FIGURE 10.3 INCARCERATION RATES PER 100,000 IN 2010

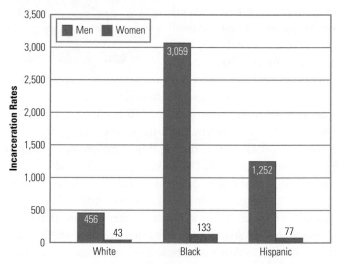

Source: Bureau of Justice Statistics (2011).

TABLE 10.2 VARIOUS HEALTH-RELATED INDICATORS

Race	Rates of HIV Infection of Persons over 13 Years of Age per 100,000 in 2008	Rates of Infant Mortality per 100,000 in 2006	Rates of Homicide per 100,000 in 2007	Death Rates for Coronary Heart Disease in 2008
White	8.2	5.58	2.7	134.2
Black	73.7	13.35	23.1	161.6
Hispanic	25.0	5.41	7.6	106.4
Asian	7.2	4.55	2.4	77.1

Source: Center for Disease Control and Prevention (2011).

The rate of HIV infection among African Americans is about 10 times the rate for whites and Asians and about 3 times the rate for Hispanics (see Table 10.2).

Many of these disparities in health are related to differences in healthcare coverage. According to the U.S. Census Bureau (2011), about 30 percent of Hispanics and 20 percent of African Americans lack a regular source of healthcare, compared to less than 12 percent of whites. As a result, African Americans and Latinos are far more likely than whites to rely on hospitals and clinics for their usual source of health care (U.S. Department of Health and Human Services 2000).

Political Participation and Representation Since the passage of the Civil Rights Act of 1964 and the Voting Rights Act of 1965, African Americans have experienced significant gains in political participation and representation. For example, between 1964 and 1972 over 2 million blacks were registered to vote in southern states, and since the 1970s close to 9,000 African Americans have been elected to political office (Marger 2003:287–288). In recent decades, black elected officials have become increasingly prominent in national politics. For example, during the 1990s and early 2000s African Americans such as Colin Powell and Condoleezza Rice occupied prominent positions in the Clinton and Bush administrations. In 2011 there were 44 black members of Congress, not to mention the fact that the president of the United States at the time of this writing, Barack Obama, is African American. However, despite the increasing visibility of African Americans in national politics, most black political officials remain predominantly at the state and local levels (Marger 2003).

Despite the gains in political participation that resulted from the civil rights movement, African Americans still face obstacles in exercising their voting rights. For example, a disproportionate number of African Americans are denied their voting rights because of felon disenfranchisement laws. *Felon disenfranchisement* refers to the loss of voting rights following a felony conviction. As noted earlier, African Americans make up a disproportionate segment of the population under criminal justice supervision. As a result, one in seven African Americans is denied the right to vote because of felon disenfranchisement laws. In some states, especially in the South, this number is as high as one in four (Manza and Uggen 2008). The disenfranchisement of such a large segment of the African American population has been shown to have significant consequences for electoral outcomes. Two scholars have estimated that if ex-felons had been allowed to vote in Florida in 2000, Al Gore would have carried the state by at least 30,000 votes and thus would have won the presidential election that year (Manza and Uggen 2008).

How have the high incarceration rates among African American men impacted their political participation?

How Do We Explain Racial Stratification?

Along almost any dimension of social and economic status, there are clearly significant gaps between different racial groups in the United States today. But how can we account for these inequalities?

Biology A century ago, American scholars would have embraced essentialist explanations that attributed nonwhites' poorer health outcomes to their natural physical inferiority, or that tied group differences in income levels to their inborn intellectual capacity. Sociologists today dismiss such biological explanations for racial disparities for several reasons. For one thing, they do not consider races to be biologically determined groupings but rather socially invented ones. For another, biologists claim that a trait like intelligence—if it were rooted in a person's genes—would probably not be distributed across the human species following the same pattern that supposedly racial traits like skin color are. And finally, attempts to measure and distinguish racial capacities or tendencies for things like intelligence, criminality, or other behavioral traits have been so obviously biased by researchers' stereotypes of nonwhites that they have provided very little in the way of a credible empirical basis on which to build essentialist theories of racial socioeconomic disparities.

How do sociologists account for racial inequalities?

Cultural Explanations Another longstanding approach to explaining racial socioeconomic inequality has been the cultural model. In the past, this meant attributing distinct and unchanging beliefs, norms, and values to separate racial groups and hypothesizing that these fixed cultures drove their members to certain behaviors that were advantageous or disadvantageous in the labor market, in school, or elsewhere in social life. Today, however, a more dynamic and complex notion of culture prevails, one where culture includes flexible worldviews and behaviors that people develop in response to their social context. In other words, this outlook connects culture and social structure as a way to explain racial stratification. In sociologist Elliot Liebow's ([1967] 2003) classic ethnography in Washington, D.C., it was found that black street-corner men's behaviors were not due to any intrinsic characteristics or to fixed cultural preferences but rather to the concrete obstacles these men faced in finding steady and adequate employment. Liebow argued black street-corner men's frequent decisions to turn down work did not reflect the cultural lack of a work ethic but rather a rational calculation concerning the marginal gains and physical stress brought by day labor. Therefore, he concludes that social policy aimed at eliminating racial inequality should not seek to reform individuals or modify cultural norms regarding traits such as persistence and patience but rather expand the structural opportunities open to them. In other words, culture may contribute to racial stratification not because it involves an unchanging set of values that group members are destined to hold but because it is largely a response to the structural obstacles certain races face in pursuing the American dream of upward mobility.

Structural Context Many sociologists explain racial stratification by pointing to opportunities and constraints that result from the structural environment—that is, from political arrangements, economic organization, and legal institutions. For example, the ebbs and flows of the U.S. economy create or restrict employment opportunities in ways that may affect racial groups differently. Early twentieth-century European immigrants were welcomed by a rapidly expanding U.S. economy. In contrast, immigrants since 1970, who are primarily from Asia and Latin America, have faced a tighter U.S. economy with higher unemployment and relatively fewer entry-level and low-skill jobs that can lead to long and stable careers. Consider too the many different ways in

which racial groups have "arrived" in the United States: Native Americans were at first forcibly excluded, then segregated in reservations; Africans were brought against their will to perform slave labor; and Mexican Americans and other Latino groups were originally incorporated through U.S. territorial conquest. And although voluntary immigration has historically fed the growth of both the Asian and European American populations, it is worth noting that the former faced an array of immigration, residential, and administrative restrictions that the latter did not. In summary, the economic, political, legal, and social roles these groups were assigned at the start of their American experience have had long-lasting effects on their socioeconomic status. The particular social, economic and political climate a group encounters when it arrives in the United States influences its initial status and potential path.

Historical Discrimination Racial inequalities created by formal and informal discrimination in the past continue to shape the stratification we see today. For example, historical legal and informal prohibitions against residential integration isolated racial minorities into underresourced neighborhoods, denying them access to quality public education, sufficient employment opportunities, and community infrastructure such hospitals or libraries that were taken for granted in white neighborhoods. Across the United States, there also existed thousands of "sundown towns," which prohibited the settlement—or even the presence overnight—of blacks, Asians, or Jews by force of law or physical threat (Loewen 2005). When blacks were able to move into certain areas, it often spurred "white flight," or the exodus of white residents. The historical residential segregation of African Americans and others has not only meant a loss of opportunities in the past that put their descendants at a disadvantage. The children and grandchildren of those who lived in underresourced neighborhoods in the past tend to live in the same places today, and they continue to suffer the same consequences in terms of education, health, and employment (Sharkey 2008).

Contemporary Discrimination We have already seen that many researchers, across different disciplines and using a wide array of techniques, have come to the conclusion that racial discrimination is alive and well in the United States. It may take the form of employment discrimination, where workers are treated differently by race when hiring, promotion, or firing decisions take place; it may show up on the housing market, when a person's race influences which neighborhoods or homes brokers and real estate agents will show them. Discrimination can be subtle or it can be blatant, and it can be intentional or unintentional. Whenever it materializes, however, it contributes to the racial

The mortgage lending crisis that emerged in 2007 hit black and Hispanic families disproportionately hard. African-American and Latino borrowers are estimated to have been nearly twice as likely as whites to lose their homes to foreclosure, like this house in Detroit.

inequality that has been a feature of U.S. society from its very beginnings.

☐ What to Do about Racial Stratification?

Racial stratification has been an enduring characteristic of the U.S. because for most of its history, white political elites expected and actively promoted such hierarchy. Moreover, the majority of the population felt it was natural and even desirable for whites to occupy the top economic, political, and social rungs. For at least the first 150 years of the nation's existence, white supremacy was effectively the law of the land, ensuring through both formal policies and informal practices that whites had unrivalled access to the best jobs, housing arrangements, education, and public facilities, among other things.

The idea that such racial stratification is unfair and undesirable has only recently been accepted by large numbers of Americans. The civil rights movement, largely a phenomenon of the 1950s through the 1970s, was at the heart of this sea change. Thanks to its strategy of large-scale, peaceful protest and of key court battles, in which Americans of all races participated, U.S. laws were rewritten or introduced to prohibit the favoritism toward whites that earlier laws had protected.

Civil rights–era laws—like the Civil Rights Act of 1964 or the 1965 Voting Rights Act—largely embraced a principle of color-blindness, forbidding the use or consideration of race in varied contexts like employment. However, a tool developed later in the fight against racial inequality is grounded instead in a color-conscious approach: the policy of **affirmative action**.

Affirmative action is a practice that involves considering individuals' race when making decisions that are likely to have an impact on existing patterns of racial inequality. The examples that have drawn most attention in the United States are those of college admissions and of employment. Should college admissions offices or employers take into account the race of the individuals who apply to their organizations in order to ensure that their student bodies or work forces are similar in racial makeup to the surrounding population?

Affirmative action is hotly debated, in part because it involves opinions on a whole series of issues that people don't often stop to tease apart. First, a person's view of affirmative action will depend on whether she believes racial inequality exists in the United States today. Second, even if she does think so, she may believe its causes cannot be addressed by social policy. If racial inequality simply reflects the biological and behavioral capacities of each race, there may be little public policy can do about it. If instead she believes that racial inequalities can be lessened by social policy, she may not think race-based affirmative action is a good instrument for doing so. Perhaps class-based affirmative action would be better. And finally, even if she thinks race-based affirmative action is the way to go, she may be unsure of how exactly to implement it. Should all institutions be required to implement it? (Currently very few are obligated by law to do so.) Should it take into account the races that people identify themselves with or the races that other people ascribe to them? And should it call for "hard" affirmative action—for example, numerical quotas or points—or "soft" affirmative action, like race-targeted college advertising or scholarships? In summary, affirmative action is a complex policy whose subtleties are often lost in raucous public debate.

After more than 150 years of racial privilege for whites, however, Americans are torn about whether we can eliminate racial stratification simply through formal, or legal, color-blindness. As President Lyndon B. Johnson famously put it in 1965: "You do not take a man who for years has been hobbled by chains, liberate him, bring him to the starting line of a race, saying, 'you are free to compete with all the others,' and still justly believe you have been completely fair."

5 How Are Race and Ethnicity Changing in the Twenty-First Century?

RACE AND ETHNICITY IN THE FUTURE

Watch the **Big Question Video** in **MySocLab**

"Interracial," "multiracial," "postracial"—is the United States on its way to becoming some, all, or none of these? One thing is clear: The face of America has changed a great deal since the nation's founding over 200 years ago. At that time, the former colony contained for the most part people from only three parts of the world: Northern Europe (especially England, Ireland, and the Netherlands); West Africa; and indigenous North America. The first U.S. census, in 1790, did not classify any races other than those covering these origins; official categories for Asians were almost a century away, and for Hispanics, closer to two. Yet by 2010, the most common ethnic ancestries among Americans were no longer limited to longstanding English or African American communities. Instead, the descendants of later European arrivals like Germans, Italians, and Poles are now among the most numerous in the nation, and "Mexican" ranks sixth on the list of the most common ancestries Americans report (Brittingham and de la Cruz 2004). An even bigger shift is apparent in the percentages of the U.S. population that the census classifies as white and black. In 1790, over 80 percent of the population was recorded as white, with the remainder labeled black (American Indians were usually not enumerated on the census at that time). By the 2010 census, however, whites' share of the total population had dropped to 64 percent, and blacks' from 19 to 12 percent. The Hispanic or Latino population is now slightly larger than the black one, at 12.5 percent, and Asians, Native Hawaiians, and other Pacific Islanders have grown to nearly 5 percent of the U.S. population. American Indians and Alaska Natives, neither of whom were carefully enumerated in the eighteenth century, together make up 0.7 percent. A final measure of change can be seen in the more than 9 million individuals (almost 3 percent of the total population) who were identified on the 2010 census with two or more races (Humes, Jones and Ramirez 2011). They exercised a right to identify with more than one race that had been available on the census only since 2000.

Changes in demographic makeup, however, are only part of the story of how race and ethnicity are changing in our lifetimes. In this concluding section, we will explore not only the factors behind transformations in the nation's population composition but also investigate how racial and ethnic stratification, identities, classifications, and conceptions are rapidly changing. In all these areas, we will take a look backward in time to see what trends have brought us to the present and to consider the predictions that social scientists make about the future.

☐ A Changing Population

In November 1993, *TIME* magazine put on its cover a beautiful young woman who smiled at readers over the title, "The New Face of America." Her tawny skin, light brown eyes, and chestnut hair gave no clue to her ethnic origins. And no wonder: The image was not a picture of a real person, but rather a morphed composition assembled from photographs of dozens of individuals from a wide array of ancestries. According to *TIME*, the morphed face was "15% Anglo-Saxon, 17.5% Middle Eastern, 17.5% African, 7.5% Asian, 35% Southern European and 7.5% Hispanic." Its purpose was to illustrate "How Immigrants Are Shaping the World's First Multicultural Society."

Although the United States is far from being the first multicultural society, the exaggeration tells us something about the story that Americans tell themselves about how the country has changed over the last two centuries. As the *TIME* magazine headlines suggest, it is a narrative about a nation whose growing tolerance leads to greater immigration and interracial mixture over time.

What this account overlooks is that the United States has always been a multiracial—not to mention multicultural—society. From its earliest beginnings as a collection of English colonies, racial intermixture was common. As far back as the 1630s and 1640s, colonial records attest to interracial sexual unions and mixed-race offspring (Williamson 1980). As the enslavement of Africans continued over the next two centuries, interracial mixing—notably through the coercion of black female slaves by white male slaveowners—was so widespread that by 1915, the U.S. Census Bureau estimated that three-quarters of the black population had some nonblack ancestry (U.S. Census Bureau 1918). Similarly, Latino people are largely of mixed European, Native American, and African descent. Yet we do not usually include Hispanics and African Americans in our picture of multiracial America because their mixed ancestry is old, dating back to the eras of slavery and colonial conquest. Instead, we prefer to think of multiraciality as something new, linked to the contemporary era in which individuals have had new freedom to enter voluntarily into interracial relationships. The artificiality of this picture of multiracial America is sharply conveyed by the writer Danzy Senna's comment on the *TIME* magazine photomorphed image: "Of course, anyone could see that women just like the computer face they had created did exist in Puerto Rico, Latin America, and Spanish Harlem" (quoted in Streeter 2003: 305).

If neither interracial unions nor multiracial people are new in the United States, what *has* changed is our attitudes toward them. In 1967, the Supreme Court struck down all state laws banning interracial marriage. In 1997, the federal government revised its official racial classifications to permit individuals to identify with more than one race. Both decisions signaled a sea change in Americans' willingness to recognize and even accept new ways of thinking about race. These policy shifts are mirrored in both public attitudes and behaviors. In 1958, 96 percent of whites surveyed disapproved of intermarriage, but nearly 40 years later, in 1997, that share had dropped to 33 percent (Schuman et al. 1997). Correspondingly, in the last 30 years, the percentage of newlyweds married to someone of a different race or ethnicity has more than doubled: Less than 7 percent of the individuals

Professional golfer Tiger Woods is of Asian, African, European, and American Indian descent. He is just one of a long list of 21st-century celebrities—like Jessica Alba, Paula Abdul, or Keanu Reeves—whose multiracial or multiethnic ancestry is widely known and accepted.

who married in 1980 had a spouse of another race or ethnicity, but in 2010, more than 15 percent did. More than a third of U.S. adults now say they have an immediate family member or close relative who is married to someone of a different race (Wang 2012). National statistics also show an increase in the mixed-race population. From 2000, when the U.S. census first counted multiracial people, to 2010, the number of people identified with more than one race rose from fewer than 7 million to more than 9 million, or nearly 3 percent of the total population (Humes, Jones and Ramirez 2011).

These statistics have several limitations. Figures on interracial marriages do not include people who live together or have other intimate relationships. Census counts of mixed-race people exclude large numbers of people who

How have attitudes toward interracial unions and multiracial people changed in the United States?

TABLE 10.3 THREE WAVES OF IMMIGRATION

Approximate Time Period	Immigration Wave	Origin Countries
1820–1870	The Frontier Expansion	• Brought over 7 million immigrants, largely Irish, German, and Scandinavian, who were drawn to homesteading and farming opportunities. • Immigration from Asia also began in this era, although efforts would soon be made to stem it, starting with the 1882 Chinese Exclusion Act designed to bar Chinese migrants from entry.
1880–1925	Ellis Island	• Brought southern and eastern Europeans in large numbers for the first time, channeling them to cities and industrial work.
1965–present	Immigration and Nationality Act	• After a long hiatus, immigration picked up in mid-twentieth century. • Immigration and Nationality Act of 1965 was designed to even out old immigration barriers that sought to exclude immigrants not from Northern Europe. • Today's immigrants are more diverse than ever, with most coming from Asia, Latin America, and the Caribbean.

Note: This table refers to the countries from which immigrants arrive in the U.S. In contrast, the discussion of "immigration eras" in Chapter 12 refers to the immigration laws that were in place at different points in U.S. history.

have multiracial ancestry—like most African Americans and Latinos—but who are not aware of or choose not to report their mixed background. These and other shortcomings make it difficult to compare the numbers of interracial unions and multiracial people today to those in the past. However, the statistics that are available do point to an upward trend underway for both.

Immigration is the other major demographic trend to reshape the racial and ethnic makeup of the United States. Here there is no question that the twenty-first century is very different from the nineteenth century. The United States has undergone three major waves of immigration since its founding, and each has left its mark on the nation's demographic composition, as indicated in Table 10.3 (Kritz and Gurak 2004). According to the Population Reference Bureau, 20 percent of the world's migrants live in the United States (Martin and Midgley 2010). And in sharp contrast to the European predominance in the two previous immigration waves, today's immigrants are overwhelmingly from Asia, Latin America, and the Caribbean. Of the foreign-born individuals who entered the United States in 2008 or later, 40 percent came from Asia and 35 percent from Latin America and the Caribbean. The top six sending countries of immigrants to the United States are Mexico, China, India, the Philippines, Vietnam, and El Salvador (Walters and Trevelyan 2011).

As remarkable as these changes are, demographic changes in the twenty-first century may be just as striking. The U.S. Census Bureau has forecast that before mid-century, the non-Hispanic white population of the United States will shrink to less than half of the total. Current Bureau projections for 2050 put the white share of the U.S. population at 46 percent, Hispanics at 30 percent, blacks at 12 percent, Asians at 8 percent, American Indians and Alaska Natives at 1 percent, and multiracial people at 3 percent. These estimates are of course based on many assumptions—about fertility, mortality, and migration—that may not hold true. These projections presume the continuation of trends that have been underway for decades now: the decrease in the white population and stability in the black and American Indian ones, compared to dynamic growth among both Hispanic and Asian Americans. However, another factor may play a role in ways that are difficult to anticipate now: namely, the choices that people will make about how to identify themselves in racial and ethnic terms and the options they are given for doing so.

How has the U.S. census adapted to the evolving shifts in how Americans identify themselves?

☐ Changing Classification and Identity

The twentieth century saw several major shifts in how Americans identified themselves—and were identified by others—in terms of race and ethnicity. And in fact, census racial and ethnic categories have changed almost every 10 years in the United States (Lee 1993). The only group that has consistently been named on the census is white; everything else was added later, anywhere from the eighteenth to the twentieth century (see Table 10.4). Will the next 100 years usher in another round of momentous change in the ways Americans classify by race and ethnicity?

TABLE 10.4 RACE CATEGORIES ON U.S. CENSUS IN 1810, 1910, AND 2010

1810: Free White Males; Free White Females; All Other Free Persons, Except Indians Not Taxed; Slaves

1910: White; Black; Mulatto; Chinese; Japanese; Indian; Other

2010: White; Black, African Am., or Negro; American Indian or Alaska Native; Asian Indian; Chinese; Filipino; Japanese; Korean; Vietnamese; Native Hawaiian; Guamanian or Chamorro; Samoan; Other Asian; Other Pacific Islander; Some other race

Sources: U.S. Census Bureau (1918); Lee (1993); Nobles (2000).

The growing demographic diversity of the United States suggests that it will become more and more common for Americans to share workplaces, schools, families, and social settings with people of different races.

Perhaps the most significant change in recent years has been the federal government's shift in 1997 to allow people to identify themselves with more than one race when filling out the census or other official documents. Although government policies are not a direct reflection of how everyday people think about racial and ethnic categories, the emergence of grassroots organizations for mixed-race people in recent decades suggests that Americans have grown increasingly accepting of the idea that a person might belong to more than one race (DaCosta 2007; Williams 2006).

A change that has yet to take place but that seems likely in the future is the inclusion of "Hispanic/Latino" as a race on government forms. At present the U.S. government considers Hispanics to constitute an ethnic group and so does not include it on the census race question. In the wider society, however, the terms *Hispanic* and *Latino* tend to be used as if they were akin to races: journalists, politicians, academics, and everyday people use phrases like "blacks, whites, and Latinos," suggesting that Hispanics are seen as a racial group like "whites" and "blacks." Moreover, the current lack of a "Hispanic or Latino" category on the census creates problems for people who would rather identify themselves using those terms instead of being forced to choose among options like "white," "black," and "American Indian or Alaska Native." As a result, large numbers of Hispanic people select "Some other race."

☐ Changing Stratification

Immigration inflows that are more diverse than ever, rising rates of interracial marriage, and new openness to multiracial identities—what impact will these demographic and social changes have on racial inequality in the United States? Some observers believe they all point the way to a more racially inclusive and egalitarian society. Consider for example these newspaper headlines: "A New Generation Is Leading the Way: What Young People of Mixed Race Can Tell Us about the Future of Our Children" (Jackson Nakazawa 2003) or "The New Face of America: Blended Races Making a True Melting Pot" (Puente and Kasindorf 1999). The basic idea is that demographic trends reveal a new openness to bridging historical racial divides, and therefore that race is growing less significant as a factor in social, political, and economic life.

A closer look, however, suggests that while race may be becoming less important for some groups, it remains a powerful barrier for others. The question, as sociologists Jennifer Lee and Frank Bean (2004: 221) put it, is "whether racial boundaries are fading for all groups or whether America's newcomers are simply crossing over the color line rather than helping to eradicate it." It is important to note, for example, that although the rate of interracial marriage overall has grown considerably in recent years, Asian and Hispanic newlyweds are more likely than blacks to have spouses of a different race (Wang 2012). In addition, individuals of mixed-race ancestry are more likely to identify themselves (or be identified) as multiracial if they have Asian ancestry but to be assigned to a single race—black—if they have African ancestry (Gullickson and Morning 2011). And as we have seen, race is still associated with pronounced differences in socioeconomic status, with blacks, Hispanics, and American Indians generally worse off than whites and Asians. These kinds of findings have led some scholars to conclude that the color line is hardly disappearing from American life; it is simply shifting from one that separated whites from nonwhites to one that distinguishes blacks from nonblacks. In other words, we may have a new "beige majority" (Lind 1995) where whites, most Asians, light-skinned Latinos, and mixed-race people can all lead lives relatively free of racial discrimination, while darker Hispanics, some Asians, Native Americans, and blacks remain stigmatized by color (Gans 1999).

Other sociologists take a more optimistic view. Over the next 20 years, the post–World War II "baby boom" generation, born between 1946 and 1966, will gradually retire from the work force. They will be replaced by a younger cohort that has a much smaller percentage of whites, thus placing larger shares of nonwhites in the relatively good jobs that the baby boomers held. In his recent analysis of the U.S. labor market, Richard Alba (2009) foresees a smooth transfer of opportunities for a comfortable middle-class life from whites to nonwhites without competitive conflict. Older whites will simply leave good jobs vacant, and a mix of younger people, white and nonwhite, will move into them. Alba stresses that this is not a foregone conclusion; for example, he calls on the nation to invest more wisely in blacks' and Hispanics' education to better prepare the future work force. His vision, however, reminds us that race and ethnicity—both as ideas and as structuring

What impact will demographic and social changes have on racial inequality in the United States?

social forces—have never been static, and that even as short a time span as a quarter-century may bring about striking changes.

CONCLUSION DEVELOPING A SOCIOLOGICAL IMAGINATION ON RACE AND ETHNICITY

In trying to uncover the cultural and structural forces that shape our lives, even when we are not aware of them, sociologists often come up with answers that are not intuitive, because they go against the grain of common sense. The study of race is a good example. It is an everyday term for Americans, and one that we usually think is a straightforward descriptor of people's physical characteristics. What sociology tells us, though, is that there are no such simple, obvious groupings of human beings based on bodily traits, and that labels like "black" and "white" tell us more about the way societies choose to classify people than it does about the individuals who get assigned to those categories. In this area as in so many others, developing a sociological imagination means looking beyond widespread beliefs that are too often taken for granted.

Watch the **Video** in **MySocLab**
Applying Your Sociological Imagination

1 What Is the Difference between Race and Ethnicity? *(p. 264)*

👁 **Watch** the **Big Question Video** in **MySocLab** to review the key concepts for this section.

More often than not, the words race and ethnicity get used interchangeably, as if they mean the same thing. In this section, we discussed how sociologists make clear distinctions between race and ethnicity and how they use the terms to describe different kinds of categories and identities.

UNDERSTANDING RACE AND ETHNICITY (p. 264)

Sociological Definitions of Race and Ethnicity (p. 264)

- **How do contemporary sociologists define race and ethnicity?**

Key Distinctions between Race and Ethnicity (p. 265)

- **Which matters more, race or ethnicity?**
- **How did race come to be used as a tool of domination?**

2 Is Race Real? *(p. 267)*

👁 **Watch** the **Big Question Video** in **MySocLab** to review the key concepts for this section.

If there's one thing academics agree on, it is that race is real. But is race anchored in deep-seated physical differences between individuals or is it an invention that is not determined by human biology but is real because it has an unmistakable impact on daily life?

THE SOCIAL CONSTRUCTION OF RACE (p. 267)

Race and Society (p. 268)

- **How have Americans' ideas about who is white changed over time?**

Race and Biology (p. 268)

- **Is race determined by biology?**

Race and Place (p. 270)

- **Why is race understood differently around the world?**

3 What Is Racist and What Isn't? *(p. 271)*

 Watch the **Big Question Video** in **MySocLab** to review the key concepts for this section.

Concern about the "political correctness" of our ideas, speech, and behavior is a prominent feature of both public and private conversations on race today. Sociologists have thought a lot about prejudice and discrimination, providing ample food for thought on racism in the contemporary United States.

CONTEMPORARY RACISM (p. 271)

What Is Racism (p. 272)

- **What is the difference between prejudice and discrimination?**

 Explore A Sociological Perspective: Who are you going to be for Halloween? in **MySocLab**

 Read the **Document** *Names, Logos, Mascots, and Flags: The Contradictory Uses of Sport Symbols* by Stanley D. Eitzen in **MySocLab.** This reading demonstrates the importance of language and symbols in society.

Why Does Racism Occur? (p. 272)

- **How can people be socialized into racism?**

Does Racism Still Exist in the United States? (p. 274)

- **Does racial prejudice and discrimination still exist in the U.S. today?**

4 Do Race and Ethnicity Matter Anymore? *(p. 276)*

 Watch the **Big Question Video** in **MySocLab** to review the key concepts for this section.

Many people today wonder whether it is fair to say that the United States has entered a "postracial" era. This section discussed how sociologists suggest that race is still closely linked to socioeconomic inequality today.

THE IMPACT OF RACE AND ETHNICTY TODAY (p. 276)

Racial Disparities in Socioeconomic Status (p. 276)

- **How do sociologists explain racial gaps in socioeconomic status?**

 Explore the **Data** on Race and Inequality in **MySocLab**

- **What patterns of educational attainment have minority groups experienced over the last 30 years?**
- **Why do disparities in health exist among racial groups?**
- **How have the high incarceration rates among African American men impacted their political participation?**

How Do We Explain Racial Stratification? (p. 281)

- **How do sociologists account for racial inequalities?**

What to Do about Racial Stratification? (p. 283)

KEY TERMS

racism *(p. 272)*

prejudice *(p. 272)*

stereotype *(p. 272)*

discrimination *(p. 272)*

genocide *(p. 272)*

individual discrimination *(p. 272)*

institutional discrimination *(p. 272)*

KEY TERMS

ghetto *(p. 280)*

affirmative action *(p. 283)*

5 How Are Race and Ethnicity Changing in the Twenty-First Century? *(p. 284)*

 Watch the **Big Question Video** in **MySocLab** to review the key concepts for this section.

The face of America today is very different from what it was 200 years ago. In this section, we explored the demographic changes in the U.S. that have impacted its racial and ethnic makeup, patterns of socioeconomic inequality, and attitudes and beliefs about race and ethnicity.

RACE AND ETHNICITY IN THE FUTURE (p. 284)

A Changing Population (p. 284)

- **How have attitudes toward interracial unions and multi-racial people changed in the United States?**
- **How has the U.S. census adapted to the evolving shifts in how Americans identify themselves?**

Changing Classification and Identity (p. 286)

Changing Stratification (p. 287)

- **What impact will demographic and social changes have on racial inequality in the United States?**

 Watch the **Video** Applying Your Sociological Imagination in **MySocLab** to see these concepts at work in the real world

13
FAMILIES and FAMILY LIFE

by KATHLEEN GERSON
with STACY TORRES

"T"hat's a typical family." We've all heard this phrase before, but is there a typical family? And how can we really know what life is like in someone else's home? Often our perceptions as outside observers are quite different from the perceptions of those who are family members. Consider the story of 24-year-old Josh, who grew up in Oceanside Terrace, a small working-class suburban community on Long Island not far from the hustle and bustle of New York City. In a survey, Josh had reported growing up with his biological parents and two brothers in a household where his mother stayed home during his preschool years. From the outside, Josh's childhood home seemed to be what Americans tend to think of as a typical, traditional family, but his family experience was much more complex than it appeared. Josh was back for a brief visit to celebrate his parents' anniversary before moving to a new job on the West Coast when I sat down with him one morning to talk about his family life.

Josh grew up with his biological parents and two brothers in the kind of household Americans like to call "traditional" (for an overview of this period, see Coontz 1992). His father was a carpenter, and his mother stayed home during his preschool years, but Josh recounts a sequence of events that left him feeling as if he lived in three different families. The first, anchored by a breadwinning father and a home-centered mother, did indeed take a traditional form. Yet this outward appearance mattered less to him than his parents' constant fighting over money, housework, and the drug habit his father developed in the army. "All I remember is just being real upset, not being able to look at the benefits if it would remain like that, having all the fighting and that element in the house," Josh tells me.

MY SOCIOLOGICAL IMAGINATION
Kathleen Gerson

My sociological imagination began when I realized I was part of—yet stood apart from—the world around me. Born in the deep South, I grew up in a community where traditional homes and worldviews were the norm. Yet my own family was headed by a single mother strongly committed to social justice. As I developed a sense of being both an insider and an outsider, I learned to see the world from several vantage points at once. A move to San Francisco during adolescence deepened my questioning of what others took for granted. By the time I reached college, these experiences had attuned me to the power of social contexts. Sociology offered a place to address the big issues facing contemporary societies. With that aim in mind, my research focuses on gender, work, and family life, with an eye to understanding the new work and family pathways emerging in the United States and other postindustrial societies. Although I rely on a range of methods, I specialize in qualitative interviewing. My goal is to uncover how personal biographies intersect with social institutions to bring about social change. I have written books and articles that offer innovative frameworks for explaining the revolution in gender, work, and family patterns, and my current research focuses on the new worlds of work and care, where occupational paths and personal relationships are increasingly uncertain.

A "one size fits all" model cannot describe the many shapes that today's families take nor the quality of the interactions among their members.

Watch the **Video** in **MySocLab**
Inspiring Your Sociological Imagination

As Josh reached school age, his home life took a major turn. His mother found a job as an administrator in a local business and, feeling more secure about her ability to support the family, asked her husband to move out and "either get straight or don't come back." Even though his father's departure was painful and unusual in this neighborhood where two-parent homes were the norm, Josh also felt relief. His parents' separation provided space for his mother to renew her self-esteem through her work outside the home. Josh missed his father, but he also came to accept this new situation as the better of two less-than-perfect alternatives.

> **A "one size fits all" model cannot describe the many shapes that today's families take, nor can it capture the quality of interactions among their members.**

Yet Josh's family changed again a year later when Josh's father "got clean" and returned home. Even more remarkable, when his parents reunited, they hardly seemed the same couple. Time away had given his father a new appreciation for the family and a deepened desire for greater involvement in his children's lives. Josh's mother displayed major changes as well, for taking a job had given her pride in knowing she could stand on her own. As his father became more attentive and his mother more self-confident, the family's spirits and fortunes lifted. In Josh's words, "that changed the whole family dynamic. We got extremely close."

In the years that followed, Josh watched his parents build a new partnership quite different from the conflict-ridden one he experienced in his earliest years. He developed a new and closer relationship with his father, whom he came to see as one of his best friends. He also valued his mother's strengthening ties to work, which not only nourished her sense of self but also provided enough additional income for him to attend college.

Josh's story exemplifies several important but often hidden truths about family life in contemporary societies. First, families are not "types" but are rather a set of dynamic processes and unfolding pathways that develop in unexpected ways over time. Despite the apparent stability and continuity his family may have shown on a survey checklist, a closer look revealed a domestic life that actually changed in fundamental ways. Second, families can look very different depending on one's point of view. Survey and census questions may reveal a snapshot of how a family looks at one or even several points in time, but an in-depth interview that charts the ups and downs of family life is more likely to reveal how family life is an unfolding pathway where crucial events often trigger unexpected transitions and unforeseen outcomes. Third, families come in all shapes and sizes, and it is misleading to assume that one type is better than another. A "one size fits all" model cannot describe the many shapes that today's families take, nor can it capture the quality of interactions among their members.

Finally, and perhaps most crucially, Josh's story reveals how the tumultuous changes of the last several decades require us to think in new ways about family life in the United States and other advanced, postindustrial societies. In a rapidly changing world, his parents were neither able nor willing to maintain a static set of arrangements for organizing their marriage or providing emotional and financial support to their children. As they developed new responses to a host of unexpected events, Josh's family changed dramatically. Its shift from a breadwinner-homemaker to a single-parent to a dual-earner home exemplifies both the growing diversity of family forms and the increasingly fluid nature of family life. These changes offer today's young adults options their parents barely imagined and their grandparents could not envision. Yet they also pose new challenges for creating and sustaining intimate relationships, for bearing and rearing children, and for integrating earning a living with caring for others. In the context of twenty-first century America, some families may thrive and others may not, but all of today's families face uncharted territory.

Families are films, not snapshots, and family life is an unfolding, unpredictable process. Actress Sandra Bullock adopted her son, Louis, just months before making the decision to divorce her husband.

THE BIG QUESTIONS

👁 **Watch** the **Big Question Videos** in **MySocLab**

To make sense of family life, both in the American context and beyond, this chapter will consider a variety of questions.

1 **What is a family?** To begin at the beginning, we first need to examine the meaning of the term *family*. What is a family, and what are the various ways to define it? Answering this question leads to the next one.

Why has family life become the topic of such heated debate? To understand the contemporary debate over "family values," we need to map out the competing views about the current state of the American family as well as how we got here and what we need to do in response. **2**

3 **What challenges do we face as we develop relationships and balance family and work?** Some pressing issues that affect American families today include the decline of permanent marriage and the new contours of adult commitment, as well as the blurring of gender divisions and the rise of work-family conflict.

What is it like to grow up in a twenty-first century family? The experiences of children growing up in twenty-first century families and transitioning to adulthood are very different than they once were. How have these changes affected children and young adults? **4**

5 **What causes inequality among families?** The causes of family inequality are complex and difficult to isolate, especially because the economy is changing and gender, race, and ethnic diversity intersect with class differences.

What social policies around the world best support changing families? Finally, we will place this overview of American family life today in a comparative perspective. By examining how other countries have experienced and tackled many of the same challenges, we will be in a better position to create the supports that American families will need to thrive in the **6**

1 What Is a Family?

THE MANY WAYS WE DEFINE *FAMILY*

👁 **Watch** the **Big Question Video** in **MySocLab**

The family is a core institution in all societies. It provides the first and most immediate context for our physical, emotional, and social development. As we age, family issues confront us with many of life's most crucial choices—whether and whom to marry, how to shape our sexual activity, whether to bear children and how many to bear, and how to raise the children we choose to have. Families influence us in ways so deep that it is difficult to exaggerate their importance. Yet their power to shape our destiny depends on their links to other institutions. Families are shaped by the societies they inhabit, but they also have the power to transform those societies.

Most of us think we know what a family is, even if we cannot always offer a precise definition. As the saying goes, we think we know a family when we see one. Yet "the family" can have many meanings. In this section we will explore how we define family, starting with a global and historical perspective.

☐ A Global and Historical Perspective

Though families are a universal social institution, their forms vary greatly across diverse social settings. Americans tend to think that the traditional family consists of an independent household anchored by a husband who concentrates on earning an income, a wife who focuses on childrearing and housekeeping, and their biological children. Yet this term is inaccurate and misleading. From a global and long-term historical perspective, it is clear that the independent home-maker-breadwinner household is a relatively rare, modern, and short-lived arrangement. Many other family forms can be found throughout human history and across diverse societies and cultures. Patterns such as arranged marriages, **polygamy** (when a person, typically a man, has multiple marital partners, typically wives), and multigenerational households, for example, were common prior to the rise of modernity in the West, and they continue to hold sway in many non-Western cultures. Some societies, especially those ruled by monarchies, have allowed marriages between cousins and even siblings among the ruling elite in order to keep the transfer of inherited power within an enclosed family system. And some cultures, deemed **patrilocal**, require a wife to live with her husband's parents and obey their authority.

The homemaker-breadwinner household that Americans often label *traditional* actually rose to prominence in the mid-twentieth century, largely as a consequence of post-World War II prosperity and the growth of the suburbs. While a majority of American households took this form for much of the 1950s, many did not. Working-class and minority communities, in particular, were more likely to find

What are some family forms that can be found throughout human history and across diverse societies and households?

the middle-class ideal of the traditional family either out of reach or unappealing. Equally important, many husbands and wives who lived in these "traditional" households found them unnecessarily stifling. When renowned feminist Betty Friedan spoke of middle-class women's confinement to domesticity as "the problem that has no name" (Friedan [2001] 1963: 57) and sociologist William Whyte (1956) referred to the conformity expected of the "organization man," they both identified a growing sense of unease about the reigning 1950s family structure.

Since that time, American families have changed in vast and unexpected ways, reminding us that the history of family life is a history of change. We have seen the rise of a diverse array of family forms, including dual-earner, single-parent, same-sex, and single-adult homes, which now vie with breadwinner-homemaker households for social and cultural support. Because these changes leave no one untouched, family life has become the site of both private struggles and public contention. If the 1950s produced a misleading belief in "the ideal family," the twenty-first century leaves us facing instead a series of puzzles and paradoxes. Is the family declining, or is it here to stay? Do families shape people, or do people shape families? Is there one best family form, or is it better to have a variety of family forms and practices? When it comes to these (and many other) questions, there are no simple answers. Instead, we need a sociological lens that allows us to see family life from a variety of perspectives, just as a prism allows us to see light in all of its hues.

☐ Kinship System or Household?

For demographers, *families* refer to groups of people who live together in households and share legal ties. Anthropologists, in contrast, see families as **kinship systems**—the social links and boundaries, defined by biology and social custom, that establish who is related to whom. In modern settings, and especially in the contemporary United States, it is common to stress the emotional bonds that connect people who care deeply about each other, whether or not they are linked by concrete bonds of law or biology. Many people today thus refer to their close friends—and even their pets—as "family" (Powell et al. 2010).

None of these definitions is either right or wrong, nor is one inherently better than another. The value of any definition depends instead on its usefulness in explaining the social world, and that can change with the social puzzle that needs solving. Sociologists thus conceive of the family as a social institution with multiple dimensions—"the familistic package," as sociologist William J. Goode once described it (Goode 1982). This package of social relationships can consist of a network of **kin**, a group of people who share a residence, or even the cultural meanings and perceptions that ordinary people use to decide which groupings they consider family and which they do not.

Since the peaking of the homemaker-breadwinner household in the mid-twentieth century, we have seen the rise of a diverse array of family forms, including single-parent homes.

Sociologists also distinguish between the families we inherit and the families we create (Streuning 2010). Our "family of orientation" consists of the people linked to us by birth—our parents, siblings, and extended kin. Our "family of procreation," in contrast, consists of the relatives we gain over the course of our lives through marriage and childbearing—our spouses, partners, and children. Yet in postindustrial societies, these terms seem overly simple and out of date. Now that openly acknowledged same-sex relationships are on the rise and many people sustain committed partnerships that do not involve legally sanctioned marriage or childbearing, the term *procreation* cannot encompass the wide range of chosen families that are emerging in the contemporary United States and elsewhere.

Our definitions also shape the questions we can pose about family life. If we define families as systems of kinship, our focus turns to questions about how kinship links and boundaries are mapped in any given society: Who counts as a member of the **nuclear family**—that is, the socially recognized parents and their dependent children—and who counts as extended kin? In premodern societies, for example, kinship lines include a number of people who extend far beyond the nuclear unit to encompass a whole clan, and in some tribal societies, the biological parents are not necessarily recognized as the social parents. For example, the work of the pioneering anthropologist Bronislaw Malinwoski found that among a tribe known as the Trobriand Islanders, a child's uncle—that is, his or her mother's brother—performed many of the social functions that modern Western societies associate with fatherhood, such as providing material support and enforcing discipline, while a child's biological father acted in a similar way toward his sister's children (Malinowski 1913).

Who do you consider to be your family? Many people today refer to their close friends (and even their pets) as "family."

Modern societies, in contrast, draw boundaries that limit kin to a much smaller number of people, rarely extending beyond cousins and second cousins (Levi-Strauss 1964). Because modern societies are large and complex, they have fewer concerns about intermarriage within kinship groups than do simple societies. Yet this complexity also requires more attention to creating legal standards for who is and is not a family member as well as for establishing the lines of responsibility and obligation among family members. The rise of divorce, remarriage, and out-of-wedlock childbearing has complicated these concerns. Equally important, the rise of reproductive technologies means that a rising number of children have both social parents and biological parents, including a sperm donor, an egg donor, or a surrogate mother. As the boundaries and definitions of parenthood blur and grow rapidly, kinship systems become more difficult to chart.

If we view families as households, our attention turns to residence patterns: Who lives together in households, and how are these households distributed geographically? The U.S. Census Bureau, for example, focuses on household units. In collecting and analyzing census data, the bureau defines *family* as a set of people living together who are connected by biological or legal ties and distinguishes these family households from nonfamily households, which consist of two or more individuals living together who are not linked by biological or legal ties—such as a group of college roommates or young singles sharing an apartment. By using this definition, moreover, the Census Bureau explicitly includes married couples (with and without children) and single parents living with their children in the category of family while excluding childless couples who are not married but living together, whether straight or gay.

Yet many people disagree with such a strict definition, preferring instead to use more subjective measures. A recent national survey found that Americans offered a variety of criteria for deciding when a household is a family (Pew 2010). Being married and having children are cited most often, with 99 percent agreeing that a married couple with children makes a family. Yet that figure drops to 88 percent for a married couple without children, to 86 percent for

singles with children, to 80 percent for an unmarried heterosexual couple with children, and to 63 percent for a same-sex couple with children. Less than half believe that same-sex couples without children (45 percent) and unmarried heterosexual couples (43 percent) are a family. These definitions are also linked to differences in ethnic and class cultures. Minority subcultures and residents of poor neighborhoods are more likely to create wide networks of caretaking and financial support that resemble the kinds of bonds we associate with kinship. We can even think of these relationships as "fictive kin"—that is, people whom we rely on, provide support for, and feel close to as if they were family members (Hill Collins 1991; Stack 1974).

Read the Document *Beyond the Nuclear Family: The Increasing Importance of Multigenerational Bonds* in **MySocLab**

How do kinship systems and residence patterns contribute to different definitions of family?

Personal and Cultural Ideals of Family Membership

To understand the varying ways that individuals define the family and decide whom they consider a member of their own family, it is necessary to investigate the ways that families embody a set of personal and cultural ideals. This perspective turns our attention to the perceptions, beliefs, norms, and values that inform multiple, and often conflicting, views of family life: What constitutes membership in our own and others' families, and how should family members treat each other? Many of the most heated controversies taking place in the United States today—from the legitimacy of gay marriage to parental rights for surrogate parents to abortion rights to employment among mothers—reflect a growing political and social divide between those who believe it is essential to maintain a relatively narrow definition of the family and those who believe it is necessary to conceive of families in much broader and more flexible ways.

Because family life has multiple aspects, sociologists strive to understand the family from a variety of vantage points. Most important, families embody a wide array of interrelated institutions that link the most intimate aspects of human experience to each other and to the wider world of public pursuits. These organized arrangements and patterned behaviors include processes of mate selection and sexual behavior; patterns of marriage, divorce, and adult commitment; patterns of fertility and childbearing; domestic activities such as housework and childrearing; the division of household labor; patterns of caregiving and breadwinning; patterns of authority relations among partners, spouses, and children; processes of social placement that link families to the class structure; and the structuring of individual development over the life course.

What does it mean to describe family life as multidimensional?

As we examine the many ways that family life unfolds—as an institution and a set of lived experiences—we first need to understand how and why family life in contemporary American society has become the topic of such heated debate (Risman 2010).

2 Why Has Family Life Become the Topic of Such Heated Debate?

CONTEMPORARY AMERICAN FAMILIES: A CONTROVERSIAL TOPIC

👁 Watch the **Big Question Video** in **MySocLab**

Given the many ways that we can define *family*, it is no surprise that the study of family life lends itself to controversy. Yet during various points in American history, the topic did not provoke nearly as much heated debate. In the mid-twentieth century, few people objected to defining the family—or at least the ideal family—as a household with a breadwinner husband, a homemaker wife, and their dependent children. Why, then, is family life so controversial today? The most obvious reason is that, unlike the post-World War II era, one family type no longer dominates others. In 1950, with the baby boom underway, almost 80 percent of U.S. households consisted of a married couple, and three-quarters of the wives in these couples did not hold a paid job. Yet recent decades have witnessed a rapid erosion of this once predominant form, which now accounts for less than 15 percent of American households. Instead, a mosaic of living arrangements—including dual-earning married couples, couples in **cohabitation** (nonmarried couples living together, both straight and gay), single-parent homes, and single adults living alone or with others—coexist side by side. Figure 13.1 shows how the composition of households has changed over the past 40 years.

The rise of diverse family forms has not only transformed the residential landscape; it has also undermined an earlier consensus about what makes a group of people into a family. Although dual-earner and single-parent homes have always existed alongside the homemaker-breadwinner home, they were a numerical minority. In the United States today, however, there is no numerical majority. The once-labeled "traditional family" must now compete with other types of relationships for social resources and cultural legitimacy. In the wake of such a vast social shift, it is perhaps inevitable that a thorny political debate would ensue. On one side are those who argue that the erosion of the traditional couple, with an earner-husband and caretaker-wife, endangers society; on the other are those who argue that supporting many different family forms is necessary for social justice and personal well-being. These differing perspectives suggest different causes and reach different conclusions about the consequences of family change (Giele 1996).

The Family Values Perspective

Some critics argue that a weakening of **family values**—the orientations people have toward family responsibilities—has created rising selfishness and unfettered individualism, which has in turn fueled the growth of nontraditional living arrangements. Proponents of this *family decline* perspective see lower marriage rates, along with rising rates of cohabitation, divorce, and premarital sex, as a decline in adult commitment. They worry that the increasing number of single mothers and out-of-wedlock pregnancies endangers children. Even in two-parent families, they are concerned about the growth in employed mothers, the blurring of gender distinctions, and the weakening of fathers' position as head of household. And they see the acceptance of same-sex partnerships as a devaluation of heterosexual marriage. Taken together, they fear that all of these changes undermine the family bonds needed to raise healthy children and create a stable society. To halt this supposed family decline, social policies should thus aim to reinvigorate "traditional marriage" and make it harder to choose other options. (Prominent proponents of the family decline perspective include Blankenhorn 1995; Blankenhorn

2009; Popenoe 1988; Popenoe, Elshtain, and Blankenhorn 1996; and Whitehead 1997. For rebuttals to the family decline perspective, see Bengston, Biblarz, and Roberts 2002; Moore et al. 2002; Skolnick 2006; and Stacey 1996).

By focusing on the central role of eroding moral values, however, the family-decline perspective ignores the many uplifting values that diverse family forms embody, such as a stress on equality and freedom to choose in intimate matters. In important ways, the cultural-decline argument thus offers an evaluation of new family forms rather than an explanation of why they have emerged.

The Economic Restructuring Perspective

In contrast, a second perspective focuses on the social-structural factors, rather than the cultural norms, that have prompted family change. This *economic restructuring* approach does not dispute the trends that signal family change, but its supporters argue that basic social and economic forces, not a decline in family values, has inevitably eroded the foundations of the breadwinner-homemaker family and required new family arrangements. Changes in men's job opportunities, such as the decline of both unionized blue-collar work and secure white-collar career paths, have left fewer men with the ability to earn enough money to support a family on their own. In a parallel development, the growth of service work has expanded the pool of jobs for women, while expanded educational opportunities have encouraged and allowed them to pursue professional careers once reserved for men. These deep-seated changes in the

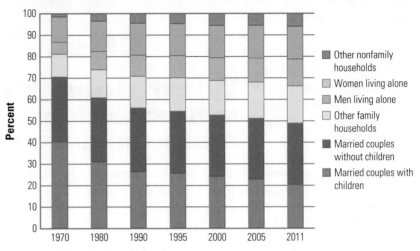

FIGURE 13.1 CHANGES IN COMPOSITION OF U.S. HOUSEHOLDS, 1970–2011

Legend:
- Other nonfamily households
- Women living alone
- Men living alone
- Other family households
- Married couples without children
- Married couples with children

Source: U.S. Census Bureau (2011).

What concerns do proponents of the family decline perspective have regarding the nature of families today?

Expanded educational opportunities have allowed and encouraged women to pursue professional careers once reserved for men.

occupational structure have allowed women to pursue more independent lives, but they have also made it more difficult for families to survive on only one income.

From an economic restructuring perspective, blurring gender boundaries, the rise of dual-earner families, and a new emphasis on individual choice and self-reliance are inescapable consequences of a new economic order. These changes have produced a mix of new opportunities and new insecurities. The financial stability that middle-class families once enjoyed is waning, replaced by a growing divide between the top tier of well-compensated, securely employed professionals and everyone else. If families are more vulnerable today, it is not because they have rejected good family values but rather because they cannot rely on a stable, predictable economic and social system to provide for their needs. In this context, social policies that try to restore the traditional family are doomed to fail. Instead, such policies should focus on broadening the safety net so that all types of families can thrive in an uncertain postindustrial economy.

By recognizing the institutional constraints over which most families have little control, the economic restructuring perspective does not assume nontraditional choices reflect poor values. Instead, family shifts stem from growing constraints on the practicality of traditional options, along with expanding desires to take advantage of new opportunities. Because these shifts are irreversible, it is shortsighted and even harmful to try to turn back the clock or to blame people for their values.

How do proponents of the economic restructuring approach explain changing family arrangements?

The Gender Restructuring Perspective

The focus on economic causes is important, but it tends to ignore the role of cultural forces and especially the growing desire among many women—and men—to live in families that do not resemble the heterosexual, gender-divided household that predominated in the mid-twentieth century. A third perspective on family change, which focuses on *gender restructuring*, adds another wrinkle to the economic restructuring approach that stresses institutional forces.

Focusing on the interdependence of paid and domestic work, the gender restructuring perspective highlights the growing mismatch between the structure of jobs (and careers) and the caretaking needs of families. While the family revolution has sent mothers into the labor force and created single-parent and dual-earner households, complementary changes have not occurred in the structure of jobs or care giving. To the contrary, employees who wish to move ahead are expected to place their job before family pursuits, yet parents, especially mothers, are expected to shower their children with attention. (see Epstein et al. 1999; Hays 1996; Moen and Roehling 2005; Williams 2000; Williams 2010). The expansion of new options is thus on a collision course with resistant institutions. Families may have changed, but the structure of the workplace and the organization of childrearing continue to presume a breadwinner-homemaker model that is no longer practical or desirable for most families.

These growing conflicts leave parents stressed, overburdened, and contending with time squeezes every bit as severe as their financial squeezes. They also create dilemmas about how to resolve a host of competing needs and values. How do adults balance the desire for personal independence with the value of lifelong commitment? How do parents trade off between the need to earn money and the need to care for their children? How do children experience growing up in diverse and changing families where new opportunities coexist with new uncertainties? How are these opportunities and uncertainties distributed across families in different class and ethnic subcultures? And is it possible to develop social policies that reconcile the growing divide between those who wish to restore the once dominant homemaker-breadwinner household and those who support more diverse and **egalitarian relationships** (where caretaking and breadwinning tasks are shared more or less equally by both partners)?

Focusing on the contradictions and dislocations of family change allows us to examine the ways that contemporary family life involves a mix of new opportunities and new insecurities. This perspective acknowledges the irreversible nature of change, but it does not assume that long-term outcomes are already determined. Instead, it draws our attention to the dilemmas and paradoxes created by inconsistent and contradictory social arrangements (Lorber 1994; Risman 1998). To make sense of modern families, we need to understand the interplay between inescapable social forces, such as the rise of a postindustrial economy with uncertain job paths, and the efforts of individuals, families,

What role do cultural and economic forces play in the gender restructuring perspective on family life?

and societies to craft innovative resolutions to the dilemmas created by incomplete change. These dilemmas take many forms, from tensions in forging adult commitments and sharing earning and caretaking tasks, to new challenges in growing up and making the transition to adulthood, to new class and ethnic inequalities. We examine each of these dilemmas in the sections that follow.

3 What Challenges Do We Face as We Develop Relationships and Balance Family and Work?

THE NEW CONTOURS OF ADULTHOOD COMMITMENT

⊙ Watch the **Big Question** Video in **MySocLab**

I n 2006, the Census Bureau reported that for the first time in U.S. history, less than half of American households contained a married couple and only 20 percent of households contained married couples with children (U.S. Census Bureau 2006). Compared to 1960, when the average age of marriage hovered around 20 for women and 23 for men, people are more likely to live together before getting married, to postpone a first marriage until their late 20s or early 30s, and to divorce or separate if the marriage proves unfulfilling (see Figure 13.2; Pew 2010).

Despite these trends, rumors of the death of marriage are greatly exaggerated. The overwhelming majority of Americans, around 90 percent, eventually marry, and most of those who divorce choose to remarry (Casper and Bianchi

2002; Cherlin 2009). Time and again, studies report that Americans consider having a good marriage as one of their most important goals (Kefalas et al. 2011). Indeed, the fight for same-sex marriage rights serves as a powerful indicator of its continuing importance. Marriage to one person for life may no longer be required, but marriage remains highly valued. Explore the Infographic on how mate preferences have changed over the years on page 360.

☐ Love and Marriage

American culture has always embodied a tension between creating lifelong commitments and retaining a measure of personal autonomy about whether and how to build intimate

FIGURE 13.2 CHANGES IN MARITAL AND LIVING PATTERNS, 1960–2008

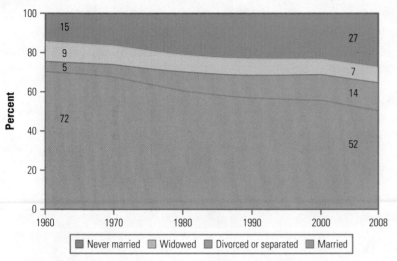

Note: Ages 18 and older. Numbers may not total to 100 percent due to rounding.

Source: Pew Research Center (2010).

relationships (Swidler 1980). These contradictory values go back as far as the nation's founding, when both individualism and community became central to national identity (Bellah et al. 1985). Yet this tension has found different expressions as social conditions have changed. Prior to industrialization, parents exercised great control over their children's mate choices, but this control subsided when the rise of industrialization in the nineteenth century demanded a socially and geographically mobile labor force. This new economic system fostered a new family unit, the "conjugal family" consisting of a relatively autonomous married couple able to seek its fortune outside the parental household (Goode 1963). The conjugal unit not only fit well with the industrial system; it also elevated the importance of emotional considerations, such as love and companionship, over parental approval as the appropriate criteria for choosing a mate.

The industrial system also produced the physical, economic, and mental separation of the home and the workplace. As many forms of work, and especially the manufacture of goods, moved outside the home to become paid jobs, the family became the site for unpaid tasks, such as childrearing and housework. This new division between the domestic and public spheres, intertwined in earlier periods, engendered a strict division—even polarization—of feminine and masculine roles. In a process that one sociologist has called "the feminization of love," women became responsible for emotional and caretaking duties, while men were

expected (and allowed) to pursue goals outside the home (Cancian 1987; see also Parsons and Bales 1954). Although these gender differences were defined as complementary, they inevitably created tensions between the ideal of individualism, which grants everyone the right to pursue autonomous goals, and the notion that women should maintain the intimate bonds of marriage and childrearing through selfless commitment to caring for others.

Today's postindustrial economy, which gathered steam in the later decades of the twentieth century, has changed the social context in which family members must balance the tension between commitment and self-development. The gender revolution, illustrated most vividly by the rise of women's employment, has created a form of economic individualism in which almost everyone, including women no less than men, expects to support him- or herself. The reproductive revolution, demonstrated by the expansion of contraceptive options, has given people more control over their reproductive choices. The sexual revolution has undermined the sexual double standard, destigmatized premarital sex, and allowed gay and other previously hidden relationships to move out of the closet. The divorce revolution has made it easier to leave a marriage without being found at fault. And the life course revolution has lengthened the lifespan, providing more time to make, unmake, and remake intimate bonds (Luker 2007; Rosenfeld

How has marriage become deinstitutionalized in today's postindustrial economy?

Americans today can cohabit prior to (or instead of) marriage, and recent estimates suggest that close to 45 percent of Americans are likely to cohabit at some point in their lives.

What Women and Men Want

What do women and men want in a mate? According to sociologist Christine B. Whelan, they generally want the same thing: mutual attraction and love. Whelan's research shows that both women's and men's rankings of desirable qualities in potential partners have changed drastically between 1939 and 2008. Of particular interest is the fact that a desire for education and intelligence in a partner has risen for both men and women.

Qualities Women Want in a Mate

RANK IN
1939

RANK IN
2008

1. Mutual attraction, love
2. Dependable character
3. Emotional stability, maturity
4. Desire for home, children
5. Education, intelligence
6. Sociability
7. Pleasing disposition
8. Ambition, industriousness
9. Good health
10. Good financial prospect
11. Similar education background
12. Good looks
13. Refinement, neatness
14. Similar religious background
15. Good cook, housekeeper
16. Favorable social status
17. Similar political background
18. Chastity

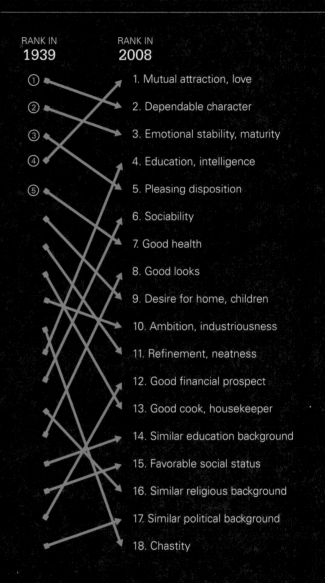

Qualities Men Want in a Mate

RANK IN
1939

RANK IN
2008

1. Mutual attraction, love
2. Dependable character
3. Emotional stability, maturity
4. Education, intelligence
5. Pleasing disposition
6. Sociability
7. Good health
8. Good looks
9. Desire for home, children
10. Ambition, industriousness
11. Refinement, neatness
12. Good financial prospect
13. Good cook, housekeeper
14. Similar education background
15. Favorable social status
16. Similar religious background
17. Similar political background
18. Chastity

Source: Based on data from Boxer, Noonan, and Whelen (forthcoming).

 Explore the **Data** on What Women and Men Want in **MySocLab** and then . . .

▉ Think About It

What do these changes in what men seek in a mate tell us about how larger social and economic changes influence personal relationships? How do you think women's mate preferences have changed?

▉ Inspire Your Sociological Imagination

What traits do you look for in a partner, and in what ways do you think they are different than the ones your parents or grandparents sought in a partner? Why do you think your preferences are different in this way?

2009; Skolnick 2006; Weitzman 1985). All of these changes have combined to deinstitutionalize marriage by creating a wide array of alternatives to traditional marriage, including cohabitation, **serial relationships** (when people enter and exit a series of intimate partnerships), gay partnerships, and permanent singlehood (Cherlin 1992; Smock 2000; Smock and Manning 2010). Recent estimates suggest, for example, that close to 45 percent of Americans are likely to cohabit at some point in their lives. Americans today can cohabit prior to (or instead of) marriage, engage in sexual activity and bear children without marrying, and leave a marriage if it seems unworkable.

The shift from a system in which getting married was a prerequisite for forming a family to one in which it is one option among many has transformed the meaning of marriage itself. Marriage is now a highly valued, but nevertheless voluntary, bond that adults may decide whether or not to make or, indeed, unmake. As they ponder this decision, contemporary adults are more likely to stress the importance of love, respect, and mutual interests than to seek relationships built around a notion of different but complementary gender roles. One recent survey found that most married adults believe that love (95 percent) and companionship (82 percent) are very important reasons to get married, compared to only 31 percent who cite financial stability, and most singles agreed. In another, 62 percent said that sharing household chores is very important for a successful marriage, while 53 percent cited an adequate income (Pew 2007a; Pew 2010). These ways of measuring a successful marriage place more stress on sharing and less on distinct spheres linked to gender. In fact, the concept of static roles can no longer adequately describe the blurring gender distinctions between women's and men's activities in the home or outside of it. These new ideals for marriage also mean that people apply new—and higher—standards when choosing a mate and deciding how to define a worthwhile relationship. Yet the stress on emotional rather than financial bonds also makes marital ties more fluid and voluntary. Now that marriage is both optional and reversible, love has conquered marriage (Coontz 2005).

Mothers, Fathers, and Work-Family Conflict

Once considered separate spheres, the relationship between the home and the workplace evokes a very different metaphor today. As women, especially mothers, have joined the paid labor force and new technologies have blurred the lines between home and work, the image of family life as a distinctly private realm—a "haven in a heartless world"—has given way to the image of families in conflict with the wider world, especially with the world of work (Shorter 1975). Mothers and fathers are now more likely to share breadwinning, but they also face daunting challenges about how to integrate their paid jobs with their families' caregiving needs (Blair-Loy 2003; Hochschild 1997; Jacobs and Gerson 2004; see also Folbre 2008). In fact, although we generally use the term *work* to refer to paid jobs, unpaid work in the home is also a form of work. **Care work**, whether it is paid or unpaid, is as essential to a household's survival as is bringing in an income. Even though we often pay others outside the household to perform care work, we tend to ignore its economic value, especially when it is performed by a family member without a wage or salary attached.

Despite the media portrayal of an "opt-out revolution," to use a term coined by journalist Lisa Belkin (2003) to portray women who leave the workplace to care for children, young women now pursue careers in unprecedented numbers (Damaske 2011; Stone 2007). According to one study, employment among college-educated women in professional and managerial occupations has increased across generations, with less than 8 percent of professional women out of the labor force for a year or more during their prime childbearing years (Boushey 2008). Even though women's labor force participation rates have stopped rising, this stall has occurred at a very high level (well over 70 percent), especially compared to several decades ago, when the rate hovered around 30 percent. Today, women's participation in the paid labor force stands at almost 73 percent, down from a peak of almost 75 percent in 2000 (compared to men, whose participation rate has dropped from a peak of 96 percent in 1953 to about 86 percent) (Percheski 2008).

While mothers with children under the age of one show a small decline in their work force participation compared to a peak in the late 1990s, mothers whose children are older than one year show no similar drop. In fact, the difference in employment rates between mothers and childless women has declined. Most mothers now hold a paid job outside the home, even when their children are very young. Almost 55 percent of married mothers with children under the age of one year are employed, and that figure rises to more than 60 percent for married mothers with children under six years and 75 percent for those with children between 6 and 18 years (Cohany and Sok 2007; Cotter, England, and Hermsen 2010). Table 13.1 provides more details.

It is clear that the image of women opting out is highly misleading. It also ignores the constraints, such as a lack of widely available childcare and employer reluctance to tailor jobs to caretaking needs, which prompt some women to pull back temporarily and make it difficult for others to return to the labor force. Women's march into the workplace may have reached a plateau, but there is no widespread exit of women (at any educational level or marital status) from the world of paid work. Moreover, despite the persisting perception that women leave work for family reasons and men because they lose their jobs, the ups and downs of women's employment, like that of men's, reflect the opening and closing of work opportunities as the economy shifts. Indeed, the recent recession

TABLE 13.1 CHANGES IN WOMEN'S LABOR FORCE PARTICIPATION, 1950–2010

Women's Labor Force Participation Rates by Marital Status, Children in the Household, Age, and Percent of Full-Time Workers, 1950–2010

	1950	1960	1970	1980	1990	2000	2010
Single	40.6%	41.8%	45.6%	52.5%	66.7%	68.9%	63.3%
Married, husband present	21.6	30.5	40.8	49.4	58.4	61.1	61.0
No children in household	30.3	34.7	42.2	46.7	52.3	54.8	54.3
Children under 6 in household	11.9	18.6	30.3	43.2	58.2	65.3	63.6
Children 6–17 in household	28.3	39.0	49.2	59.1	74.7	79.0	77.5
Aged 20–24	46.0	46.1	57.7	67.7	71.3	73.1	68.3
25–34	34.0	36.0	45.0	65.4	73.5	76.1	74.7
35–44	39.1	43.4	51.1	65.5	76.4	77.2	75.2
45–54	37.9	49.8	54.4	59.6	71.2	76.8	75.7
55–64	27.0	37.2	43.0	41.7	45.2	51.9	60.2
Percent of women workers who work year-round full-time	–	36.9	40.7	43.7	57.5	59.9	58.6

Sources: Gerson (1985); United States Census Bureau (2012); Bureau of Labor Statistics (2010). For presence of children, 2010 data are from 2008.

has been dubbed a "man-cession" because men (who are more likely to work in declining sectors, such as blue-collar work) lost jobs at a higher rate than did women. Whether women's earnings contribute to a dual-earner partnership or provide the sole support for a household, they are integral both to the economy and to the financial well-being of their families. Indeed, according to one study of contemporary women's work paths, employed women now see their decision to work at paid jobs as "for the family" (Damaske 2011).

Despite women's movement out of the home, the organization of work remains largely based on the principle that each employee can count on someone else to take care of a family's domestic needs. Indeed, the pressure to put in longer hours at the workplace has intensified, with over a quarter of men and more than 10 percent of women workers putting in more than 50 hours a week and 60 percent of married couples working a combined total of at least 82 hours (Jacobs and Gerson 2004). While part-time jobs are available, they often require working inconvenient schedules and provide neither sufficient income nor sufficient opportunities for advancement (Presser 2003). Indeed, many of those holding part-time jobs actually work at more than one. The best jobs remain reserved for those who work full time and overtime for an uninterrupted span of decades.

In what ways does the clash between family needs and work pressures affect family life?

The clash between family needs and workplace pressures spills over into family life in a variety of ways. It has produced an unequal **second shift**, a phrase coined by sociologist Arlie Hochschild, where employed mothers are more likely than fathers to add the lion's share of domestic duties to their already crowded work schedules (Hochschild 1989; Hochschild 1997). This inequality produces marital tensions, or what Hochschild calls "a scare economy of gratitude" in which everyone feels unappreciated and shortchanged. Faced with these tensions, couples may develop strategies that help them cope, but these strategies do not—and cannot—change the underlying conditions from which the tensions stem. Hochschild thus recounts the efforts of Nancy and Evan Holt, who decide to split tasks by their location in the house—with Evan responsible for outside duties, such as taking care of the dog and cleaning the garage, while Nancy remains responsible for everything else. While the Holts hope this arrangement will ease tensions in the household, it instead allows the couple to create a family myth of equality that actually contributes to strains. Paradoxically, the growth of employment among mothers (in both dual-earner and single-parent families) has occurred alongside increased pressure for parents, especially mothers, to give their children more time and attention. This norm of

Fathers' parental involvement still lags behind mothers', but men are doing more domestic work than their fathers and grandfathers.

intensive motherhood conflicts with the countervailing norm that everyone should work hard and contribute financially, leaving women to face a "damned if you do and damned if you don't" set of options (Hays 1996). If a mother takes a job, she faces accusations of neglecting her children, but if she does not, she must defend her position as a stay-at-home mom, a social status whose symbolic value and social support have declined sharply. Research in this area reports that employed and nonemployed mothers both expressed unease about not meeting their mothering obligations or living up to the standards expected of mothers (see Hays 1996).

The blurred boundary between home and work produces time crunches and cultural contradictions, but it also creates new opportunities and possibilities. Women and men are both more likely to say they want to integrate earning and caring in their own lives and to establish a more flexible, egalitarian relationship with a lifelong partner. Fathers' parental involvement still lags behind mothers', but men are doing more domestic work than their fathers and grandfathers (Coltrane 2004; Deutsch 1999; Sullivan and Coltrane 2008). The gender gap in parenting is shrinking, and couples with more equal sharing express higher levels of satisfaction and are less likely to break up (Cooke 2006). More surprising, despite the image of the stressed, neglectful parent, parents today actually spend more time with their children than their counterparts did several decades ago. Mothers and fathers may both hold paid jobs, but they are also focusing more on their children when they are not at work (Bianchi 2000; Bianchi, Robinson, and Milkie 2006).

Work-family conflicts nevertheless remain difficult to manage, largely because the organization of jobs and childcare has not changed to accommodate shifts in gender relationships and the family economy. Individual workers, especially among professionals and other well-paid occupations, face growing pressures to put in long days at the office, while less educated workers increasingly take jobs with nonstandard schedules and little long-term security. In addition, the *combined* working time of whole families has risen dramatically (see Figure 13.3), with dual-earning and single parents feeling most caught between the demands of work and the needs of domestic life (Gornick and Meyers 2003; Williams 2010). These types of households have always been stretched thin, but many more Americans live in them today. The future of family well-being will thus depend on restructuring jobs and childcare to help workers resolve the time squeezes created by widespread, deeply anchored, and irreversible social changes to the nature of the economy and the structure of families (Esping-Anderson 2009; Hochschild 1989).

FIGURE 13.3 CHANGES IN COUPLES' COMBINED WORKING TIME, 1970 AND 2000 (MARRIED COUPLES AGES 18–64)

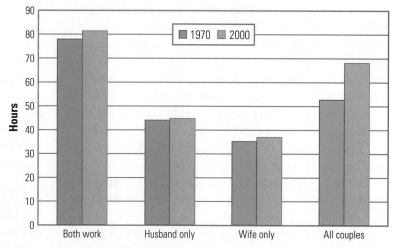

Source: Jacobs and Gerson (2004).

4 | What Is It Like to Grow Up in a Twenty-First Century Family?

GROWING UP IN TODAY'S FAMILIES

👁 Watch the **Big Question** Video in **MySocLab**

The rise of family diversity has also transformed the experience of childhood as well as the transition to adulthood. A growing percentage of children now grow up in a home with either two employed parents or a single parent or a same-sex-couple (Galinsky et al. 2009; Johnson et al. 2005; U.S. Census Bureau 2006; U.S. Census Bureau 2007). Children are also more likely to live in homes that change shape over time. While children have always faced predictable turning points as they move from infancy to adulthood, more children today experience unpredictable family changes as well. Compared to their parents or grandparents, they are more likely to see married parents break up or single parents remarry. They are more likely to watch a stay-at-home mother join the work force or an employed mother pull back from work when the balancing act gets too difficult. And they are more likely to see their financial fortunes rise or fall as a household's composition changes or parents encounter unexpected shifts in their job situations. Growing up in an era of fluid marriages, unpredictable finances, and mothers with new work ties shapes the contemporary world of childhood, even for those children whose own parents remain steadfastly traditional.

The transition to adulthood, like the experience of childhood, is also not what it used to be. Major events, such as graduating from school, getting a job, and getting married, now take place at later ages. In 1960, by age 30, 65 percent of men and 77 percent of women had completed all of the major life transitions that form the historic benchmarks of adulthood, including leaving home, finishing school, becoming financially independent, getting married, and having

a child. By 2000, however, only 46 percent of women and 31 percent of men by age 30 had completed these transitions (Furstenberg et al. 2004); Newman (2009) also reports that these trends are not confined to the United States, as many European countries are also witnessing even greater increases in the number of 20-somethings still living with their parents. Let's explore how these changes have affected children and young adults.

☐ The Changing Face of Childhood

Among all children in 2000, only 21 percent lived in a two-parent household with an employed father and a nonemployed mother, while 59 percent lived with an employed mother, including 41 percent who lived with two employed parents, 3 percent with an employed mother and nonworking father, and 15 percent with an employed single mother (Johnson et al. 2005). Table 13.2 displays these results. It shows that the remaining children lived with either a single mother who did not have a paid job (5 percent), a married couple where neither were employed (4 percent), a father-only household (6 percent), or with neither parent (5 percent). The proportion of children born to unmarried mothers is at an all-time high of almost 37 percent, although about half of these nonmarital births are to cohabiting couples (U.S. Census Bureau 2006; U.S. Census Bureau 2007).

How have these changes affected children? Fortunately, worries about the harmful effects of having an employed mother or even experiencing a parental breakup are overstated. Decades of research have found that, on the whole,

TABLE 13.2 PROFILE OF PARENTS LIVING WITH CHILDREN UNDER 18

	All parents	Married	Unmarried	Among unmarried parents		
				Divorced/ Separated	Living with a partner	Never married
	%	%	%	%	%	%
Men	45	50	23	22	42	14
Women	55	50	77	78	58	86
18–29	19	15	32	14	40	52
30–49	73	76	61	76	56	46
50–64	8	9	6	10	4	2
65+	<1	<1	<1	<1	<1	<1
Whites	65	68	52	63	59	36
Blacks	11	7	24	16	13	41
Hispanics	17	16	19	16	24	19

Note: Hispanics are of any race. Whites and blacks include only non-Hispanics.

Source: Pew Research Center (2010).

children do not suffer when their mothers work outside the home. Instead, a mother's satisfaction with her situation, the quality of care her child receives, and the involvement of a father and other caretakers are more important than whether or not a mother holds a paid job (Galinsky 1999; Harvey 1999; Hoffman, Wladis, and Youngblade 1999; Waldfogel 2006). The children of employed mothers do just as well in their cognitive development and, among children in low-income families, they do better (Burchinal and Clarke-Stewart 2007). Those who see a mother's employment as harmful generally point to thin research results showing small, temporary, and nonsignificant negative effects of being in day care for a small number of children (Crouter and McHale 2005). Indeed, despite the difficulties of balancing work and family, employed mothers and two-income homes are, in the words of Rosalind Barnett and Caryl Rivers, "happier, healthier, and better off" (see Barnett and Rivers 1996; 2004).

In the case of one- versus two-parent homes, children living with both biological parents do fare better on average, but this difference declines substantially after taking account of a family's financial resources and the degree of parental conflict prior to and after a breakup. Most of the negative consequences of divorce can be traced to the high conflict and emotional estrangement preceding a breakup, along with the hostility and loss of economic support that often follows in its aftermath (Cherlin et al. 1991; Furstenberg and

Cherlin 1991; Hetherington and Kelly 2002; McLanahan and Sandefur 1994). The effects of divorce on children vary greatly, with one researcher concluding that "while certain divorces harm children, others benefit them" (Li 2007). Children in high-conflict families whose parents divorce fare better, for example, than children raised in high-conflict families whose parents do not divorce (Amato and Booth 1997; Rutter 2010). While some analysts argue that all divorces are harmful in the long run, with a "sleeper effect" emerging many years later (Marquardt 2005; Wallerstein et al. 2000), others point to the large variation in divorce's consequences. One study found that over one-third of grown children felt their parents' marriage was more stressful than the divorce, which came as a relief when it reduced the long-term daily conflict between parents (Ahrons 2006). All in all, the effects of parental breakups—both negative and positive—vary with and depend on the circumstances that surround the divorce before and after it takes place.

What does research indicate about the effects of divorce on children?

Most research demonstrates that the diversity within family types, however defined, is as large as the differences between them. Some researchers show, for example, that family composition does not predict children's well-being (Acock and Demo 1994), while others make the same case for different forms of parental employment (Parcel and Menaghan 1994). In my own research, I found that almost four out of five young adults who had work-committed mothers believed this was the best option, while half of those whose mothers did not have sustained work lives wished they had. Similarly, a slight majority of those who lived in a single-parent home wished their biological parents had stayed together, but almost half believed it was better for their parents to separate than to continue to live in a conflict-ridden or silently unhappy home. In addition, a majority of children from intact homes thought this was best, but two out of five felt their parents might have been better off splitting up (Gerson 2011).

Children can thrive in a variety of domestic circumstances, but family process is more important than family form. What matters is how well parents and other caretakers meet the challenges of providing economic and emotional support rather than the specific forms in which these challenges are met. Children care about how their families unfold, not what they look like at any one point in time. Family life is dynamic, as families are not a stable set of relationships frozen in time but rather involve situations that can change daily, monthly, and yearly as children grow. All families experience change, and even the happiest ones must adapt to these changes if they are to remain so. Family pathways can move in different directions as some homes become more supportive and others less so.

What explains why some family pathways remain stable or improve, while others stay mired in difficulty or take a downward course? My study of "the children of the gender revolution," who grew up during the recent period of family change, finds that flexibility in earning and caregiving provides a key to understanding how and why some families are able to provide for children's well-being while others are not (Gerson 2011). Flexible family strategies can take different forms. In two-parent homes, children fared well when couples shared breadwinning and caretaking fairly equally or when they took turns and traded places as mothers pursued committed careers or fathers encountered roadblocks at the workplace. Chris, for example, tells how his family life improved dramatically when his mother's promotion at a hospital, where she worked as an intensive care nurse, allowed his father to quit a dissatisfying job as a printer and retrain for work as a machine technician, which he found much more satisfying.

In single-parent, divorced, and remarried households, children fared better when mothers were able to find jobs that kept the family afloat and fathers remained closely involved in their children's day-to-day care. Letitia thus recounts how her home life changed for the better when her father became the primary caretaker, providing emotional support that her inattentive and often absent mother could not. In the wake of her parents' separation and her father's remarriage, she also gained a more nurturing stepmother (in her words, "my real mother") whose commitment to work also contributed to the family's financial stability.

Despite the differences in family circumstances, all of these responses involved breaking through rigidly drawn gender boundaries between women as caretakers and men as breadwinners. In a world where parents may not stay together, where men may not be able or willing to support wives, and where women may need and want to pursue sustained work ties, most families will encounter unexpected challenges, whether they take the form of financial crises or uncertainties in parental relationships. When families are able to respond by rejecting narrow roles in favor of more expansive and flexible family practices, they are better positioned to create more financially stable and emotionally supportive homes for children. Flexible approaches to breadwinning and caretaking help families adapt, while inflexible ones leave them ill prepared to cope with the economic and marital challenges that confront twenty-first century families.

☐ Becoming an Adult

The markers used to decide who is—and who is not—an adult are very different today than they were several decades ago, with people much more likely to stress economic achievements over family commitments. In 2002, 90 percent of Americans considered completing one's education and achieving financial independence to be quite or extremely important to being considered an adult, followed by working full time (84 percent), supporting a family (82 percent), and becoming financially independent (81 percent; see Figure 13.4). In contrast, less than one third of Americans considered such family events as getting married and having a child (33 percent and 29 percent respectively) as requirements for adulthood (General Social Survey 2002; Furstenberg et al. 2005).

The extended time it takes to complete the transition to adulthood has produced a new life stage that some call "delayed adulthood" and others see as "the age of independence" (Rosenfield 2009). Like most social changes, this expanding period of early adulthood—after adolescence but before making lifelong commitments—can contain benefits and drawbacks. Sociologist Christian Smith (2011), for example, argues that young adults now get "lost in transition" without a moral compass to guide them, while Michael

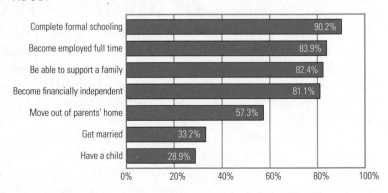

FIGURE 13.4 PERCENT WHO SAY AN EVENT IS QUITE IMPORTANT OR EXTREMELY IMPORTANT TO BECOMING AN ADULT

Complete formal schooling — 90.2%
Become employed full time — 83.9%
Be able to support a family — 82.4%
Become financially independent — 81.1%
Move out of parents' home — 57.3%
Get married — 33.2%
Have a child — 28.9%

Source: Figure created based on data from GSS (2002); Furstenberg et al. (2004).

Kimmel (2008) points to the emergence of a place he calls "guyland," where young men engage in potentially self-destructive pursuits such as excessive drinking and partying. Others, however, see notable benefits in the emergence of a period when young adults are freed from childhood (and parental) controls and have an opportunity to develop a more independent self. The research of sociologist Michael Rosenberg (2009) has found that the rise of new kinds of relationships, including interracial and same-sex couples, reflects new opportunities for young adults to forge a life that is less constrained by the prejudices of earlier eras and more in tune with the realities of contemporary life.

Whatever the viewpoint, young adults now have more time to pursue independent goals before making major lifelong commitments and to develop ways of living that diverge from their parents' paths. This new period has also fueled a gender revolution in young women's and men's aspirations and plans. National surveys and my own in-depth interviews find that a majority of young people hope ultimately to create a lasting relationship, but not one that is based on separate spheres for mothers and fathers. Instead, most women and men want to create a flexible, generally equal partnership where they share paid work and family caretaking while also reserving considerable room for personal independence (Pew 2007b). In my interviews with young adults aged 18 to 32, I found that four-fifths of the women want an egalitarian relationship, and so do two-thirds of the men (Gerson 2011). In addition, three-fourths of those reared in dual-earner homes report wanting to share breadwinning and caretaking fairly equally with a partner, and so do more than two-thirds of those from traditional homes and close to nine-tenths of those with single parents.

Yet young women and men also fear their goals will be hard to achieve and may prove out of reach. Worried about finding the right partner and integrating family with work, they are pursuing fallback strategies in young adulthood. Young women and men both emphasize the importance of work as a central source of personal identity and financial well-being, but this outlook leads them to pursue different strategies. Women are more likely to see paid work as essential to their own and their family's survival and to prefer self-reliance over economic dependence within a traditional marriage (see Figure 13.5). Men, in contrast, are more likely to worry about the costs of equal sharing and to prefer a neo-traditional arrangement that allows them to put work first and rely on a partner for the lion's share of caregiving.

Images of young people avoiding adulthood and "failing to launch" cannot capture the complex experiences of today's young women and men. New generations do not wish to create a brave new world of disconnected individuals. In the long run, they hope to balance autonomy with a satisfying, committed relationship. However, they also believe they need to take time to create a financial base, discover their own strengths and needs, prepare for an uncertain economy that demands more education and higher levels of training, and find a partner whose family vision meshes with their own.

What are the benefits and drawbacks of the expanding period of early adulthood experienced by U.S. young adults?

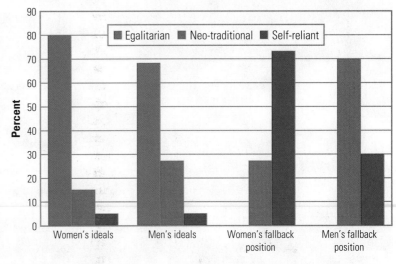

FIGURE 13.5 IDEALS AND FALLBACK POSITIONS OF YOUNG WOMEN AND MEN

Legend: ■ Egalitarian ■ Neo-traditional ■ Self-reliant

(Y-axis: Percent, 0 to 90)

Categories: Women's ideals, Men's ideals, Women's fallback position, Men's fallback position

Source: Gerson (2011).

The extended time it takes to complete the transition to adulthood has produced a new life stage, where young adults can pursue independent goals, such as work and leisure pursuits, before making lifelong commitments.

5   What Causes Inequality among Families?

FAMILIES AND SOCIAL INEQUALITY

Watch the Big Question Video in **MySocLab**

Families of all classes and ethnicities are changing, but different groups are changing to different degrees and in different ways. Single-parent families, for example, are more likely to be found among African American households, where 65 percent of children live with either one parent or neither parent, compared to 34 percent of non-Hispanic white children, 24 percent of Hispanic children, and 17 percent of Asian children (Blow 2008). And while the overwhelming majority of Americans eventually marry, marriage rates have declined most steeply for the less educated and for members of racial minorities, where men's school and work opportunities are especially squeezed (Porter and O'Donnell 2006). Because economic inequality is linked to family differences, with a disproportionate number of poor and economically disadvantaged families found among single-parent families, it follows that ethnic minorities are also more likely to be overrepresented in lower income levels (see Figure 13.6).

The causes of family inequality are complex and difficult to isolate. Does inequality reflect different family values,

FIGURE 13.6 SHARE OF NEVER MARRIED, BY RACE, ETHNICITY, AND EDUCATION

(A)

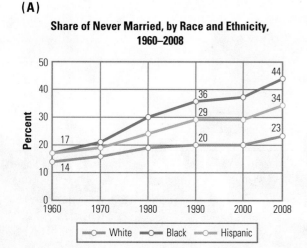

Share of Never Married, by Race and Ethnicity, 1960–2008

(B)

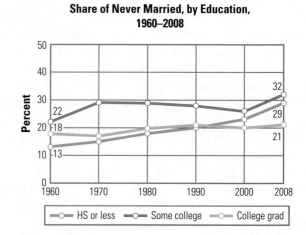

Share of Never Married, by Education, 1960–2008

Note: Ages 18 and older. Hispanics are of any race. Whites and blacks include only non-Hispanics.

Source: Pew Research Center (2010).

Many middle class parents engage in a form of intensive parenting that some call "concerted cultivation," involving a high degree of scheduled activities.

or does it stem from unequal access to economic and social resources? Sociologist Annette Lareau (2003) proposes a circular link between class cultures, especially childrearing practices, and the transmission of inequality from one generation to the next. She argues that middle-class parents engage in a form of intensive parenting called "concerted cultivation," which involves a high degree of scheduled activities, a stress on the acquisition of language skills, and a sense of entitlement when interacting with social institutions such as schools. In contrast, working-class families engage in "natural growth," which involves unstructured play and leisure activities, a more informal approach in conversations, and more deference to authority figures such as teachers and doctors. While all families strive to provide their children with love and nurturance, she argues that different childrearing styles leave middle-class children better equipped to succeed in high-pressure, well-compensated jobs and occupations, thus continuing the cycle of inequality.

Yet diverse class and ethnic subcultures also share many values and practices. Sharon Hays (1996; 2003) finds that standards of intensive mothering, which bear a strong resemblance to Lareau's notion of concerted cultivation, exist in all classes. Studies of poor and middle-class single mothers find many similarities in their reasons for choosing motherhood over marriage as well as their strategies for raising children (Edin and Kefalas 2005; Hertz 2006). Poor single mothers are more likely to begin childbearing in late adolescence or early adulthood, while middle-class single mothers are more likely to postpone until their late 30s and early 40s as biological deadlines near, but both groups offer similar reasons for having a child while not being married. In separate studies of unmarried mothers in poor neighborhoods and middle-class single mothers by choice, both sets of researchers found that all these women valued motherhood highly and were not willing to forgo the experience simply because the right partner could not be found (Edin and Kefalas 2005; Hertz 2006). Though they possessed vast differences in financial resources, both groups relied on a support network of friends and relatives, including some men, to help rear their children.

People who grow up in the same class or ethnic subculture also vary greatly, and many move up and down the class ladder over the course of their lives. Some children are able to move to a higher class position than that of their parents, while others are not. Mobility across the generations has declined in recent years, but most children born into the bottom quintile of the income distribution are likely to move higher to some degree. One researcher reports that among children born into bottom fifth of the income distribution, 42 percent will stay there, but 24 percent will move to the fourth quintile, 15 percent will move to up to third quintile, 12 percent will move up to second quintile, and 7 percent will make it to top quintile. Among children born into the top quintile, 40 percent will remain there, but 54 percent will fall (Furstenberg 2007). Even siblings who grow up in the same family may follow different paths. Another researcher reports that the income differences among adult siblings are greater than the average income differences between families (Conley 2004). Because children who grow up in the same households are likely to diverge as adults, it is difficult to attribute their trajectories to a shared class or family culture.

In addition, the uncertainty of the twenty-first century economy makes it increasingly difficult to draw clear class boundaries. While there are many ways to define class, the most typical definition focuses on occupation. People are generally classified as middle class or upper middle class when at least one family member is employed in a professional, managerial, or similar occupation, while they are deemed working class if the adult earners are employed in blue-collar, pink-collar, or other service or wage work not requiring a college education. The poor encompass those families that fall at or below the official poverty level, although the official level often underestimates the number of people whom many would agree live in poverty. More important, many working-class and middle-class American families now find themselves facing financial uncertainty, knowing that the loss of a job or a family member would trigger a downward slide. These families live on a "fault line," precariously balanced between maintaining a class position and dropping below it (Newman and Tan 2007; Rubin 1994; Warren and Tyagi 2003).

Complicating matters even more, race and ethnic diversity intersects with class and gender inequality. Sociologist Patricia Hill Collins (1991) points out that class, race, and gender combine in ways that make it difficult to separate their distinct effects. Not only are African Americans and Latinos more likely than whites and Asians to be concentrated at lower income levels, but so are women of all races

How do race, ethnicity, and gender intersect with class to create inequality among families?

and ethnicities. None of these categories can be considered alone. On the other side of the class divide, an emerging black middle class signals growing diversity among African Americans, just as the rise of women professionals has created similar diversity among women.

In the long run, a range of factors—including supports and obstacles provided by neighborhoods, schools, and jobs in addition to the family environment—structure children's experiences and shape their life chances. All in all, family differences, such as poor people's tendency to marry less often than other income groups, stem more from differences in resources and opportunities than from differences in values.

6   What Social Policies around the World Best Support Changing Families?

THE UNITED STATES
IN COMPARATIVE PERSPECTIVE

👁 **Watch** the **Big Question Video** in **MySocLab**

Alleviating the difficulties created by inconsistent change depends on accepting the irreversibility of family change and creating a range of institutional supports for this new reality. Individual families cannot make these adjustments on their own. Only collective social policies can create the supports that twenty-first century families need to thrive or even survive.

☐ Social Policy around the World

The United States lags far behind many other postindustrial societies in adopting social policies that support new family forms. France, for example, allows any two people to form a civil union that bestows all the legal rights and responsibilities of a married couple. France, along with all the Scandinavian countries, also offers universal childcare, and Scandinavian countries guarantee paid parental leave for everyone (Gornick and Myers 2009). In Sweden, Iceland, and Norway, these leave policies not only support employed mothers; they also encourage fathers' parental involvement by specifying that a father cannot transfer his leave time but must "use it or lose it." Most Europeans can also build their families without regard to such considerations as health-care and educational access, which are available to everyone whether or not they are married or employed full time.

In thinking about how the United States approaches family change, it is helpful to compare it with other nations at a similar level of economic development. From Europe to the Far East, all the postindustrial nations have experienced similar social shifts, including a rise in women's labor force participation, the postponement of marriage and childbearing, and the proliferation of diverse family forms. Yet the policy responses to these shared demographic trends are quite distinct.

Some countries, especially in Scandinavia, have developed policies based on the principle of providing universal family supports regardless of who you are. This egalitarian approach covers a range of specific policies, including paid parental leaves, universal day care, and antidiscrimination workplace policies along with universal health care and free education. Taken together, this approach aims to reduce both gender and class inequality while providing for children's well-being regardless of the kind of family they live in.

In contrast, other countries, such as Italy, have adopted an approach that encourages maternal care but does not support women's employment or more egalitarian family forms. This familistic approach offers mothers with children, even if they are single, economic incentives for bearing children and staying home to rear them. It does not, however, stress day care, antidiscrimination at work, or others measures that would facilitate employment among mothers, encourage fathers to share in caretaking, or generally acknowledge the rise of new family and gender arrangements. Ironically, in Italy, Japan, and other countries that have resisted the incorporation of women in the public sphere, many women have responded by resisting marriage and motherhood, creating a shortage of births not seen in societies with more egalitarian policies. Explore *A Sociological Perspective* on page 372 for a closer look at social policies around the world.

FIGURE 13.7 PARENTAL LEAVE FOR TWO-PARENT FAMILIES IN 21 COUNTRIES

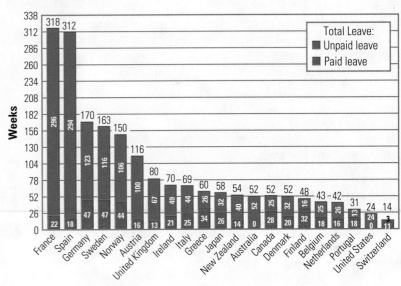

Source: Ray, Gornick, and Schmitt (2009).

How do government policies **towards families differ** around the world?

☐ Social Policy in the United States

Where does the United States fit in this picture? Unlike either egalitarian or familistic approaches, U.S. social policies stress the principle of individual opportunity. This individualistic approach stresses policies aimed at providing a chance to succeed—or fail—in the labor market but not at creating programs of family support for everyone. Unlike familistic approaches, there is less concern for recreating the traditional family through maternal support; but unlike egalitarian approaches, there is less concern with equality of outcomes or facilitating the inclusion of mothers into the labor force or the inclusion of fathers in caring for dependents (see Figure 13.7). In practice, this means that American social policy has focused more on whether and how to prevent discrimination and far less on creating universal family support programs. Indeed, we continue to debate the advantages and disadvantages of the family revolution rather than accepting its irreversibility and restructuring other institutions to better fit the new realities.

☐ Where Do We Go from Here?

What, then, would a more effective, inclusive policy approach look like? In an era of massive family change, we need to think more broadly about what equal opportunity really means. Individuals live in families, and we cannot separate

A SOCIOLOGICAL PERSPECTIVE

Is childcare the same around the world?

United States: Parents often struggle to find affordable, high-quality childcare for the most part without help from the government. Low-income families, in some cases, can find subsidized childcare if they meet certain criteria but higher income families are not eligible for such services. Census figures show that 48 percent of children four years and younger with working mothers were cared for by relatives and the number of stay home mothers (5 million) has declined since 2008.

Japan: A chronic childcare shortage makes finding daycare slots a competitive process. Worried that women would choose either a career or motherhood, Japan, in 2008, announced a 10-year goal of providing working parents with daycare for children ages 1-5.

If the Unites States offered the same level of parental leave for fathers as offered in Sweden, how could the father-child relationship change?

Sweden: Policies like the "use it or lose it" paid parental leave encourage greater involvement of fathers because leave days cannot be transferred. Parents may take up to 480 total parental leave days when a child is born or adopted, and the government subsidizes childcare for its citizens.

France: The state provides free preschool for children from two years of age. A system of "child minders" helps to supplement its daycare centers. A child minder receives training, undergoes regular inspections, and can care for up to five children at a time.

Can you think of some possible benefits for governments to provide subsidized childcare for all of its citizens?

How would affordable and available access to childcare affect mothers' contributions to the workplace?

 Explore A Sociological Perspective in **MySocLab** and then …

■ Think About It

The U.S. lags far behind many other postindustrial societies in adopting social policies that support new family forms. What enables other countries to adopt different, more supportive approaches to accommodating families with children, including paid parental leave and universal daycare?

■ Inspire Your Sociological Imagination

What are the long-term implications of these different approaches for both the economic development of each country and for the well-being of families and individuals?

Workplace antidiscrimination policies need to cover "family responsibilities" discrimination, which will help protect all of those who shoulder responsibilities for caring for others. Here, workers in Belgium are demonstrating in support of giving fathers two weeks fully paid paternity leave.

the fate of individuals from the well-being of their families. We thus need family policies that reaffirm classic American values, such as equal opportunity, tolerance of diversity, and individual responsibility, but do so in the context of collective support for the diverse needs of the new family arrangements that are essential pieces of modern social life.

More concretely, this means a host of specific policies in diverse arenas: family support policies, workplace policies, and legislation to protect the vulnerable of all ages, family statuses, and sexual orientations. Legislative efforts need to encompass equal opportunities for all kinds of families and interpersonal relationships, including single parents, same-sex couples, dual-earner families, and single adults. At the workplace, antidiscrimination policies need to be expanded to include what Joan Williams (2007) calls "family responsibilities" discrimination, so that those who shoulder responsibilities for caring for others will not face huge penalties for devoting time to this essential but undervalued task. Family-support

What would a more effective, inclusive policy approach to family support in the United States look like?

policies should thus aim to reduce poverty and inequality along with creating a wider institutional framework for dependent care, including the care of children, the elderly, and anyone in need of it. Community childcare supports, in particular, will help employed parents and nurture the next generation. Jobs that offer flexible avenues for working and career building will not only help families integrate paid work and care work but also help employers attract and retain committed workers.

Antidiscrimination policies that protect the rights of all parents with caregiver responsibilities will not only even the playing field for employed mothers but also create fairer workplaces for men (of all sexual orientations and class positions) who wish to be involved as caretakers. No one policy can address all the challenges that twenty-first century families face, but taken as a whole, these approaches will go a long way toward helping families develop their own strategies for meeting the challenges that await them in the decades to come.

CONCLUSION THE FUTURE OF FAMILIES

Despite the rapid pace of change, most Americans remain quite upbeat about the future of the family. According to a recent Pew survey, 67 percent say they are optimistic about the future of marriage and the family. Yet Americans are also concerned about some family trends, such as the rise in divorce and unwed childbearing, and politically divided over others, such as gay marriage, abortion, and the growth of paid childcare (Pew 2010). Another Pew survey thus found that 71 percent believe the growth of unwed motherhood is a big problem (Pew 2007b).

The focus of attention may shift from employed mothers to abortion rights to single motherhood to gay marriage, but underlying political cleavages remain between those who support diversity in family life and those who would like to restore the breadwinner-homemaker family that predominated a half century ago.

The uneven and inconsistent character of family change means not only that people will live in different types of families but also that they will have different outlooks on family life. Those who are pioneering new family forms have good reasons to favor social policies, such as supports for employed parents and same-sex couples, that will help ease their dilemmas. But those who favor traditional family arrangements are more likely to view such policies as unwarranted support for options they consider unpalatable and even unacceptable. These differences play an important role in national elections, where a sizable "marriage gap" has emerged alongside the highly publicized gender gap. Married couples, and especially those who depend only on a man's income, are more likely to vote for conservative candidates, while single women and men are more likely to vote for candidates who identify themselves as liberals (Edlund and Pande 2002).

To complicate matters, those who oppose family change are not immune to it. Regions of the country with the highest rates of unwed motherhood and divorce are more likely to lean toward conservative views on family life that stress the role of cultural decline in creating new challenges. In contrast, regions with the lowest rates are more likely to take a liberal approach that is less concerned with individual values and more focused on economic restructuring (Cahn and Carbone 2010). It appears that those most susceptible to the uncertainties of family change are also the most unsettled by it.

These ambivalent and conflicting views make it difficult to assess the prospects for the future. Family diversity is here to stay, but so is the debate over family diversity. There is, however, another approach that takes seriously the feminist view that gender restructuring is not only at the heart of family change but also represents a set of values worth enacting. Because family change is inevitable and offers new possibilities for equality, this view argues that the challenge is to accept the growing need for more egalitarian arrangements and restructure society to make that possible (Ferree 1990).

There are some signs that the family values debate may be cooling. New generations, who watched their parents and other adults invent a mosaic of new living arrangements, now take for granted options that earlier generations barely imagined. Jason's story is instructive. Although he grew up in a white, working-class suburb where traditional views predominated, he watched his parents struggle with unexpected crises and experienced changes that broadened his views on family life. Like his peers throughout the United States, the experience of growing up in a changing family prompted a rejection of older certainties and a more tolerant perspective on his own family options and the choices of others. These more tolerant outlooks among those who came of age amid the family and gender revolution may result in a decline in the resonance of politically divisive cultural wedge issues (DiMaggio et al. 1996; Jayson 2007; Teixeira 2009). Even among young adults who identify as highly traditional and very religious, a growing number say they "are tired of the culture wars [and] want to broaden the traditional evangelical agenda" (Banerjee 2008).

Facing their own conflicts about marriage, sexuality, work, and parenthood, young adults are increasingly weary of a divisive political rhetoric that blames families for conditions beyond their control. Most say they prefer a politics that avoids finger-pointing in favor of a more tolerant vision that stresses similar needs rather than putting social groups in conflict. These aspirations point toward the possibility of a more inclusive politics that focuses on the common needs of diverse families and replaces an image of moral decline with a concern about realigning our social institutions to better fit the new circumstances of twenty-first-century families.

Yet without social supports for more versatile ways of constructing families, new generations have good reason to remain skeptical about their chances of achieving these ideals. In the absence of institutional supports, American families face uncharted territory. The rise of alternatives to permanent marriage means that sexual partnerships are necessarily more optional and fluid. And economic shifts, such as the rise of service-sector jobs and the decline of blue-collar ones, make women's participation in the world of paid work inevitable. These intertwined and reinforcing changes create a host of new options, but they are also on a collision course with other social institutions that remain based on a mid-twentieth century model of static family forms. If families are films, not snapshots, then we need public discussions and social policies that see family life as an unfolding, unpredictable process in which anyone, at any time, may need some kind of help. In the context of this irreversible but unfinished family revolution, people need social supports for the diverse and changing families that exist today.

Watch the Video in MySocLab
Applying Your Sociological Imagination

What Is a Family? *(p. 352)*

 Watch the **Big Question Video** in MySocLab to review the key concepts for this section.

To begin this chapter, we first needed to examine the meaning of the term family. What is a family, and what are the various ways to define it?

THE MANY WAYS WE DEFINE *FAMILY* (p. 352)

A Global and Historical Perspective (p. 352)

- **What are some family forms that can be found throughout human history and across diverse societies and households?**

Kinship System or Household? (p. 353)

- **How do kinship systems and residence patterns contribute to different definitions of family?**

Read the **Document** *Beyond the Nuclear Family: The Increasing Importance of Multigenerational Bonds* by Vern Bengston in **MySocLab**. This reading examines the changes in multigenerational bonds that have emerged as family forms have changed.

Personal and Cultural Ideals of Family Membership (p. 354)

- **What does it mean to describe family life as multidimensional?**

KEY TERMS

polygamy *(p. 352)*

patrilocal *(p. 352)*

kinship system *(p. 353)*

kin *(p. 353)*

nuclear family *(p. 353)*

Why Has Family Life Become the Topic of Such Heated Debate? *(p. 355)*

 Watch the **Big Question Video** in MySocLab to review the key concepts for this section.

To understand the contemporary debate over "family values," this section mapped out the competing views about the current state of the American family, how we got here, and what we need to do in response.

CONTEMPORARY AMERICAN FAMILIES: A CONTROVERSIAL TOPIC (p. 355)

The Family Values Perspective (p. 356)

- **What concerns do proponents of the family decline perspective have regarding the nature of families today?**

The Economic Restructuring Perspective (p. 356)

- **How do proponents of the economic restructuring approach explain changing family arrangements?**

The Gender Restructuring Perspective (p. 357)

- **What role do cultural and economic forces play in the gender restructuring perspective on family life?**

KEY TERMS

cohabitation *(p. 355)*

family values *(p. 356)*

egalitarian relationship *(p. 357)*

What Challenges Do We Face as We Develop Relationships and Balance Family and Work? *(p. 358)*

👁 **Watch** the **Big Question Video** in **MySocLab** to review the key concepts for this section.

This section examined the decline of permanent marriage and the new contours of adult commitment, as well as the blurring of gender divisions and the rise of work-family conflict.

THE NEW CONTOURS OF ADULTHOOD COMMITMENT (p. 358)

Love and Marriage (p. 358)

- **How has marriage become deinstitutionalized in today's postindustrial economy?**

 Explore the **Data** on What Women and Men Want in **MySocLab**

Mothers, Fathers, and Work-Family Conflict (p. 361)

- **In what ways does the clash between family needs and work pressures affect family life?**

What Is It Like to Grow Up in a Twenty-First Century Family? *(p. 364)*

👁 **Watch** the **Big Question Video** in **MySocLab** to review the key concepts for this section.

In this section, we discussed how the experiences of children transitioning into adulthood are very different from how they once were and what this means for today's children and young adults.

GROWING UP IN TODAY'S FAMILIES (p. 364)

The Changing Face of Childhood (p. 364)

- **What does research indicate about the effects of divorce on children?**

Becoming an Adult (p. 366)

- **What are the benefits and drawbacks of the expanding period of early adulthood experienced by U.S. young adults?**

5 What Causes Inequality among Families?
(p. 368)

 Watch the **Big Question Video** in **MySocLab** to review the key concepts for this section.

The causes of family inequality are complex and difficult to isolate, especially because the economy is changing and gender, race, and ethnic diversity intersect with class differences.

FAMILIES AND SOCIAL INEQUALITY (p. 368)

- **How do race, ethnicity, and gender intersect with class to create inequality in families?**

6 What Social Policies around the World Best Support Changing Families? *(p. 370)*

 Watch the **Big Question Video** in **MySocLab** to review the key concepts for this section.

Finally, we placed American family life today in a comparative perspective. This section examined how other countries have approached social policies for families and how we can learn from their tactics.

THE UNITED STATES IN COMPARATIVE PERSPECTIVE (p. 370)

Social Policy around the World (p. 370)

- **How do government policies towards families differ around the world?**

 Explore A Sociological Perspective: Is childcare the same around the world? in **MySocLab**

Where Do We Go from Here? (p. 371)

- **What would a more effective, inclusive policy approach to family support in the United States look like?**

 Watch the **Video** Applying Your Sociological Imagination in **MySocLab** to see these concepts at work in the real world

17

SOCIAL MOVEMENTS and REVOLUTIONS

by JEFF GOODWIN

O n September 17, 2011, several hundred people marched to Wall Street in lower Manhattan with the goal of occupying public space in front of or near the Stock Exchange. The ultimate goals of the protesters were unclear, but they were clearly opposed to the tremendous economic and political power of banks, financial institutions, and corporations generally. They claimed to speak for the 99 percent of the population who have no control over these institutions. Wall Street was blocked by police, but the protesters occupied a small park—known as Zuccotti Park—not far away. Many of the protesters began to sleep overnight in the park, which became a site for political discussions and for organizing marches and other protests. Thus began the so-called Occupy Wall Street movement.

The protesters were evicted by police from Zuccotti Park just two months after they occupied it. In the meantime, however, the movement organized several demonstrations in New York City with thousands of participants, including a demonstration in Times Square on October 15 in which perhaps 50,000 people participated. The mass media began to focus on the movement, and politicians began speaking about inequality and the economic problems of the "99 percent." Protesters unexpectedly began to occupy public parks and other public spaces in dozens of cities and towns across the United States—in Washington, Boston, Chicago, New Orleans, Portland (Oregon), Oakland, and beyond. Police eventually evicted protesters from virtually all the parks they had occupied, but these evictions did not end the movement, even if they made it less visible. Activists continued to meet and organize a range of protest activities against banks and corporations.

Occupy Wall Street raises a number of questions that have preoccupied sociologists interested in social movements and revolutions. Why did this movement develop when it did? Who participated in it? Why did the protesters use certain tactics and not others? What changes has the movement brought about? What might cause it to decline or disappear? Is this a revolutionary movement? Is a revolution possible or likely in a country like the United States? Or are other countries, with different problems and political institutions, more likely to have revolutions in the future?

MY SOCIOLOGICAL IMAGINATION
Jeff Goodwin

I grew up at a time when the U.S. government was trying hard to destroy domestic social movements, especially the black power and the anti–Vietnam War movement, as well as revolutions overseas, particularly in Cuba, Vietnam, and Chile. I remember vividly the killing of students at Kent State University who were protesting the invasion of Cambodia, something that was pretty scary for a young kid. I was also scared and anxious when my older brother was drafted into the military, but fortunately he was not sent to Vietnam. All this made me interested in why people protest and rebel, sometimes violently, and why governments sometimes use violence against their opponents. I came to understand how the sociological imagination which C. Wright Mills described—the capacity, that is, to see how seemingly personal grievances are in fact linked to social structures and shared with others—is a prerequisite of political protest. While I was studying rebels in college and graduate school at Harvard, I also joined the ranks of movements that were trying to stop the U.S. government from supporting brutal armies in Central America and the racist government in South Africa. I have been studying social movements (and occasionally participating in them) as well as revolutions ever since.

The Occupy Wall Street movement grew in size and spread very rapidly across the United States in the fall of 2011.

Watch the **Video** in **MySocLab**
Inspiring Your Sociological Imagination

THE BIG QUESTIONS

👁 Watch the Big Question Videos in MySocLab

Scholars and activists themselves have asked four key sets of questions about social movements and revolutions. This chapter examines how sociologists have answered these questions.

1 **What are social movements?** Social movements play a crucial role in contemporary societies. Through them we can learn about the world around us. We start the chapter by defining social movements and exploring what we can learn by studying them.

Why do movements emerge, and who joins them? The most frequently asked question about social movements is why they emerge when they do. In this section we examine how movements take shape and look at who joins or supports social movements.

2

3 **What do movements accomplish?** Why do movements use certain tactics and not others? Why do movements decline or disappear? In this section we look at what movements do and what changes and outcomes movements bring about, including unintended consequences.

What are revolutions, and why do they occur? Finally, we look at why some social movements are revolutionary and what causes revolutionary situations to occur. When and why have revolutionary movements been able to take state power? We conclude the chapter by examining how democracy shapes social conflict and the prospects for revolution.

4

1 What Are Social Movements?

STUDYING SOCIAL MOVEMENTS

👁 Watch the **Big Question Video** in **MySocLab**

Throughout history, people have complained about the things they disliked. Sometimes they do more than complain; they band together with others to try to change things. In modern societies, more than ever before, people have organized themselves to pursue a dizzying array of goals, and they have used a wide variety of tactics to attain those goals. There are the strikes, pickets, and rallies of the labor movement, aimed at unionization and better wages but also (sometimes) at political goals. The women's movement has tried to change family life and gender relations through persuasion and lawmaking. Animal rights activists have broken into labs and "liberated" experimental animals. And there have been many conservative and right-wing movements as well, from Americans opposed to immigrants in the 1840s (and today) to those who have bombed abortion clinics in recent years.

Some of these movements have looked for opportunities to claim new rights while others have responded to threats or violence. Some have sought political and economic emancipation and gains, while others have fought against lifestyle choices they disliked or feared. Some have created formal organizations, others have relied upon informal networks, and still others have used more spontaneous actions such as **riots**, which are unplanned collective protests, loosely organized at best, involving attacks on property and (sometimes) persons. Movements have regularly had to choose between violent and nonviolent activities, illegal and legal ones, disruption and persuasion, radical and moderate demands, reform and revolution.

Social movements are conscious, concerted, and sustained efforts by ordinary people to change (or preserve) some aspect of their society by using extrainstitutional means. *Extrainstitutional means* are collective actions undertaken outside existing institutions, like courts and legislatures, although movements may also work through such institutions at least part of the time. Movements are more conscious and organized than fashions or **fads** (behavior that spreads, often rapidly, among a specific population and is repeated enthusiastically for some period of time before disappearing, often rapidly). They last longer than a single protest or riot. There is more to them than formal organizations, although such organizations usually play a part. They are composed mainly of ordinary people as opposed to wealthy elites, politicians, or army officers. They need not be explicitly political, but many are. Movements protest against something, either explicitly as in antiwar movements or implicitly as in the back-to-the-land movement that is disgusted with modern urban and suburban life.

Why do we care about social movements? Examining protesters and their points of view is certainly a good way to comprehend human diversity. For example, why do some people think animals have rights, or others that the United Nations is part of a sinister conspiracy? But aside from studying social movements to understand a diverse array of viewpoints, movements are also windows onto a number of aspects of social life. These include politics, human action, social change, and the moral basis of society.

Politics, Human Action, and Social Change

Social movements are a main source of political conflict and change. They often articulate *new* political issues and ideas. As people become attuned to some social problem they want solved, they often form some kind of movement to push for a solution. Political parties and their leaders rarely ask the most interesting questions or raise new issues; bureaucracy sets in, and politicians spend their time in routines. It is typically movements outside a society's political institutions that force insiders to recognize new fears and desires among specific social groups. During the Obama administration, for example, politicians were generally not discussing growing inequality in the United States or the power of corporations; it took the Occupy Wall Street movement to initiate a public discussion about these issues.

Scholars of social movements ask why and how people do the things they do, especially why they do things *together*; this is also the question that drives sociology in general, especially sociological theory. Social movements raise the famous question asked by philosopher Thomas Hobbes regarding social order: Why do people cooperate with each other when they might get as many or more benefits by acting selfishly or alone? The study of social movements makes the question more manageable: If we can see why and how people voluntarily cooperate in social movements, we can understand why and how they cooperate in general. Political action sheds light on action in other spheres of life. It gets at the heart of human motivation. For example, do people act to maximize their material interests like wealth and power? Do they act out rituals that express their beliefs about the world or simply reaffirm their place in that world? What is the balance in movements between symbolic action—which is intended to spread a message—and instrumental (i.e., goal-oriented) action—which is intended to bring about some specific change? What is the balance between selfish and altruistic behavior?

Social movements are also a central source of social and political change. In the United States, movements are at least partly responsible for most of the progressive laws of the past century, including women's right to vote, the right to organize unions, and civil rights for African Americans and other minorities, including homosexuals. Of course, there are other sources of social change, including corporations, which are out to make a profit: they invent new technologies that change our ways of working and interacting. Corporations are always inventing new ways of extracting profits from workers and inventing new products to market. These changes typically disrupt people's ways of life: A new machine may throw people out of work or make them work harder. Toxic wastes may be disposed of near a school. People react to these changes, and resist them, by forming social movements.

But while corporations are the main source of technical change, they are rarely a source of change in values or in

social arrangements. Why? In modern societies with tightly knit political and economic systems, the big bureaucracies demand economic and political control and stability. So they try to routinize social life in order to prevent the unexpected. They resist changes in property relations, for example, which are one of the key components of capitalism.

So innovation in values and political beliefs often arises from the discussions and efforts of social movements. Why don't societies just endlessly reproduce themselves intact? It is often social movements that develop new ways of seeing society and new ways of directing it. They are a central part of what has been called "civil society" or the "public sphere," in which groups and individuals debate their own futures (Cohen and Arato 1992).

What can movements teach us about social life?

Moral Sensibilities

Social movements are similar to art: They are efforts to express sensibilities that have not yet been well articulated, that journalists or novelists have not yet written about, and that lawmakers have not yet addressed. We all have moral sensibilities—including unspoken intuitions as well as articulated principles and rules—that guide our actions or at least make

These students from Oberlin College are protesting hydraulic fracking in Ohio. Why are students so often involved in social movements?

us uneasy when they are violated. Social movements are good ways to understand these moral sensibilities. For example, movements have challenged ideas about who deserves legal rights, including the right to vote. Radical abolitionists like Frederick Douglass fought to end slavery and give rights to African Americans; women's movements have fought for the right to vote and for reproductive rights (including access to contraceptives and abortions); antiabortion activists argue that human fetuses have rights; and many people now believe that certain animals have at least some rights, like the right not to be used in scientific experiments. It's safe to say that many fewer people (and other species) would have rights today were it not for social movements, which have dramatically changed the moral sensibilities of societies over the past two centuries.

Social movements play a number of crucial roles in contemporary societies. We learn about the world around us through them. They encourage us to figure out how we feel about government policies and social trends and new technologies. In some cases they even inspire the invention of new technologies or new ways of using old technologies. Most of all, they are one means by which we work out our moral visions, transforming vague intuitions into principles and political demands.

Understanding Social Movements Today

Sociologists and other scholars have emphasized different aspects of social movements at different historical moments. They once largely feared movements, seeing them as dangerous mobs. Later scholars were much more sympathetic, emphasizing that movements are quite rational, carefully weighing the costs and benefits of their actions. Others stressed the political nature of movements. The **political process perspective** emphasizes that movements are primarily concerned with politics, not individual psychological states, and are a normal response, under certain circumstances, to routine political processes. Movements emerge and may be successful if those political processes create opportunities for certain kinds of collective protest. Still other scholars emphasize the cultural side of movements, exploring the work that goes into creating powerful symbols, convincing people that they have grievances that can be remedied, and building a sense of solidarity or connectedness among certain people.

What aspects of movements are contemporary sociologists interested in?

Recently sociologists have begun to recognize and study even more aspects of social movements. For example, many movements have a global reach, tying together protest groups and networks across many countries and even forming international organizations. The environmental movement and the protest against the World Trade Organization and the unregulated globalization of trade are examples. Yet most of our models still assume a national movement interacting with a single national state.

Our understanding of social movements has grown as movements themselves have changed. Like everyone else, scholars of social movements are influenced by what they see happening around them. Much protest of the nineteenth century took the form of riots, so it was natural to focus on the nature of crowds and "mobs." Scholars who examined the labor movement and the American civil rights movement recognized that claims of new rights necessarily involve the state, so it was natural for them to focus on the political dimensions of protest. Social scientists who came of age in the 1960s and after were often favorably disposed toward the social movements around them and so portrayed protesters as reasonable people. Many of the movements of the 1960s and after were not about rights for oppressed groups but about lifestyles and cultural meanings, so it was inevitable that scholars sooner or later would turn to this dimension of protest.

Likewise in recent years, several important social movements have become more global in scope. The so-called alter-globalization movement against the power of multinational corporations and international lending agencies is one example. Many movements are also interested in changing our emotional capacities, especially movements influenced by the women's movement, which argued that women were disadvantaged by the ways in which different emotions were thought appropriate for men and for women. Research on social movements will undoubtedly continue to evolve as social movements themselves evolve.

These protesters in Seattle are opposed to the politics of the World Trade Organization. Why has unregulated global trade led opponents to forge ties across the borders?

2 Why Do Movements Emerge, and Who Joins Them?

MOVEMENT ORIGINS AND RECRUITMENT

👁 Watch the Big Question Video in **MySocLab**

The most frequently asked question about social movements is why they emerge when and where they do. Where we think a movement comes from colors the way we view its other aspects, too: its goals, participants, tactics, and outcomes.

☐ How Movements Take Shape

In general, theories of movement origins focus either on the characteristics of participants or on conditions in the broader environment which potential participants face. It is also possible to link these two perspectives.

Scholars have discovered a wide range of factors that explain why a movement emerges when and where it does: political factors such as divisions among authorities or lessened repression from the police and army; economic conditions such as increased income, especially among those sympathetic to a movement's cause, or alternatively an economic crisis that throws many people out of work; organizational conditions such as social-network ties or formal organizations among aggrieved populations (such as churches, schools, and athletic leagues); demographic conditions such as the increased population density and human connectedness that comes with industrialization (if you live a mile from your nearest neighbor, it is hard to organize collectively); and cultural factors such as moral intuitions or sensibilities that support the movement's

What factors explain why movements emerge when and where they do?

cause. And of course potential protesters must understand factors such as these as real opportunities for collective protest before they can take advantage of them.

Resource Mobilization and Political Process Approaches
In the 1960s and 1970s, a group of researchers noticed that social movements usually consist of formal organizations (McCarthy and Zald 1977). Known as the **resource mobilization approach**, this theoretical perspective emphasizes the importance of resources, like labor and money, for generating and sustaining social movements. The more resources a movement is able to employ or mobilize, the more successful it is likely to be. This school argues that there are always enough discontented people in society to fill a protest movement, but what varies over time—and so explains the emergence of movements—is the resources available to nourish it. These researchers accordingly focused on how movement leaders raise funds, sometimes by appealing to wealthy people, sometimes through direct-mail fundraising from thousands of regular citizens. As a society grows wealthier, moreover, citizens have more money to contribute to **social movement organizations (SMOs)**—the formal organizations that support and sometimes initiate movements—and so there are more movements than ever before. With this point of view, the focus shifted decisively away from the kinds of individuals who might join a movement and toward the organization and resources necessary to sustain a movement. Today, scholars

still consider resources an important part of any explanation of movement emergence.

The theoretical paradigm that has concentrated most on movement emergence is the political process approach mentioned earlier (e.g., McAdam 1982). According to this perspective, economic and political shifts occur, usually independently of protesters' own efforts, that open up a space or opportunities for the movement. Because this approach views movements as primarily political, making demands of the state and asking for changes in laws and policies, it regards changes in the government or state as the most important opportunity a movement needs. Most often, this consists of a slackening in the repression that organizers are otherwise assumed to face, perhaps because political authorities are divided (the movement may have found some allies within the government) or because powerful political and economic actors have divergent interests. There may be a general crisis in the government, perhaps as a result of fighting (or losing) a foreign war, which distracts leaders and may bankrupt the government. In many versions of this perspective, the same factors are seen as explaining both the rise of the movement and its relative success.

Resources, organization, and a sense of new opportunities all undoubtedly encouraged the civil rights movement that grew rapidly beginning in 1955. By then, the migration of African Americans out of the rural South provided them with more resources and denser social ties; churches and organizations through which money could be channeled to civil rights work; and a new, more optimistic cultural outlook. These factors encouraged more extensive political mobilization, especially through the National Association for the Advancement of Colored People (NAACP), which in turn won inspiring legal victories, especially *Brown v. Board of Education* in 1954, which held that racially segregated schools violated the Constitution.

is recruited, the very existence of social ties among potential recruits is seen as a prerequisite for the emergence of a movement. If most political process theorists emphasize conditions in the external environment (especially the government) that allow a movement to emerge, network theorists look at the conditions within the community or population of those who might be recruited. Those people with dense ties, or who belong to certain formal organizations, find it easier to reach, persuade, and mobilize other people and thereby build a movement.

Scholars who have studied the 1969 Stonewall rebellion in New York City and the subsequent development of a militant gay and lesbian movement emphasize the critical importance of social networks. The Stonewell rebellion involved violent confrontations between police and gay men and lesbians over the course of several days following the arrest of gay patrons at a bar called the Stonewall Inn in Greenwich Village. This rebellion, apparently a spontaneous eruption of gay militancy, in fact marked the public emergence of a long-repressed, covert urban subculture. The gay movement was also able to draw upon preexisting networks of activists in the radical movements then current among American youth. The "gay liberation" movement recruited from the ranks of both the anti–Vietnam War movement and the women's movement. It also borrowed its confrontational tactics from these movements. Many lesbians and gay men had already been radicalized and educated in the arts of protest by the feminist and antiwar movements.

The theoretical approaches discussed thus far redefined somewhat the central question of movement emergence. Scholars began to see movements as closely linked to one another because leaders and participants shifted from one to the other or shared social networks, or because the same political conditions encouraged many movements to form

Social Networks Alongside resource mobilization and political process approaches, a number of sociologists have emphasized the **social networks** through which people are mobilized into social movements. Social networks are the webs of ties or connections that link individuals (and organizations) to one another, thereby facilitating communication and other exchanges. Although networks have been used primarily to explain *who*

This march in New York City occurred on the first anniversary of the Stonewall rebellion, then known as "Gay Liberation Day."

at the same time. So researchers began to ask what caused entire waves or "cycles" of social movements to emerge rather than asking about the origins of single movements. One cannot fully understand any one of the movements of the 1960s cycle of protest, for example—including the civil rights movement, the women's movement, the farm workers' movement, and the anti–Vietnam War movement—without knowing something about the other movements in this cycle.

Cultural Approaches In recent years, some sociologists who take a cultural approach have linked social movements to broad historical developments, especially the shift from an industrial or manufacturing society to a postindustrial or knowledge society in which fewer people process physical goods and more deal with symbols and other forms of knowledge. Social movements are seen as efforts to control the direction of social change largely by controlling a society's symbols and self-understandings.

In cultural approaches, the goals and intentions of protesters are taken very seriously. For instance, the origin of the animal protection movement has been linked to broad changes in sensibilities over the last 200 years that have allowed citizens of the industrial world to recognize the suffering of nonhuman species—and to worry about it. Such concerns would simply not have been possible in a society

Here, an animal rights advocate has just thrown blood on a fur coat worn by actress Kim Cattrall. Why have some people become so concerned with the suffering of animals in recent decades?

where most people worked on farms and used animals both as living tools (horses, dogs, dairy cows) and as raw materials (food, leather, etc.). The point is to observe or ask protesters themselves about their perceptions, desires, and fantasies without having a theory that predicts in advance what protesters think and feel. Perceptions are crucial in this view.

From this perspective, the work of sociologist Charles Kurzman (1996) helped change the way scholars think about shifts in political opportunities for protest. Political process theorists had insisted that these were objective changes, independent of protesters' perceptions, but Kurzman's research shows that the perceptions may matter as much as the underlying reality. Kurzman's research on the Iranian Revolution (1978–1979), in which the monarch (or shah) was overthrown by a popular uprising, indicates that there were no objective political changes on the eve of the revolution that suddenly weakened the monarchy or created new opportunities for protest. Indeed, despite considerable police repression and expressions of U.S. support for the monarchy, protest against the shah continued to grow and people gradually came to believe they could topple the regime. A movement can sometimes succeed, apparently, if it thinks it can. In other words, cultural perceptions can play as important a role as changes in the state or society. Political process theorists had apparently not tested their model in cases where perceptions and objective realities diverged: Protesters may fail to see (or seize) opportunities, and they may imagine opportunities for protest when none seems to exist. The slackening of police repression, divisions among wealthy elites and politicians, and so on (the "opportunities" of political process theorists) may only have an effect if they are perceived as such. And people may sometimes rebel (and sometimes win), as in Iran, even when the political environment does not at first seem promising.

Cultural sociologists have reached different conclusions than resource mobilization and political process theorists in part because they have examined different kinds of social movements. Most political process theorists, for example, have focused on movements of groups who have been systematically excluded from political power and legal rights, in other words groups that are demanding the full rights of citizenship. Cultural approaches have been more likely to examine movements of those who already have the formal rights of citizens—who can vote, pressure legislators, and run for office—but who nonetheless feel they must step outside normal political institutions to have a greater impact. Resource mobilization theorists also assume that people know what they want and simply need the resources and organization to pursue it; cultural sociologists recognize that in many cases people only gradually figure out what they want, often because movement organizers persuade them of it (e.g., that animals can suffer like humans, that marijuana should be legal, that the U.S. government is the tool of Satan).

Cultural sociologists have reasserted the importance of perceptions, ideas, emotions, and grievances, all of which resource mobilization and political process theorists once thought did not matter very much or could simply be taken for granted. But these are examined today in the context of broader social and political changes, not in isolation from them. It is not as though people first develop goals and then decide to go out and form movements to pursue them; there is an interaction among ideas, mobilization, and the broader environment. Some people get pulled into movements by friends or family and are only slowly converted to the movement's cause; their political beliefs are a consequence, not a cause, of joining the movement. Research suggests, for example, that over 40 percent of committed antiabortion activists had ambiguous views about abortion or even considered themselves "pro-choice" when they initially joined the movement; it was only after they spent some time in the movement, interacting with long-term activists, that they came to emphatically oppose abortions (Munson 2008).

Recruitment: Joining or Supporting Movements

Once activists form groups or networks and begin to think of themselves as a movement (or at least a potential movement), their next step is usually to try to expand their ranks by recruiting others to their cause. Like accounts of movement origins, sociological theories of recruitment have evolved over time from an emphasis on individual traits to one on availability, and finally toward a synthesis of these dimensions.

Individual Traits among Protesters   Scholars once tended to see protesters as swept up in crowds, acting in abnormal and sometimes irrational ways because of frustration with their individual circumstances. In some theories marginal and alienated members of society were seen as most likely to join social movements; in others it was those who were insecure or dogmatic. Such claims were usually demeaning to protesters, who were thought to be compensating for some sort of personal inadequacy or psychological problem, but subsequent empirical research did not generally support the image of protesters as more angry or alienated than others.

The economist Mancur Olson (1965) suggested that protesters are perfectly rational, arguing that they do not join groups if they think they can gain the benefits that these groups pursue without taking the time to participate. In other words, people may become "free riders" on the efforts of others, letting others protest while benefitting from their successes. You don't have to join the environmental movement to enjoy the clean air that it wins for all of us—so why join it? Another reason to free ride is that your own participation in or contribution to a collective effort won't make a noticeable difference once the group consists of more than a few dozen people. What can a group of 101 people accomplish that a group of 100 can't? So to attract participants, Olson argues, movements must provide "selective incentives" that are enjoyed only by those who participate, such as interesting political discussions, the possibility of making new friends, insurance for trade union members, and the like. Olson challenged scholars to show how organizers manage to overcome the free rider problem.

Olson helped inspire the resource mobilization paradigm, which shifted attention from what kinds of *people* protest to what kinds of objective *conditions* facilitate protest. Attitudes and grievances were dismissed as insufficient to cause protest, for many people had the right attitudes and interests but did not participate. As part of this new agenda, **biographical availability** was seen as necessary for participation: People with few family or work obligations—especially young people without children—were particularly available to devote time to movement activities (McAdam 1988).

Recruitment via Social Networks   Researchers have found that the best predictor of who will join a movement, in addition to biographical availability, is whether an individual knows someone already in that movement. In many movements, a majority of participants are recruited this way. Social networks are thus usually a precondition for the emergence of a movement as well as the explanation for who was subsequently recruited to it. Physically scattered or socially isolated people are the least likely to join a movement. In the extreme case of "bloc recruitment," organizers bring a whole social network or organization virtually intact into a movement. This suggests that—contrary to Olson's view—people do not make decisions to join movements (or not) as isolated, self-regarding individuals but in concert with others in their networks.

Different kinds of social networks can be used for recruitment. They may not be political in origin or intent. Black churches and colleges were crucial to the Southern civil rights movement in the 1950s, fundamentalist churches helped defeat the Equal Rights Amendment in the 1980s, and mosques facilitated the Iranian Revolution. Networks developed for earlier political activities can also aid recruitment into a movement that develops later—one reason why

How do movements recruit supporters?

a history of previous activism makes someone more likely to be recruited. The clustering of movements in waves or cycles makes this mutual support especially important, as one movement feeds into the next. Because of these networks, prior activism and organizational memberships help predict who will be recruited (and who will not be).

Social media like Facebook and Twitter can also be used to recruit people to political protests, as was seen during the so-called Arab Spring of 2011 as well as in the Occupy Wall Street movement later that year. These media allow multitudes of people who have never met before and who have no other connections to communicate with one another. They make it possible to organize huge protests in a much shorter span of time and over greater distances than was previously possible. They allow activists to direct people to assemble at specific places and at specific times before the authorities have time to react. This can be especially important where authoritarian regimes are likely to break up protests violently. On the other hand, government authorities may also monitor social media—or attempt to shut them down altogether—in their attempts to control protest. So social media can be used to organize as well as disrupt movements.

Without denying the importance of personal contacts and communication networks, recent studies have also examined the cultural messages transmitted across these networks. For example, "suddenly imposed grievances" that are produced by dramatic and unexpected events may be important for recruitment. The partial nuclear meltdown in 1979 at the Three Mile Island power plant in Dauphin County, Pennsylvania, which led to the evacuation of nearly 200,000 people, alerted the public to the risks of nuclear energy, giving a big boost to the antinuclear movement (Walsh 1981). Recruitment is also more likely when people feel that they have a chance of success. This sense of optimism and efficacy has been called "cognitive liberation" (McAdam 1982). People may have lots of grievances as well as ties to individuals in a movement seeking to redress those grievances, but they are unlikely to join that movement if don't think it can succeed.

Scholars view direct personal contacts as important because they allow organizers and potential participants to achieve a common definition of a social problem and a common prescription for solving it. In successful recruitment, organizers offer ways of seeing a social problem that resonate with the views and experiences of potential recruits. The Occupy Wall Street movement, for example, spread very rapidly across the country in 2011 because its message about the power of banks and corporations and the plight of the "99 percent" resonated with people during a time of economic crisis and home foreclosures. Networks are important *because* of the cultural meanings they transmit. Networks and meanings are not rival explanations;

they work together. Explore the Infographic on page 485 to learn more about who makes up the Occupy Wall Street movement.

How Framing and Cultural Attitudes Shape Recruitment

Scholars of movements have also emphasized the framing work involved in recruiting people to movements. **Framing** generally refers to the specific ways that ideas and beliefs are presented to other people. Scholars of movements focus on how activists try to frame or present their ideas so that they make sense to or resonate with the beliefs of potential recruits and supporters. Scholars have distinguished three successive types of framing that are necessary for successful recruitment: *diagnostic*, in which a movement convinces potential converts that a problem needs to be addressed; *prognostic*, in which it convinces them of appropriate strategies, tactics, and targets; and *motivational*, in which it exhorts them to get involved in these activities (Snow and Benford 1988). Frames are more likely to be accepted if they fit well with the existing beliefs of potential recruits, if they involve empirically credible claims, if they are compatible with the life experiences of the audiences, and if they fit with the stories or narratives the audiences tell about their lives. Frames, in short, must resonate with the salient beliefs of potential recruits. When the frames of activists and potential recruits fit together in this way, scholars speak of "frame alignment."

Collective identity is another concept used to get at the mental worlds of people which helps explain recruitment to movements. A **collective identity** is one's belief that one belongs to a certain group (or groups) with distinctive characteristics and interests (for example, women, the working class, feminists). In order to devote time and effort to protest, people must usually feel part of a larger group they think they can help. Not all identities come easily to people; they may have to be consciously created, which is one of the things that some movements do. The gay and lesbian movement, for example, still devotes a lot of its energy to making it possible for gays and lesbians to feel comfortable with themselves and to identify themselves publicly as gay or lesbian (i.e., to "come out of the closet"). Obviously, people who for whatever reason find it difficult to identify themselves publicly with a certain group are unlikely to become politically active on its behalf.

Another cultural approach emphasizes how attitudes and worldviews matter. Political scientist Ronald Inglehart (1977) has argued that new "postmaterial" values and beliefs have emerged in the advanced industrial nations since the 1960s. Through most of human history, in his view, people have been forced to worry about basic material needs such as food, shelter, and security, but since World War II the advanced industrial world has been largely spared traditional privations. Those born after World War II—at least the college-educated and affluent middle class—were "freed" to

Constructing a profile of the typical participant in the Occupy Wall Street movement, as for any movement, can be quite difficult. Participants in movements are like the layers of an onion. At the core are the devoted, full-time (or nearly full-time) leaders and activists who do most of the strategic thinking and planning for the movement. Then there are the part-time activists who do a lot of the difficult but necessary work involved in recruiting participants and organizing meetings and protests. Then there are movement's "foot soldiers," the people who show up at meetings and protests—and who must show up if the movement is to come to the attention of the public, the media, and the authorities. And then there are people who express support for the movement in public opinion polls and may contribute money to it.

Sources: Based on data from Fast Company (2011); Panagopoulos and Costas (2011); Pew Research Center (2011).

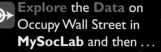
Explore the **Data** on Occupy Wall Street in **MySocLab** and then . . .

■ Think About It

How might the views of OWS activists about the President and Congress lead them to use "extra-institutional" political tactics?

■ Inspire Your Sociological Imagination

What do you think is behind the reasoning that younger people tend to support the OWS movement while older people tend to oppose it?

What do supporters of the O.W.S. Movement look like?

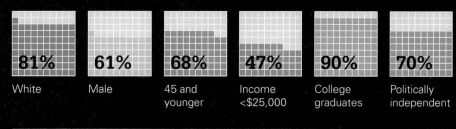

81%	61%	68%	47%	90%	70%
White	Male	45 and younger	Income <$25,000	College graduates	Politically independent

Political views of those active in the movement in N.Y.C.

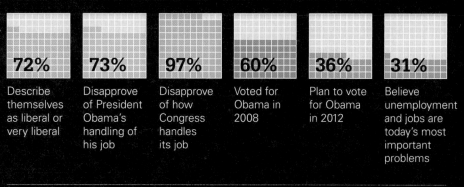

72%	73%	97%	60%	36%	31%
Describe themselves as liberal or very liberal	Disapprove of President Obama's handling of his job	Disapprove of how Congress handles its job	Voted for Obama in 2008	Plan to vote for Obama in 2012	Believe unemployment and jobs are today's most important problems

What does the public think of the Occupy movement?

Percentage in each group that supports or opposes the movement. Figures may not add to 100 because of rounding.

		Supports	Opposes	Neither/ don't know
	Overall	44	35	22
Politics	Republican	21	59	20
	Independent	46	34	21
	Democrat	60	21	19
Age	18-29	49	27	24
	30-49	45	32	23
	50-64	45	38	17
	65+	33	47	20
Education	College graduate	48	40	12
	Some college	50	33	17
	High school or less	39	33	28
Family income	$150,000+	36	55	10
	$100,000-$150,000	46	43	11
	$75,000-$100,000	49	37	14
	$30,000-$75,000	48	34	18
	<$30,000	43	30	27

pursue "higher" goals such as control over their lives, environmental protection, and satisfying work rather than worrying primarily about their paychecks. The spread of mass communication and higher education contributed to the same trends. The result has been less emphasis on economic redistribution, class-based political organizations, or the pursuit of political power—again, at least where the affluent middle class is concerned. Instead we have seen movements critical of large bureaucracies, meaningless work, complex technologies, and many different forms of oppression. One can certainly better understand who is likely to support the environmental movement or the animal-rights movement by using the concept of postmaterial politics. These movements have a primarily middle-class social base, even though they are not pursuing the narrow economic interests of this class. So the growth of a postindustrial sector of the economy can help explain not only changes in political concerns over time but also different sympathies across parts of the population at any given time.

It turns out that another contemporary movement has a primarily well-educated and middle-class social base: the followers of the late Osama bin Laden (Kurzman 2002). While many Westerners assume that the Islamic world is mired in religious superstition and rejects modern rationality, bin Laden's followers are much better educated than their peers and use the latest technologies and media. They are not motivated by narrow class or economic interests but by their opposition to the policies of the U.S. government in the Middle East, even as they use religious language and look nostalgically backward to a golden age of Islam. Attitudes and worldviews matter for recruitment, but they are not always what we assume them to be.

Recruitment, however, involves more than ideas about how the world works. Its moral and emotional dimensions are equally important. In fact, all the key factors that explain recruitment depend heavily on their emotional impact on people. Social networks, for example, are often grounded in the emotional bonds among their members: We pay attention to people in our networks, and what they say, because we are fond of them or trust them. The term **moral shock** is also meant to incorporate some of the moral and emotional dimensions of recruitment to movements. A moral shock is an unexpected event that surprises, distresses, and outrages people, often to the point of motivating them to join a movement to eliminate the source of their outrage. Moral shocks may be so strong that they lead people without social ties to activists to seek out or even form a group to redress their grievances (Jasper 1997). An example of a moral shock is the impact of the *Roe v. Wade* Supreme Court decision of 1973, which legalized abortions under certain circumstances, on many religious Americans, especially Catholic women. For these women, it was as if the Supreme Court had legalized the murder of certain kinds of children. Although they had not been politically active previously and knew no political activists, these women formed the core of the early antiabortion movement (Luker 1984).

Recent scholarship on movements pays more attention to what goes on inside people's heads (and hearts) than previously. Protest is no longer seen as a compensation for some psychological problem but part of an effort to impose meaning and morality on the world, to forge and express a collective identity, to create or reinforce emotional bonds with others, and to define and pursue collective interests. These are things that all humans desire and seek. There is today considerable consensus that positions in networks and cultural orientations (cognitive, moral, and emotional) are equally important in recruitment. But there are also cases in which cultural messages can be used to recruit people in the absence of social networks, relying on moral shocks instead of personal ties. For virtually all social movements, only a small fraction of potential recruits actually join, and it takes all the factors we have considered to understand who does and does not sign up.

While many Westerners assume that the Islamic world is caught up in religious superstition and rejects modern rationality, it is known that the followers of the late Osama bin Laden are actually much better educated than their peers and use the latest technologies and media.

3 What Do Movements Accomplish?

MOVEMENT TACTICS AND OUTCOMES

👁 Watch the **Big Question Video** in **MySocLab**

If you are in a social movement, the most pressing question you face is: *What is to be done?* How do you choose tactics that will help your cause? How do you recruit more people, attract the news media, put pressure on the rich and powerful, or favorably impress decisionmakers? Tactical decisions are the real "stuff" of social movements. Fortunately, a few sociologists have looked at how these decisions are made, how and when protesters innovate in their tactics, and what the tradeoffs are between different kinds of tactics. Practitioners as well as academics have also addressed these issues.

The Strategies and Tactics of Movements

The tactical choices of activists are usually made in the heat of conflict and so can be hard to explain in a rigorous fashion. These choices depend in part on the instincts of movement leaders, who themselves may not always be able to explain why they made one choice rather than another. Decisions are sometimes made quickly, and it may be difficult to reconstruct the process later—when being interviewed by a sociologist, for instance.

Tactical choices are usually made during the course of interactions with other decisionmakers: with one's opponents, of course, but also with the police, the media, the

Why do movements use certain tactics and not others?

legislators, potential allies, and many others. To take just one example, before most rallies or marches today, leaders negotiate with the police over where they will go, what they will do, how many will be arrested (if any), and so on. Leaders must also make tactical choices with regard to their own followers as well as opponents: how to placate disaffected factions, how to keep members coming back to future events, how to increase or simply maintain the membership. As a result, any given action is probably designed for several different audiences at the same time. But an action that satisfies one may not please another.

With regard to their opponents, protesters hope to change their behavior through persuasion, intimidation, or imposing costs (financial or otherwise) upon them. Raising the costs of "business as usual" is generally necessary when movements confront powerful elites (especially the wealthy) who have not been elected. They can simply ignore protesters or try to repress them if they become threatening. Strikes and boycotts, however, hurt the wealthy economically and may lead them to make concessions to protesters so that their factories and farms can continue to make profits.

Movements also seek to undermine their opponents' credibility with the public, media, and government officials. With regard to such officials, protesters hope to change laws, policies, regulatory practices, and administrative rules and to avoid repression. From the courts, protesters typically strive to have unfavorable laws struck down or at least interpreted

FIGURE 17.1 WHICH SMOs HAVE RECEIVED THE MOST MEDIA ATTENTION DURING THE TWENTIETH CENTURY?

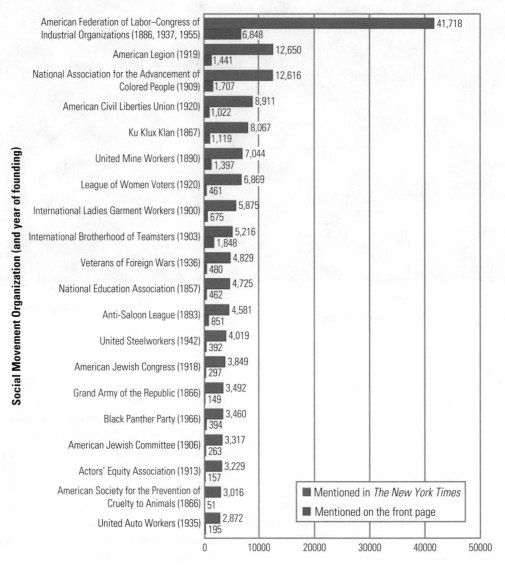

Source: Based on data from Amenta et al. (2008).

in a new way. With both courts and police, they hope for tolerance of their protests. Social movements seek to use the news media to spread their message and sometimes to undermine their opponents (see Figure 17.1). Protesters may also approach professional groups, such as engineers, to change their standards. They may seek allies in other protest groups. And from the public at large, they may hope for new recruits, sympathy, contributions, or at least changes in awareness. Finally, they even have goals for their own members: personal transformations and continued fervor for the cause. In other words, movements have a lot of goals to balance in their tactics, and striking the right balance is sometimes extremely difficult.

Movement leaders, moreover, are only familiar with a limited number of tactics. The sociologist Charles Tilly (1986) developed the concept of a "repertoire of contention"

to describe the range of tactics available to protesters in any given society in a particular period. Most social movements in that society draw on the same repertoire because it is largely fixed and unchanging, at least in the short run. There are many possible tactics that movement leaders are not familiar with or do not have the knowledge to utilize, including (hypothetically) tactics that might be extremely beneficial to the movement. Tilly was interested in explaining how repertoires of contention changed over long stretches of time, while other scholars have been concerned with explaining why particular leaders choose certain tactics and not others from the existing repertoire: Why a march rather than a letter-writing campaign? Why wait a week before responding to your opponents' actions rather than acting immediately? Why choose one cultural frame rather than another for a speech or website?

Shown here, the sit-in protest in support of affirmative action has taken over the steps of the Michigan state capitol building. Why are some protest tactics used repeatedly over the years?

Saul Alinsky, one of the greatest community organizers of the twentieth century, wrote a great deal about tactics in the course of trying to improve the living conditions of poor neighborhoods, particularly in Chicago (Alinsky 1971). Alinsky developed tactical principles that are not unlike those of army generals: Try to take your opponents by surprise, and try to make them think you are more powerful than you are. Try to use tactics your own followers enjoy and are familiar with. The idea of keeping the pressure on one's opponents is important because you never know where and when your opponent will be vulnerable or will make a blunder. The greater the pressure, the greater the chance you will trip them up. Alinsky also recognized that it is usually necessary to portray your enemy as an utter villain, a real flesh-and-blood person who can be blamed, not an abstract principle. Thus, protest movements during the Arab Spring of 2011 demonized dictators like Hosni Mubarak in Egypt. Protesters called for the replacement of the authoritarian regime in Egypt with democracy, but they usually called simply for the overthrow of Mubarak, who symbolized all that was wrong in the country. Such demonization can lead to strong emotions and polarization. Alinsky's rules are quite general, but they can be helpful reminders to social movement leaders.

In describing civil-rights sit-ins, sociologist Aldon Morris (1984) exemplifies the resource mobilization approach to tactics. He is not so much concerned with the origins of the sit-in tactic or the strategic thinking behind its use. Rather, he is concerned with revealing the indigenous organizations and social networks through which the sit-ins rapidly spread, arguing against a view of the sit-ins as spontaneous eruptions. Morris also touches on another important issue: the emergence of "movement centers" with resources, social ties (especially preachers and NAACP activists), and regular meetings (usually at churches). Other theorists have called these "free spaces," places relatively free from surveillance where oppositional ideas and tactics can develop and spread.

Other scholars have looked at the use of violent strategies by social movements and have tried to dispel some of the myths surrounding these. They point out that guerrilla warfare and terrorism are rational political responses to state violence and conflicts over territory, not the handiwork of psychopaths or religious fanatics, as the media often suggest.

Scholars as well as journalists are often hesitant to emphasize the rationality or achievements of political violence, in part because of their moral discomfort with it. In the case of the antiapartheid movement in South Africa, this has led some scholars to avoid discussing violence altogether and to portray the movement, misleadingly, as an entirely nonviolent civil-rights struggle like that in the United States. But political violence, like war, is routine politics by other means. That said, recent research indicates that nonviolent movements may be twice as likely to succeed as violent movements, even against very repressive regimes (Chenoweth and Stephan 2011). This is because ordinary people usually find it much easier to participate in nonviolent movements, so they tend to be much larger than violent movements, and because government officials and soldiers are more likely to defect to nonviolent movements.

Although social movements are defined, in part, by their use of extrainstitutional tactics (that is, outside existing political institutions) to pursue their political goals, protest can

We often think of protests as occurring "in the streets," but they can occur within institutions as well. Here gay rights advocates call for the repeal of the "don't ask, don't tell" policy during a Senate hearing.

also take place *within* institutions. For example, gays and lesbians in the U.S. military have fought with allies outside the military to overturn the so-called "don't ask, don't tell" policy that prohibited them from serving as openly gay or lesbian. Thus, free spaces *outside* regular institutions are not always enough for movements to flourish; sometimes they can also thrive *within* dominant institutions.

The choice of strategies and tactics is certainly an area in which additional research is needed. One limitation of existing research has been that most scholars have thought about the movement as their unit of analysis: how each grows, operates, and affects the world around it. But tactical choices are made in close interaction with other actors in the same "field of conflict," including opponents and allies, actual and potential. These interactions are like a game of chess: Each player's tactical moves are shaped as much by the moves of the other players as by one's preferred or ideal course of action. So movements often end up doing things they would rather not do but feel they must—such as killing civilians. But this is not surprising. In an ideal world, after all, people would not need to make hard choices about political tactics; they would already have the things their movements are fighting for.

Why do movements decline or disappear?

☐ The Decline and Disappearance of Movements

Not surprisingly, scholars have had much more to say about why social movements arise than why they decline or disappear altogether. Nonetheless, several hypotheses about movement decline have attained some prominence.
📖 **Read** the **Document** *The Rise and Fall of Aryan Nations* in **MySocLab**

Changing Political Environments Most explanations for movement decline focus on the surrounding political environment, which may constrain as well as facilitate movements. Of course, the very success of a movement in changing laws or government policies may undermine the motivations that many people had for participating in that movement. Movement organizations may also be legally

recognized by the government, leading to their institutionalization and declining reliance upon disruptive protest. Government concessions of this type, even if they do not redress all the grievances and concerns of movement participants, may nevertheless be sufficient to satisfy or placate many people, who will then drift away from the movement or from protest tactics. Social movements, in short, may become victims of their own limited successes. The U.S. labor movement is a prime example of this dynamic. After militant and sometimes deadly strikes in the 1930s led to the legal recognition of trade unions and the right to collective bargaining, unions gradually turned away from strikes and the aggressive recruitment of new members. As a result, the proportion of workers who belong to unions has been declining since the 1950s. Explore *A Sociological Perspective* on page 491 to learn more about the U.S. labor movement.

Internal Dynamics and Evolution Movements may also decline as a result of their own internal dynamics and evolution. The women's movement, for example, has gradually lost its radical vision and militancy (Epstein 2001). This was a result in part of intense ideological conflicts among radical feminists within the movement, who had provided much of the movement's activist core and ideological inspiration. Gradually, and partly because of its own success in opening up new professional careers for women, the women's movement as a whole took on a middle-class outlook. It became more concerned with the career opportunities and material success of individual women than with the group solidarity of women or addressing the concerns of poor and working-class women. A number of women's organizations have now been successfully institutionalized, including the National

A SOCIOLOGICAL PERSPECTIVE

Will the labor movement revive?

Why do movements decline or disappear? Sometimes they become victims of their own limited success, as was the case with the American labor movement. After decades of internal divisions and repression by private armies and government officials, an industrial labor movement emerged in the United States in the 1930s. New tactics like sit-down strikes (in which striking workers occupied their factories), as well as divisions among employers, allowed workers to win significant concessions, including the right to unionize and bargain collectively.

These concessions encouraged union officials to focus less on mass mobilization and more on reaching deals with employers. When profits were threatened beginning in the late 1960s, however, business groups became more aggressively anti-union. Since the 1970s, workers' rights and protections have been steadily undermined and many industries have been de-unionized. After a long decline, many workers and activists hope Occupy Wall Street's direct-action tactics will reinvigorate the American labor movement.

Sit-down strikes like this one at a GM factory in 1936 resulted in expanded rights for workers. How did a changing political environment impact this movement?

How might an alliance with the Occupy movement help to revive the American labor movement?

Encouraged by the loss of unions' capacity to mobilize, business leaders pushed to erode collective bargaining rights, an effort that continues to this day. Shown here, air-traffic controllers march during a 1981 strike. After 12,000 controllers went on strike, President Reagan fired all the workers who did not return to work. What other factors were responsible for the decline of the labor movement?

 Explore A Sociological Perspective in **MySocLab** and then ...

■ Think About It

What factors contributed to the union victories of the 1930s? Is it likely that conditions like those of the 1930s will happen again?

■ Inspire Your Sociological Imagination

Think of the people you know in the full-time workforce. How many are members of unions? Are those who are in unions satisfied with their union? Why or why not? How many of those who are not in a union wish they were? Why?

Organization for Women (NOW), but they have not been able, and most have not been concerned, to bring about gender equality within the larger society.

The sociologist Joshua Gamson (1995) emphasizes yet another way in which a movement's internal dynamics may lead to break up and decline. As we have seen, movements typically require—or themselves attempt to create—clear and stable collective identities. How can we make claims and demands upon others, after all, if we do not know who "we" and "they" are? Many recent movements have been centrally concerned with establishing, recasting, or defending collective identities, including previously stigmatized identities. But collective identities, sociologists argue, are not "natural" or given once and for all; they are culturally constructed and continually reconstructed. Some identities, moreover, may obscure or devalue other identities that people have. As a result, people have often attempted to blur or reconfigure certain identities. Hence, Gamson's question: Must movements organized around a particular identity self-destruct?

Gamson shows how the gay and lesbian movement has been shaken in recent years by "queer" theorists and activists who have challenged fixed sexual identities like "gay," "lesbian," and "straight." Queer activists have also challenged the assimilationist goals of mainstream (and generally older) gay and lesbian activists, some of whom object to the very use of a stigmatized label like "queer." To some extent, Gamson points out, queer activism developed out of the growing organization of bisexual and transgendered people, whose very existence challenges the notion of fixed sexual and gender identities.

Ultimately, the gay and lesbian movement, and indeed all movements, face a dilemma: To be politically effective they may feel a need to emphasize exclusive and secure collective identities, but this may paper over and effectively ignore important differences among movement participants—differences based on race and class, for example, which may later erupt in a way that weakens the movement. How movements handle this dilemma in order to avoid self-destruction—how they weigh and balance competing and potentially disruptive identity claims—is an important question for future research.

Repression   Movements may also decline because the political opportunities and the free space that have helped give rise to them begin to contract or disappear. Divisions among the wealthy and powerful may be resolved or (perhaps because of such unity) authorities may decide to harshly repress or crack down on a movement. Both of these factors are usually invoked to explain the violent demise of the democracy movement in China in 1989. A number of scholars have also pointed to repression as a key factor in the decline of the U.S. labor movement since the 1950s. More specifically, union decline is largely explained by aggressive employer opposition to unions, which has been facilitated by laws and policies that favor employers over workers. One does not see the same type of employer resistance to unions in much of Europe (or Canada), mainly because laws discourage it. As a result, unions have held their own in these countries or even become stronger. American unions have also been hurt by factory closings in recent years; many businesses have transferred their operations to parts of the country (mainly the South) or to other countries where unions are weak and wages relatively low.

A primary reason for the existence of a legal framework in the United States that encourages business opposition to unions is the long-standing *political* weakness of the American labor movement. Unlike all other developed capitalist countries, the United States has never had a strong labor or leftist political party (although some scholars have suggested that the Democratic Party briefly functioned like one during the 1930s and 1940s). Scholars refer to the historical weakness of labor and socialist parties in the United States as "American exceptionalism." The precise reasons for this exceptionalism continue to be debated, with factors such as the two-party system, racial and ethnic antagonisms among workers, and the American creed of individualism receiving considerable emphasis.

Many scholars point out that while repression usually works, it does sometimes fail. Police violence sometimes demobilizes protesters and crushes insurgents, but it sometimes backfires, spurring even more people to take to the streets or to take up arms. What explains this? Research on Central America during the 1970s and 1980s (Brockett 1993) suggests that ruthless repression was most effective when authorities used it before movements had become strong—before a cycle of protest had begun. However, after such a cycle of protest was underway—when people were already active and organized—repression tended to backfire. Organized activists redoubled their efforts, went underground, and often turned to violence, joined by others seeking protection, justice, and sometimes revenge.

U.S. counterinsurgency efforts in Iraq failed because they were based on a misunderstanding of insurgent social movements (Roxborough 2007). U.S. officials assumed that popular attitudes towards insurgents and the government are based on short-term cost-benefit calculations, failing to see how insurgencies are deeply rooted in class, ethnic, or religious conflicts. Accordingly, attempts by the United States to win over the "hearts and minds" of the Iraqi population by providing material benefits proved insufficient. Insurgent movements are less interested in popularity or legitimacy per se than in monopolizing political control at the grassroots; such movements constitute an alternative government. Effective counterinsurgency, then, requires establishing local political control, a project that requires a great deal of time and manpower—something that outside powers may be unwilling to commit.

One of the unintended consequences of the bombing of a federal building in Oklahoma City in 1995 (shown here during a memorial service two weeks after the bombing, which killed 168 people) was a decline in the activities of right-wing militia groups.

☐ Outcomes

Social movements have a number of effects on their societies, some of them intended and others quite unintended. A few movements attain many or most of their goals, while others at least manage to gain recognition or longevity in the form of protest organizations, but many if not most are suppressed or ignored. While sociologists used to talk about the success or failure of movements, today they are more likely to talk about movement *outcomes* in recognition of the unintended consequences of movements. Some movements affect the broader culture and public attitudes, perhaps paving the way for future movements. Others leave behind social networks, tactical innovations, and organizational forms that later movements can adopt and use. At the extreme, some movements may simply arouse such a backlash against them that they lose ground. For example, the mobilization of far-right militia groups against the U.S. government which led to the Oklahoma City bombing in 1995 inspired closer surveillance and repression of these groups than had previously existed—not to mention extremely negative media coverage. Their number and activities declined sharply after the bombing.

Measuring a Movement's Success and Achievements

When thinking about what movements can achieve, it is useful to distinguish between *acceptance* (or recognition) and the winning of *new advantages* (Gamson 1990). Acceptance occurs when a movement or SMO comes to be regarded as a legitimate representative of a group by its opponents. Acceptance is generally crucial for the stability and longevity of a protest group, especially when its main opponent is the state. New advantages are the benefits a movement or SMO achieves for its constituency, such as old-age pensions, voting rights, clean air, or healthcare. These are the things that most ordinary participants—as well as free riders—are looking to attain from movements.

Acceptance and new advantages don't necessarily go together; a movement can attain one but not the other (or neither). The sociologist William Gamson has described four general types of movement outcomes based on whether a

How can we measure a movement's success or achievements?

movement is fully accepted or not and whether it wins many new advantages or none (see Table 17.1). Movements that win a "full response" (i.e., full acceptance and many new advantages) are the most successful; the least successful movements are those that "collapse" by failing to win acceptance or any new advantages. There are also two outcomes that fall somewhere between success and failure. A movement is "preempted" when it wins new advantages but fails to win acceptance; and a movement is "coopted" when it is accepted by its opponents but fails to win any new advantages for its constituents. Of the 53 groups Gamson studied, 20 received a full response and 22 collapsed, while 5 were subject to cooptation and 6 to preemption (Gamson 1990:37).

Explaining movement outcomes is complicated by the fact that success in the short and the long term may not coincide. In some cases, these even conflict with each other, as when a movement's initial successes inspire strong countermobilization on the part of those under attack. The prochoice movement, for example, was quite successful in liberalizing abortion laws in a number of states and then seemed to win a huge victory with the *Roe v. Wade* Supreme Court decision in 1973. But this decision, as we have seen, which legalized certain types of abortion, sparked a formidable countermobilization by the antiabortion movement. This countermobilization has succeeded in making it more difficult to attain an abortion in many parts of the United States, especially if one is a minor. On the other hand, movement efforts that are unsuccessful in the short run may

TABLE 17.1 FOUR TYPES OF MOVEMENT OUTCOMES

		Acceptance	
		Full	None
New Advantages	Many	**1. Full Response** Examples: American Federation of Labor American Federation of Teachers	**2. Preemption** Examples: American Free Trade Tobacco Night Riders
	None	**3. Cooptation** Examples: Bull Moose (Progressive) Party American Association of University Professors	**4. Collapse** Examples: International Workingmen's Association National Student League

Source: Gamson (1990:29 and Appendix A).

turn out to have big effects in the long run, as in the case of martyrs who inspire outrage and additional mobilization.

Cultural Consequences   Overall, researchers have shown that only a few large and enduring movements have had profound effects on their societies. The labor movement won the 40-hour work week and the right to collective bargaining with employers. The civil rights movement eliminated laws enforcing racial segregation and won voting rights for African Americans, and the women's movement won laws against sex discrimination and forever changed the way people think about gender differences. A large number of movements have met with considerable repression. Others have attained some acceptance for their own organizations without obtaining tangible benefits for those they represent (i.e., they have been coopted). Still others have pushed the government to establish a new agency or regulator in response to their demands, only to discover later that this agency was ineffectual or taken over by the movement's opponents. Scholars of social movements would like to believe that the movements they study affect the course of history, but they have often had to assert this without much good evidence.

The cultural and personal consequences of activism—many of them unintended—have received considerable attention from sociologists in recent years. The activist identity is itself an important effect of social movements, just one of many cultural effects of movements. These cultural effects are perhaps the hardest movement impacts to study, yet they may be some of the most profound and longest-lasting outcomes. Many movements help articulate new ways of thinking and feeling about the world. Thus, animal

protectionists developed widespread sympathy for nonhuman species into an explicit ideology of outrage at the harm done to animals. Other movements raise issues for public debate, forcing informed citizens to think about a topic and decide how they feel about it. The pro-choice and pro-life movements are prime examples. Today, citizens are virtually expected to have an opinion on the abortion issue. A majority may reject a movement's perspective, but it can still cause them to think more deeply about their own values and attitudes. Even those who disagree with antiabortionists still have to decide *why* they disagree. Still other social movements inspire scientific research or technological change, as the environmental movement has.

There may be even broader cultural effects of social movements. On the one hand, they give people a moral voice, helping them to articulate values and intuitions and think through issues that they do not have time to think about in their daily lives. (Should women be able to have abortions? Should lesbians and gay men be able to marry and adopt children? Should the government provide a job to everyone who wants one?) This is extremely satisfying for most movement participants as well as the general public (see Table 17.2). On the other hand, social movements can also generate extremely technical, scientific, and practical knowledge. They engage people in politics in an exciting way—rare enough in modern society. Unfortunately, some movements may go too far, when instead of trying to be artists they try to be engineers, telling others what is good for them rather than trying to persuade them. This has often happened when movements have taken state power and tried to impose their views on others, which brings us to the topic of revolutions.

TABLE 17.2 WHAT DO AMERICANS THINK OF SOCIAL MOVEMENTS AND THEIR GOALS?

The Labor Movement:

30 percent want it to have more influence.

42 percent want it to have less influence.

The Civil Rights Movement:

52 percent of blacks think that new laws are needed to reduce discrimination.

15 of whites think such laws are needed.

The Women's Movement:

69 percent of women think it has improved their lives.

27 percent of women disagree.

The Gay and Lesbian Movement:

50 percent support same-sex marriage.

45 percent oppose it.

The Pro-Choice and Pro-Life Movements:

41 percent consider themselves pro-choice.

50 percent consider themselves pro-life.

The Environmental Movement:

62 percent think it has done more good than harm.

36 percent think it has done more harm than good.

The Occupy Wall Street Movement:

44 percent support it.

35 percent oppose it.

The Tea Party Movement:

20 percent agree with it.

27 percent disagree with it.

Sources: Based on data from Jones (2011); Newport (2011); Alfano (2009); Silver (2012); Saad (2012); Pew Research Center (2011a; 2011b).

☐ Revolutionary Movements and the Seizure of State Power

These two conditions, when combined, would seem to be sufficient to produce a revolutionary situation. If ordinary people are thrust into collective action because of the erosion of the regulatory capacity of key institutions, and upper-class divisions lead to a collapse in the state's infrastructural power, a powerful insurrection would seem likely. However, Lenin raises a third condition. The final ingredient that he has in mind is the *capacity* of a social movement to take advantage of the institutional shock and state collapse in order to place radical transformation on the national agenda. Simply stated, an existing regime is likely to weather a weakening of state institutions and pressures from below if the lower classes prove incapable of organizing into a radical social movement that can effectively topple it.

Consider the case of Morocco during the Arab Spring. Morocco is one of the poorest countries in North Africa and the Middle East—poorer than Tunisia and Egypt—and the vast majority of its people are struggling economically. But while there were some protests calling for political reforms in Morocco following the revolutions in Tunisia and Egypt, they were comparatively small and intermittent. As a result, Morocco's King Mohammed VI was easily able to hold onto power after enacting a few modest reforms.

Requirements for Organizing a Revolutionary Movement

For a strong revolutionary movement to take shape, two requirements must be met. First, ordinary folk must possess considerable collective leverage over the rich and powerful. This condition is met when ordinary people play important roles in crucial institutions—roles that are necessary or highly valued, which gives their threats of withdrawing their contributions to such institutions disruptive force. Important industries, for example, depend upon the labor of ordinary workers in order to function; when workers withdraw that labor during a strike, these industries shut down, and their owners cannot make profits. Thus, when the lower classes enjoy structural power rooted in their essential institutional roles, their capacity for generating costly disruptions is enhanced (Schwartz 1976). In the context of shock and crisis, elite vulnerability to such disruptions grows. The central point is that the institutional roles of the lower classes must translate into a capacity to undertake collective actions that challenge the power of the upper classes.

Most accounts of the Egyptian uprising in 2011 focus on the occupation of Tahrir Square in central Cairo by thousands of people. But the dictatorship of Hosni Mubarak may have been more shaken by the strikes and work stoppages that occurred during the occupation, culminating in a general strike in the days before Mubarak's resignation (Schwartz 2011). (A general strike occurs when workers in an entire city or country refuse to work, as opposed to workers in a single industry or factory.) The strikes hurt many businesses across the country—the tourist industry was already reeling from the loss of business caused by the political unrest—which may have convinced military officers (many of whom are also businessmen) that Mubarak had become a threat to their own interests. The military refused to disperse the protesters in Tahrir Square, urged Mubarak to resign, and took power for themselves.

A second requirement for what Lenin called "independent historical action" by the masses is the political and ideological resources necessary to convert increased political activity and leverage into decisive collective action. This means ideas, organization, and tactics as well as the ability of activists to obtain, process, produce, and deploy information among followers. Clearly, ideas and ideology play an important role in the origins and outcomes of revolutions. However, they do not operate as autonomous forces that drive the contenders in a revolutionary situation. After all, radical ideologies have existed and appealed to many people in most if not all modern societies. They have seldom, however, given rise to strong revolutionary movements, much less to revolutions.

Culture, broadly understood, matters in revolutionary situations when particular ideologies are able to shift the balance of forces, weakening authorities and upper classes. When social dislocations and state crises offer openings for radical social movements, the tactical decisions and framing work of activists can be decisive. When the strategies and ideologies promoted by radical activists resonate with ordinary people—that is, when "frame alignment" occurs—and when they are not only consistent with but also promote increased popular mobilization, thereby maximizing its disruptive impact, they can be the final necessary ingredient that provides such mobilization with the capacity to overthrow a regime. In fact, Lenin ended his famous statement on revolutionary situations with an important qualification: "Not every revolutionary situation," he explained, "gives rise to a revolution; revolution arises only out of a situation in which the above-mentioned objective changes are accompanied by a subjective change, namely, the ability of the revolutionary class to take revolutionary mass action strong enough to break (or dislocate) the old government, which never, not even in a period of crisis, 'falls', if it is not toppled over" (Lenin 1915:213). Revolutions, in other words, are only possible when there are strong social movements that can topple governments in deep crisis.

Political Environments that Encourage Revolutionary Movements

Revolutionary situations are much more likely to arise in authoritarian and repressive political contexts than in democratic and liberal ones. In fact, no popular revolutionary movement has ever overthrown

Vladimir Lenin (1870–1924), shown here in October 1917, was not only the most famous leader of the Russian Revolution but also studied and wrote about revolutions more generally. What did he consider the main causes of revolution?

a long-consolidated democratic regime. The great social revolutions of the twentieth century, for example, toppled kings and dictators (as in Russia, China, Cuba, Iran, and Nicaragua), extremely repressive colonial regimes (as in Vietnam and Algeria), and the Soviet-imposed single-party regimes of Eastern Europe. But none overthrew a regime that even remotely resembled a democracy. In fact, revolutionary movements tend to prosper when governments sponsor or defend—with violence when necessary—economic and social arrangements that are widely regarded as unjust. In certain societies, economic and social arrangements may be widely viewed as unjust (i.e., as not simply unfortunate or inevitable), yet unless state officials are seen to sponsor or protect those arrangements—through legal codes, taxation, conscription, and, ultimately, force—revolutionary movements aimed at overthrowing the state are unlikely to become strong. People may blame their social "superiors" or employers for their plight, for example, or even whole classes of such elites, yet the government itself may not be challenged unless there exists a widely shared perception that it will stand behind and defend those elites at all costs.

Indiscriminate, but not overwhelming, violence by weak states against social movements and oppositional politicians and activists unintentionally helps revolutionaries. For reasons of simple self-defense, people who are targeted by the state may join clandestine groups or even arm themselves. People whose families or friends have been victimized by the state may also join or support revolutionary movements in order to seek revenge against the perpetrators. Social movements and political parties have generally turned to disruptive strategies, including armed struggle, only after their previous efforts to secure change through legal means were violently repressed. Under repressive conditions, ordinary people often view mass disruption, including armed struggle, as a legitimate and reasonable means of political contestation.

Authoritarian and repressive states, in sum, unintentionally facilitate the development of revolutionary social movements by generating or reinforcing popular grievances, contributing to widespread feelings of moral outrage, focusing those feelings on the government (or dictator), foreclosing possibilities for peaceful reform, enhancing the plausibility and legitimacy of revolutionary ideologies, and (often) compelling people to employ disruptive and even violent strategies in order to defend themselves and to pursue effectively their collective interests and ideals.

The connection between repressive authoritarianism and revolution is clearly illustrated by the Arab Spring of 2011. The six countries that experienced broad popular uprisings—Tunisia, Egypt, Libya, Bahrain, Yemen, and Syria—are dissimilar in many ways. These countries have different levels of economic development and urbanization; some are ethnically divided, others more homogenous; some have been very close allies of Western powers, others not. But what they all had in common were longstanding dictators (or a monarch, in the case of Bahrain) who would not tolerate threats to their continued rule. Their violence and intransigence forced their political opponents to give up their dreams of incremental reforms and take to the streets. Only disruptive mass movements, most concluded, could bring an end to the reign of these autocrats. And of course they were right. Mass protests in Tunisia and Egypt convinced the armed forces in those countries to abandon their support for dictators. In Libya, Yemen, and Syria, mass protest led to divisions in and defections from the armed forces, resulting in much bloodier conflicts. Only the king in Bahrain has managed to retain the solid support of his military forces—supplemented by troops from neighboring Saudi Arabia—in the face of a broad popular uprising.

How does democracy shape social conflict?

Democracy and Social Conflict   By contrast with authoritarian regimes, more liberal and democratic governments tend to pacify and institutionalize, but hardly do away with, class and other forms of social conflict. Elections have been aptly described as a "democratic translation of the class struggle." Democracy channels a variety of social conflicts—including, but not limited to, class conflicts—into party competition for votes and the lobbying of representatives by interest groups. The temptation to rebel against the government, which is rarely seized without trepidation under any circumstances, is generally quelled under democratic regimes by the knowledge that new elections are but a few years off, and with them the chance to cast out unpopular rulers. In addition, democracies have generally provided a context in which social movements can win concessions from economic and political elites, although this often requires a good deal of disruption. But movements that aim at overthrowing elected governments rarely win much popular support unless such governments (or the armies that they command) effectively push people into rebellion by indiscriminately repressing protesters. By and large, however, the ballot box has been the coffin of revolutionaries. This explains why there have been so few large-scale attempts to overthrow long-established democracies in Western Europe and North America.

This does not mean that political radicalism and militancy go unrewarded in democratic societies. Democracy, to repeat, by no means eliminates social conflict; in fact, in many ways democracy encourages a flowering of social conflict by providing the political space within which those groups outside ruling circles can make claims on political authorities and economic elites. Not just political parties, then, but a whole range of social movements, trade unions, interest groups, and professional associations can become the organizational vehicles of political life in democratic polities. These institutions of civil society, however, are generally just that—civil. Their repertoires of contention include electoral campaigns, lobbying, strikes, boycotts, demonstrations, and civil disobedience—forms of collective action that may be quite disruptive and undertaken for quite radical ends but that are not aimed at bringing down the government.

Democracy, then, dramatically reduces the likelihood of revolutionary change, but not because it brings about social justice. Formal democracy is fully compatible with widespread poverty, inequality, and popular grievances of all sorts. This is why movements for social justice so often arise in democratic contexts. But, again, these movements almost always view the state as an instrument to be pressured and influenced, not as something to be seized or smashed. Revolutionary movements, for their part, develop not simply because people are angry or aggrieved but because the government under which they live provides no other mechanisms for social change, violently repressing those who peacefully seek incremental reforms. This said, the spread of democracy will not necessarily render revolution *passé* as a form of political struggle. Radical leaders and parties have sometimes been able to amass a broad following in democratic contexts and to win elections (for example, Salvador Allende in Chile in 1970, and Hugo Chavez in Venezuela in 1998, 2000, and 2006). Perhaps during the twenty-first century we will see some democratically elected governments attempt to revolutionize economic and political institutions. As yet, however, the democratic route to revolution has never been successfully traveled.

TABLE 17.4 WHAT DO AMERICANS THINK ABOUT THE RICH AND ABOUT CLASS CONFLICT?

77 percent think there's too much power in the hands of a few rich people and large corporations.
19 percent disagree.
76 percent think there is a wider gap between the rich and middle class compared to 10 years ago.
16 percent think the gap is narrower.
46 percent think rich people are wealthy because they know the right people or were born into wealthy families.
43 percent think rich people are wealthy because of their own hard work, ambition, or education.
66 percent think there are strong or very strong conflicts between rich and poor.
30 percent think there are no or not very strong conflicts between rich and poor.
71 percent of people between 18 and 34 think there are strong or very strong conflicts between rich and poor.
55 percent of people over 65 there are strong or very strong conflicts between rich and poor.

Sources: Based on data from Pew Research Center (2011); Teixeira (2012); Morin (2012).

CONCLUSION THE FUTURE OF MOVEMENTS AND REVOLUTIONS

We began this chapter by looking at the Occupy Wall Street movement. Like other social movements, the Occupy movement did not emerge spontaneously but grew out of the planned actions of preexisting networks of activists. The movement's tactics were not spontaneous either. Activists in the Occupy movement, like activists before them, chose tactics with which they were already familiar. The tactic of occupying public spaces was inspired by the occupation of Tahrir Square during the revolution in Egypt earlier in the year. And the movement spread rapidly across the country, like movements before it, because it framed its ideas about inequality and the power of banks and corporations in a way that appealed to a great many people during a time of economic crisis. There were also networks of activists in cities and towns across the country, most of whom had been active in previous movements, who could spread the movement's ideas and organize occupations of their own. None of this would surprise sociologists who have studied past movements.

What about the future of the Occupy movement? Police repression—expelling the occupiers from public spaces—has undoubtedly weakened the movement by reducing its visibility. But many people remain active in the movement's "working groups" and other informal networks. By the time you read this, the movement may have declined or disappeared, grown even larger, or transformed itself into a movement (or set of movements) with a different name and focus. Much will depend on whether the movement is able to discover or innovate upon tactics that will energize and unite its followers, including fresh recruits, and win concessions from the rich and powerful. If the movement continues to talk about the power of the wealthy "1 percent" but is unable to do anything about it, participants will likely tire of the movement and move on (see Table 17.4). Because the United States is a liberal democracy, we can predict with some certainty that there is very little chance that the Occupy movement will become a revolutionary movement. The movement will also find it very difficult—should it try—to convince a great many people that the U.S. government should be overthrown, violently or nonviolently, although it may convince many people (and probably already has) that the government has been corrupted by money. This could lay the foundation for another anti-corporate movement (or movements) in the future.

We will undoubtedly see many more social movements and revolutions in the years ahead. As long as ordinary people feel that the rich and powerful are oppressing them (or at least ignoring their needs and interests), and as long as people can safely connect with one another and find ways to pressure (or overthrow) the rich and powerful, movements and revolutions will remain part of the human condition.

Watch the **Video** in **MySocLab**
Applying Your Sociological Imagination

Study and **Review** in **MySocLab**   **Watch** the **Video** Inspiring Your Sociological Imagination in **MySocLab**

What Are Social Movements? *(p. 477)*

 Watch the **Big Question Video** in **MySocLab** to review the key concepts for this section.

We began this chapter by defining social movements and exploring what we can learn by studying them.

STUDYING SOCIAL MOVEMENTS (p. 477)

Politics, Human Action, and Social Change (p. 478)

- **What can movements teach us about social life?**

Moral Sensibilities (p. 478)

Understanding Social Movements Today (p. 478)

- **What aspects of movements are contemporary sociologists interested in?**

KEY TERMS

riot *(p. 477)*

social movement *(p. 477)*

fad *(p. 477)*

political process perspective *(p. 479)*

Why Do Movements Emerge, and Who Joins Them? *(p. 480)*

 Watch the **Big Question Video** in **MySocLab** to review the key concepts for this section.

The most frequently asked question about social movements is why they emerge when they do. In this section we examined how movements take shape and looked at who joins or supports social movements.

MOVEMENT ORIGINS AND RECRUITMENT (p. 480)

How Movements Take Shape (p. 480)

- **What factors explain why movements emerge when and where they do?**

Recruitment: Joining or Supporting Movements (p. 483)

- **How do movements recruit supporters?**

 Explore the **Data** on The Occupy Wall Street Movement in **MySocLab**

KEY TERMS

resource mobilization approach *(p. 480)*

social movement organization *(SMO) (p. 480)*

social network *(p. 481)*

biographical availability *(p. 483)*

framing *(p. 484)*

collective identity *(p. 484)*

moral shock *(p. 486)*

3

What Do Movements Accomplish? *(p. 487)*

Watch the **Big Question Video** in **MySocLab** to review the key concepts for this section.

Why do movements use certain tactics and not others? Why do movements decline or disappear? In this section we examined what movements do and what changes and outcomes movements bring about, including unintended consequences.

MOVEMENT TACTICS AND OUTCOMES (p. 487)

The Strategies and Tactics of Movements (p. 487)

- **Why do movements use certain tactics and not others?**

The Decline and Disappearance of Movements (p. 490)

- **Why do movements decline or disappear?**

 Explore A Sociological Perspective: Will the labor movement revive? in **MySocLab**

 Read the **Document** *The Rise and Fall of Aryan Nations* in **MySocLab**. In this reading, Robert Balch uses participant observation and interviews to study Aryan Nations, an Idaho-based white separatist movement that disintegrated in 2000.

Outcomes (p. 493)

- **How can we measure a movement's success or achievements?**

4

What Are Revolutions, and Why Do They Occur? *(p. 496)*

Watch the **Big Question Video** in **MySocLab** to review the key concepts for this section.

KEY TERMS

revolution *(p. 496)*
revolutionary movement *(p. 497)*
revolutionary situation *(p. 498)*

This section explored why some social movements are revolutionary and what causes revolutionary situations to occur. When and why have revolutionary movements been able to take state power? We concluded the chapter by examining how democracy shapes social conflict and the prospects for revolution.

UNDERSTANDING REVOLUTIONS (p. 496)

Defining "Revolution" (p. 496)

- **What makes some social movements revolutionary?**

Revolutions, Violence, and Other Forms of Conflict (p. 497)

Revolutionary Situations (p. 498)

- **What causes revolutionary situations?**

Revolutionary Movements and the Seizure of State Power (p. 500)

- **How does democracy shape social conflict?**

 Watch the **Video** Applying Your Sociological Imagination in **MySocLab** to see these concepts at work in the real world

REFERENCES

CHAPTER 1

Abbott, Andrew. 2001. *The Chaos of the Disciplines*. Chicago: University of Chicago Press.

Arum, Richard and Josipa Roksa. 2011. *Academically Adrift*. Chicago: University of Chicago Press.

Chodorow, Nancy. 1978. *The Reproduction of Mothering*. Berkeley: University of California Press.

Comte, Auguste. [1839–1853] 2009. *The Positive Philosophy of Auguste Comte*. Ed. and trans. Harriet Martinaeu. New York: Cambridge University Press.

Duster, Troy. 1990. *Backdoor to Eugenics*. New York: Routledge.

Jerolmack, Colin. 2013. *The Global Pigeon*. Chicago: University of Chicago Press.

Mills, C. Wright. 1959. *The Sociological Imagination*. New York: Oxford University Press.

Molotch, Harvey and Laura Noren, eds. 2010. *Toilet: Public Restrooms and the Politics of Sharing*. New York: New York University Press.

Saperstein, Aliya and Andrew Penner. 2010. "The Race of a Criminal Record: How Incarceration Colors Racial Perceptions." *Social Problems* 57:92–113.

Sharkey, Patrick. 2010. "The Acute Effect of Local Homicides on Children's Cognitive Performance." *Proceedings of the National Academy of Sciences* 107:11733–11738.

CHAPTER 5

Anderson, Benedict. 1991. *Imagined Communities: Reflections on the Origin and Spread of Nationalism*. Revised ed. London and New York: Verso.

Appadurai, Arjun. 1996. *Modernity at Large: Cultural Dimensions of Globalization*. Minneapolis: University of Minnesota Press.

Barnum, P.T. [1880] 1999. *Art of Money Getting*. Bedford, MA: Applewood Books. P. 68.

Blethen, Frank A. 2002. "American Democracy at Risk: Can American Democracy Survive the Loss of an Independent Press and a Diversity of Voices?" Speech delivered to the School of Journalism and Communications at the University of Oregon, The Ruhl Symposium on Ethics in Journalism, May 14.

Bourdieu, Pierre. 1984. *Distinction: A Social Critique of the Judgement of Taste*. Translated by Richard Nice. Cambridge, MA: Harvard University Press.

Bourdieu, Pierre. 1992. *The Logic of Practice*. Translated by Richard Nice. Cambridge: Polity Press.

Boyd, Danah. 2008. "Why Youth (Heart) Social Network Sites: The Role of Networked Publics in Teenage Social Life." Pp. 119–42 in *MacArthur Foundation Series on Digital Learning: Youth, Identity, and Digital Media Volume*, edited by David Buckingham. Cambridge, MA: MIT Press.

Burgess, Jean and Joshua Green. 2009. *YouTube: Online Video and Participatory Culture*. Cambridge, MA: Polity Press.

Castells, Manuel. 2009. *Communication Power*. Oxford, UK: Oxford University Press.

Clarke, John, Stuart Hall, Tony Jefferson, and Brian Roberts. 1975. "Subcultures, Cultures and Class: A Theoretical Overview." Pp. 9–74 in *Resistance through Rituals: Youth Subcultures in Post-War Britain*, edited by Stuart Hall and Tony Jefferson. New York and London: Routledge.

Cresswell, Tim. 1996. *In Place/Out of Place: Geography, Ideology, and Transgression*. Minneapolis: University of Minnesota Press.

Eliasoph, Nina and Paul Lichterman. 2003. "Culture in Interaction." *American Journal of Sociology* 108(4):735–94.

Elliot, Michael A. 2007. "Human Rights and the Triumph of the Individual in World Culture." *Cultural Sociology* 1(3):343–63.

Fischer, Claude S. 1975. "Toward a Subcultural Theory of Urbanism." *American Journal of Sociology* 80(6):1319–41.

Frank, Thomas. 2004. *What's the Matter with Kansas? How Conservatives Won the Heart of America*. New York: Metropolitan Books.

Fraser, Nancy. 1992. "Rethinking the Public Sphere: A Contribution to the Critique of Actually Existing Democracy." Pp. 109–42 in *Habermas and the Public Sphere*, edited by Craig Calhoun. Cambridge, MA, and London: MIT Press.

Gans, Herbert J. 1999. *Popular Culture and High Culture: An Analysis and Evaluation of Taste*, 2nd ed. New York: Basic Books.

Geertz, Clifford. 1972. "Deep Play: Notes on the Balinese Cockfight." *Daedalus* 101(1):1–37.

Gitlin, Todd. 1980. *The Whole World Is Watching: Mass Media in the Making and Unmaking of the New Left*. Berkeley: University of California Press.

Gitlin, Todd. 2007. *Media Unlimited: How the Torrent of Images and Sounds Overwhelms Our Lives*, Revised ed. New York: Metropolitan Books.

Graber, Doris. 2003. "The Media and Democracy: Beyond Myths and Stereotypes." *Annual Review of Political Science* 6:139–60.

Habermas, Jürgen. 1962. *The Structural Transformation of the Public Sphere: An Inquiry into a Category of Bourgeois Society*. Translated by Thomas Burger with Frederick Lawrence. Cambridge, MA: MIT Press.

Hall, Stuart and Tony Jefferson, eds. 1975. *Resistance through Rituals: Youth Subcultures in Post-War Britain*. New York and London: Routledge.

Herman, Edward S. and Noam Chomsky. 1988. *Manufacturing Consent: The Political Economy of the Mass Media*. New York: Pantheon.

Hindman, Matthew. 2008. *The Myth of Digital Democracy*. Princeton, NJ: Princeton University Press.

Hofstadter, Richard. 1960. *The Age of Reform*. New York: Vintage.

Holt, Douglas B. 1997. "Distinction in America? Recovering Bourdieu's Theory of Tastes from Its Critics." *Poetics* 25:93–120.

Holt, Douglas B. 1998. "Does Cultural Capital Structure American Consumption?" *The Journal of Consumer Research* 25(1):1–25.

Horkheimer, Max and Theodor W. Adorno. [1947] 2002. *Dialectic of Enlightenment: Philosophical Fragments*. Translated by Edmund Jephcott and edited by Gunzelin Schmid Noerr. Stanford, CT: Stanford University Press.

Hunter, James Davison. 1991. *Culture Wars: The Struggle to Define America*. New York: Basic Books.

Innis, Harold A. 1951. *The Bias of Communication*. Toronto: University of Toronto Press.

Jenkins, Henry. 2006. *Convergence Culture: Where Old and New Media Collide*. New York: NYU Press.

Johnson, Steven. 2005. *Everything Bad Is Good for You*. New York: Riverhead.

Klein, Naomi. 2000. *No Logo: Taking Aim at the Brand Bullies*. New York: Picador.

Klinenberg, Eric. 2007. *Fighting for Air: The Battle to Control America's Media*. New York: Metropolitan Books.

Klinenberg, Eric. 2012. *Going Solo: The Extraordinary Rise and Surprising Appeal of Living Alone*. New York: Penguin Press.

Lamont, Michèle. 1992. *Money, Morals, and Manners: The Culture of the French and the American Upper-Middle Class*. Chicago: University of Chicago Press.

Lareau, Annette. 2003. *Unequal Childhoods: Class, Race, and Family Life*. Berkeley: University of California Press.

Lippmann, Walter. 1922. *Public Opinion*. New York: Harcourt, Brace and Company.

Marx, Karl and Frederick Engels. [1845] 1972. "The German Ideology: Part 1." Pp. 146–200 in *The Marx-Engels Reader*, edited by Robert C. Tucker, translated by S. Ryazanskaya. New York: W.W. Norton & Company.

McChesney, Robert W. 1999. *Rich Media, Poor Democracy*. New York: New Press.

McLuhan, Marshall. 1964. *Understanding Media: The Extensions of Man*. Cambridge, MA: MIT Press.

Meyer, John W., John Boli, George M. Thomas, and Francisco O. Ramirez. 1997. "World Society and the Nation-State." *American Journal of Sociology* 103(1):144–81.

Nielsen. 2011. *Television Audience Report 2010-2011*. http://researchticker.com/wp-content/uploads/2011/12/2010-2011-nielsen-television-audience-report.pdf.

Norris, Pippa. 2001. *Digital Divide: Civic Engagement, Information Poverty, and the Internet Worldwide*. Cambridge, UK: Cambridge University Press.

Palfrey, John and Urs Gasser. 2008. *Born Digital: Understanding the First Generation of Digital Natives*. New York: Basic Books.

Park, Robert E. 1923. "The Natural History of the Newspaper." *American Journal of Sociology* 29(3):273–89.

Peterson, Richard A. and Roger M. Kern. 1996. "Changing Highbrow Taste: From Snob to Omnivore." *American Sociological Review* 61(5):900–07.

Pew Research Center. 2012. "State of the News Media 2011." http://stateofthemedia.org/2011/network-essay/data-page-5/.

Postman, Neil. 1985. *Amusing Ourselves to Death: Public Discourse in the Age of Show Business*. New York: Penguin.

Schudson, Michael. 2003. *The Sociology of News*. New York: Norton.

Sewell, William H., Jr. 2005. *Logics of History: Social Theory and Social Transformation*. Chicago: University of Chicago Press.

Swidler, Ann. 1986. "Culture in Action: Symbols and Strategies." *American Sociological Review* 51(2):273–86.

Swidler, Ann. 2003. *Talk of Love: How Culture Matters*. Chicago: University of Chicago Press.

Takhteyev, Yuri, Anatoliy Gruzd, and Barry Wellman. 2012. "Geography of Twitter Networks." *Social Networks* 34(1):73–81.

Tobin, Joseph J., David Y. H. Wu, and Dana H. Davidson. 1989. *Preschool in Three Cultures: Japan, China and the United States*. New Haven, CT: Yale University Press.

Van Der Bly, Martha C. E. 2007. "Globalization and the Rise of One Heterogeneous World Culture: A Microperspective of a Global Village." *International Journal of Comparative Sociology* 48(2–3):234–56.

Weber, Max. [1905] 2002. *The Protestant Ethic and the "Spirit" of Capitalism*. Edited and translated by Peter Baehr and Gordon C. Wells. London: Penguin.

Williams, Raymond. 1976. *Keywords: A Vocabulary of Culture and Society*. Oxford, UK: Oxford University Press.

Willis, Paul. 1977. *Learning to Labor: How Working Class Kids Get Working Class Jobs*. New York: Columbia University Press.

CHAPTER 10

"race, n.6". OED Online. March 2012. Oxford University Press.

Alba, Richard D. 2009. *Blurring the Color Line: The New Chance for a More Integrated America*. Cambridge, MA: Harvard University Press.

Allport, Gordon. 1954. *The Nature of Prejudice*. Cambridge, MA: Addison-Wesley Pub. Co.

American Sociological Association. 2003. "The Importance of Collecting Data and Doing Social Scientific Research on Race." Washington, DC: American Sociological Association.

Bertrand, Marianne and Sendhil Mullainathan. 2004. "Are Emily and Greg More Employable than Lakisha and Jamal: A Field Experiment on Labor Market Discrimination." *American Economic Review* 94: 991–1013.

Bonilla-Silva, Eduardo. 1996. "Rethinking Racism: Toward a Structural Interpretation." *American Sociological Review* 62(3):465–80.

Bonilla-Silva, Eduardo. 2002. "The Linguistics of Color Blind Racism: How to Talk Nasty about Blacks without Sounding 'Racist'." *Critical Sociology* 28(1–2):41–64.

Bonilla-Silva, Eduardo. 2006. *Racism without Racists: Color-Blind Racism and the Persistence of Racial Inequality in the United States*. Lanham, MD: Rowman & Littlefield, Inc.

Bourdieu, Pierre. 1986. "The Forms of Capital." Pp. 241–258 in *Handbook of theory of research for the sociology of education*, edited by J.E. Richardson. New York: Greenwood Press.

Brittingham, Angela, and G. Patricia de la Cruz. 2004. "Ancestry: 2000." *Census Brief* C2KBR-35 (June). Washington, DC: U.S. Census Bureau.

Brown, Michael K., Martin Carnoy, Elliott Currie, Troy Duster, David B. Oppenheimer, Marjorie M. Schultz, and David Wellman. 2003. *Whitewashing Race: The Myth of a Color-Blind Society*. Berkeley, CA: University of California Press.

Carnoy, Martin and Henry M. Levin. 1985. *Schooling and Work in the Democratic State*. Stanford: Stanford University Press.

Center for Disease Control and Prevention. 2011. "CDC Health Disparities and Inequalities Report—2011." *Morbidity and Mortality Weekly Report* Vol. 60 (Supplement): 1-113. Retrieved February 20, 2012 (http://www.cdc.gov/mmwr/pdf/other/su6001.pdf).

Conley, Dalton. 1999. *Being Black, Living in Red: Race, Wealth, and Social Policy in America*. Berkeley, CA: University of California Press.

Cornell, Stephen, and Douglas Hartmann. 2004. "Conceptual Confusions and Divides: Race, Ethnicity, and the Study of Immigration." Pp. 23–41 in *Not Just Black and White: Historical and Contemporary Perspectives on Immigration, Race, and Ethnicity in the United States*, edited by Nancy Foner and George M. Fredrickson. New York: Russell Sage Foundation.

—. 2007. *Ethnicity and Race: Making Identities in a Changing World*. Thousand Oaks, CA: Pine Forge Press.

DaCosta, Kimberly McClain. 2007. *Making Multiracials: State, Family, and Market in the Redrawing of the Color Line*. Stanford, CA: Stanford University Press.

Dikötter, Frank. 2008. "The Racialization of the Globe: An Interactive Interpretation." *Ethnic and Racial Studies* 31(8):1478–96.

Evett, Ian, Peter D. Gill, John K. Scranage, and B.S. Weir. 1996. "Establishing the Robustness of Short-Tandem-Repeat Statistics for Forensic Applications." *American Journal of Human Genetics* 58:398–407.

Fischer, Claude S., Michael Hout, Martín Sánchez Jankowski, Samuel R. Lucas, Ann Swidler and Kim Vos. 1996. *Inequality by Design: Cracking the Bell Curve Myth*. Princeton: Princeton University Press.

Frankenberg, Ruth. 1993. *White Women, Race Matters: The Social Construction of Whiteness*. Minneapolis, MN: University of Minnesota Press.

Fredrickson, George M. 2002. *Racism: A Short History*. Princeton, NJ: Princeton University Press.

Gans, Herbert J. 1999. "The Possibility of a New Racial Hierarchy in the 21st Century United States." Pp. 371–90 in *The Cultural Territories of Race: Black and White Boundaries*, edited by Michèle Lamont. Chicago and New York: University of Chicago Press and the Russell Sage Foundation.

Gould, Stephen Jay. 1996. *The Mismeasure of Man*. New York: W.W. Norton and Co.

Graham, Hugh Davis. 2002. "The Origins of Official Minority Designation." Pp. 288–99 in *The New Race Question: How the Census Counts Multiracial Individuals*, edited by Joel Perlmann and Mary C. Waters. New York and Annandale-on-Hudson, NY: Russell Sage Foundation and the Levy Economics Institute of Bard College.

Gullickson, Aaron, and Ann Morning. 2011. "Choosing Race: Multiracial Ancestry and Identification." *Social Science Research* 40:498–512.

Hall, Bruce S. 2011. *A History of Race in Muslim West Africa, 1600-1960*. Cambridge: Cambridge University Press.

Hannaford, Ivan. 1996. *Race: The History of an Idea in the West*. Washington, DC: The Woodrow Wilson Center Press.

Helgren, David M., and Robert J. Sager. 2000. *World Geography Today*. Austin, TX: Holt, Rinehart and Winston.

Herrnstein, Richard J. and Charles Murray. 1994. *The Bell Curve*. New York: The Free Press.

Humes, Karen R., Nicholas A. Jones, and Roberto R. Ramirez. 2011. "Overview of Race and Hispanic Origin: 2010." *Census 2010 Brief* C2010BR-02 (March). Washington, DC: U.S. Census Bureau.

Jackson Nakazawa, Donna. 2003. "A New Generation is Leading the Way: What Young People of Mixed Race Can Tell Us About the Future of Our Children." Pp. 4–5 in *Parade*: July 6.

Jacobson, Matthew Frye. 1998. *Whiteness of a Different Color: European Immigrants and the Alchemy of Race*. Cambridge, MA: Harvard University Press.

Jensen, Arthur R. 1969. "How much can we boost I.Q. and scholastic achievement?" *Harvard Educational Review* 33: 1–123.

Kim, Nadia Y. 2008. *Imperial Citizens: Koreans and Race from Seoul to LA*. Stanford, CA: Stanford University Press.

Kochlar, Rakesh, Richard Fry, and Paul Taylor. 2011. *Wealth Gap Rises to Record Highs Between Whites, Blacks and Latinos*. Washington DC: Pew Research Center.

Kritz, Mary M., and Douglas T. Gurak. 2004. *Immigration and a Changing America*. New York and Washington, DC: Russell Sage Foundation and Population Reference Bureau.

Landry, Bart and Krish Marsh. 2011. "The Evolution of the New Black Middle Class." *Annual Review of Sociology* 37: 373–394.

Lee, Jennifer, and Frank D. Bean. 2004. "America's Changing Color Lines: Immigration, Race/Ethnicity, and Multiracial Identification." *Annual Review of Sociology* 30:221–42.

Lee, Sharon M. 1993. "Racial Classifications in the U.S. Census: 1890–1990." *Ethnic and Racial Studies* 16(1):75–94.

Lewis, Bernard. 1990. *Race and Slavery in the Middle East*. New York: Oxford University Press.

Lewis, Oscar. 1966. *La Vida: A Puerto Rican Family in the Culture of Poverty—San Juan and New York*. New York: Random House.

Liebow, Elliott. [1967] 2003. *Tally's Corner: A Study of Negro Streetcorner Men*. 2nd ed. Lanham, MD: Rowman & Littlefield.

Lind, Michael. 1995. *The Next American Nation: The New Nationalism and the Fourth American Revolution*. New York: The Free Press.

Liptak, Adam. 2008. "U.S. Prison Population Dwarfs that of Other Nations." *New York Times*, April 23. Retrieved March 19, 2010 (http://www.nytimes.com/2008/04/23/world/americas/23iht-23prison.12253738.html).

Loewen, James. 2005. *Sundown Towns: A Hidden Dimension of American Racism*. New York: The New Press.

Manza, Jeff, and Christopher Uggen. 2008. *Locked Out: Felon Disenfranchisement and American Democracy*. New York: Oxford University Press.

Marger, Martin N. 2003. *Race and Ethnic Relations: American and Global Perspectives*, 6th Edition. Belmont, CA: Wadsworth.

Marks, Jonathan. 2002. *What it Means to be 98% Chimpanzee: Apes, People, and their Genes*. Berkeley: University of California Press.

Martin, Philip, and Elizabeth Midgley. 2010. *Immigration in America 2010*. Population Bulletin Update (June). Washington, DC: Population Reference Bureau.

Massey, Douglas S. 1995. "The New Immigration and Ethnicity in the United States." *Population and Development Review* 21(3):631–52.

Massey, Douglas S., and Nancy A. Denton. 1993. *American Apartheid: Segregation and the Making of the Underclass*. Cambridge, MA: Harvard University Press.

Morning, Ann. 2008. "Ethnic Classification in Global Perspective: A Cross-National Survey of the 2000 Census Round." *Population Research and Policy Review* 27(2):239–72.

—. 2011. *The Nature of Race: How Scientists Think and Teach about Human Difference*. Berkeley, CA: University of California Press.

National Center for Education Statistics. 2011a. "Table 8." *Digest of Educational Statistics: 2010*. Retrieved February 22, 2012 (http://nces.ed.gov/programs/digest/d10/tables/dt10_008.asp?referrer=list).

National Center for Education Statistics. 2011b. "Table 115." *Digest of Educational Statistics: 2010*. Retrieved Feburary 22, 2012 (http://nces.ed.gov/programs/digest/d10/tables/dt10_115.asp?referrer=list).

Nelkin, Dorothy, and M. Susan Lindee. 1995. *The DNA Mystique: The Gene as Cultural Icon*. New York: Freeman.

Nobles, Melissa. 2000. *Shades of Citizenship: Race and the Census in Modern Politics*. Stanford, CA: Stanford University Press.

Oliver, Melvin L., and Thomas M. Shapiro. 1997. *Black Wealth, White Wealth: A New Perspective on Racial Inequality*. New York and London: Routledge.

Omi, Michael and Howard Winant. 1994. *Racial Formation in the United States: From the 1960s to the 1990s*. New York: Routledge.

Pager, Devah. 2003. "The Mark of a Criminal Record." *American Journal of Sociology* 108(5):937–75.

Pager, Devah. 2007. *Marked: Race, Crime, and Finding Work in an Era of Mass Incarceration*. Chicago, IL: University of Chicago Press.

Pager, Devah, Bruce Western, and Bart Bonikowski. 2009. "Discrimination in a Low-Wage Labor Market: A Field Experiment." *American Sociological Review* 74(5): 777–779.

Portes, Alejandro and Jozsef Borocz. 1989. "Contemporary Immigration: Theoretical Perspectives on Its Determinants and Modes of Incorporation." *International Migration Review* 87(23): 606–630.

Puente, Maria and Martin Kasindorf. 1999. "The New Face of America: Blended Races Making a True Melting Pot." Pp. 1A, 13A in *USA Today*: September 7.

Rockquemore, Kerry Ann, and David L. Brunsma. 2002. *Beyond Black: Biracial Identity in America*. Thousand Oaks, CA: Sage.

Royster, Deirdre A. 2003. *Race and the Invisible Hand: How White Networks Exclude Black. Men from Blue-Collar Jobs*. Berkeley: University of California Press.

Sacks, Karen. 1994. "How Did Jews Become White Folks?" Pp. 78–102 in *Race*, edited by Steven Gregory and Roger Sanjek. New Brunswick, NJ: Rutgers University Press.

Schuman, Howard, Charlotte Steeh, Lawrence Bobo, and Maria Krysan. 1997. *Racial Attitudes in America: Trends and Interpretations*. Cambridge, MA: Harvard University Press.

Sharkey, Patrick. 2008. "The Intergenerational Transmission of Context." *American Journal of Sociology* 113(4):931–69.

Smedley, Audrey. 2007. *Race in North America: Origin and Evolution of a Worldview*. Boulder, CO: Westview Press.

Snowden, Frank M., Jr. 1983. *Before Color Prejudice: The Ancient View of Blacks*. Cambridge, MA: Harvard University Press.

Stevens, Jacqueline. 2003. "Racial Meanings and Scientific Methods: Changing Policies for NIH-Sponsored Publications Reporting Human Variation." *Journal of Health Politics, Policy and Law* 28(6):1033–87.

Streeter, Caroline A. 2003. "The Hazards of Visibility: 'Biracial' Women, Media Images, and Narratives of Identity." Pp. 301–22 in *New Faces in Changing America: Multiracial Identity in the 21st Century*, edited by Herman DeBose and Loretta Winters. Thousand Oaks, CA: Sage.

Steinberg, Stephan. [1989] 2001. *The Ethnic Myth: Race, Ethnicity, and Class in America*, 3rd Edition. Boston, MA: Beacon Press.

Swidler, Ann. 1986. "Culture in Action: Symbols and Strategies." *American Sociological Review* 51(2):273-286.

U.S. Bureau of Justice Statistics. 2011. "Prisoners in 2010." Washington D.C: U.S. Government Printing Office. Retrieved February 18, 2012 (http://www.bjs.gov/content/pub/pdf/p10.pdf).

U.S. Bureau of Labor Statistics. 2011. "Labor Force Characteristics by Race and Ethnicity, 2010." Report 1032, Washington DC: U.S. Government Printing Office. Retrieved February 13, 2012 (http://www.bls.gov/cps/cpsrace2010.pdf).

U.S. Bureau of Labor Statistics. 2012. "Economic News Release: The Employment Situation-January 2012." Retrieved February 12, 2012 (http://www.bls.gov/news.release/pdf/empsit.pdf).

U.S. Census Bureau. 1918. "Negro Population 1790–1915." In *Census Bureau*, edited by U.S. Department of Commerce. Washington, DC: Government Printing Office.

U.S. Census Bureau. 2011. "Income, Poverty, and Health Insurance Coverage in the United States: 2010." Current Population Reports, P60-23., Washington, DC: U.S. Government Printing Office. Retrieved February 10, 2012 (http://www.census.gov/prod/2011pubs/p60-239.pdf).

U.S. Department of Health and Human Services. 2000. "Addressing Racial and Ethnic Disparities in Health Care Fact Sheet." AHRQ Publication No. 00-PO41, February 2000. Rockville, MD: Agency for Healthcare Research and Quality. (http://www.ahrq.gov/research/disparit.htm)

U.S. Kerner Commission. 1968. "Report of the National Advisory Commission on Civil Disorders." Washington: U.S. Government Printing Office.

Van Ausdale, Debra and Joe R. Feagin. 2001. *The First R: How Children Learn Race and Racism*. Lanham, MD: Rowman and Littlefield.

Walters, Nathan P., and Edward N. Trevelyan. 2011. "The Newly-Arrived Foreign-Born Population of the United States: 2010." *American Community Survey Brief* ACSBR/10-16. Washington, DC: U.S. Census Bureau.

Wang, Wendy. 2012. "The Rise of Intermarriage: Rates, Characteristics Vary by Race and Gender." *Social and Demographic Trends*, February 12. Washington, DC: Pew Research Center.

Waters, Mary C. 1990. *Ethnic Options: Choosing Identities in America*. Berkeley, CA: University of California Press.

Weber, Max. 1978. *Economy and Society*. Berkeley: University of California Press.

Western, Bruce. 2006. *Punishment and Inequality in America*. New York: Russell Sage Foundation.

Williams, Kim M. 2006. *Mark One or More: Civil Rights in Multiracial America*. Ann Arbor, MI: University of Michigan Press.

Williamson, Joel. 1980. *New People: Miscegenation and Mulattoes in the United States*. New York: The Free Press.

Wolfe, Patrick. 2001. "Land, Labor, and Difference: Elementary Structures of Race." *The American Historical Review* 106(3):866–905.

CHAPTER 13

Acock, Alan C. and David H. Demo. 1994. *Family Diversity and Well-Being*. Thousand Oaks, CA: Sage.

Ahrons, Constance. 2006. "Family Ties after Divorce: Long-Term Implications for Children." *Family Issues* 46:53–65.

Amato, Paul R. and Alan Booth. 1997. *A Generation at Risk: Growing Up in an Era of Family Upheaval*. Cambridge, MA: Harvard University Press.

Banerjee, Neela. 2008. "Taking Their Faith, but Not Their Politics, to the People." *New York Times*, June 1.

Barnett, Rosalind C. and Caryl Rivers. 1996. *She Works/He Works: How Two-Income Families Are Happier, Healthier, and Better-Off*. San Francisco: Harper San Francisco.

Barnett, Rosalind C. and Caryl Rivers. 2004. *Same Difference: How Gender Myths Are Hurting Our Relationships, Our Children, and Our Jobs*. New York: Basic Books.

Belkin, Lisa. 2003. "The Opt-Out Revolution." *New York Times Magazine*, October 26.

Bellah, Robert N., Richard Madsen, William M. Sullivan, Ann Swidler, and Stephen M. Tipton. 1985. *Habits of the Heart: Individualism and Commitment in American Life*. Berkeley and Los Angeles: University of California Press.

Bengston, Vern L., Timothy J. Biblarz, and Robert E. L. Roberts. 2002. *How Families Still Matter: A Longitudinal Study of Youth in Two Generations*. New York: Cambridge University Press.

Bianchi, Suzanne M. 2000. "Maternal Employment and Time with Children: Dramatic Change or Surprising Continuity?" *Demography* 37(4):401–14.

Bianchi, Suzanne M., John P. Robinson, and Melissa A. Milkie. 2006. *Changing Rhythms of American Family Life*. New York: Russell Sage Foundation.

Blair-Loy, Mary. 2003. *Competing Devotions: Career and Family among Women Executives*. Cambridge, MA: Harvard University Press.

Blankenhorn, David. 1995. *Fatherless America: Confronting Our Most Urgent Social Problem*. New York: Basic Books.

Blankenhorn, David. 2009. *The Future of Marriage*. New York: Encounter Books.

Blow, Charles M. 2008. "Talking Down and Stepping Up." *New York Times*, July 12.

Boushey, Heather. 2008. "'Opting Out'? The Effect of Children on Women's Employment in the United States." *Feminist Economics* 14(1):1–36.

Burchinal, Margaret and Alison Clarke-Stewart. 2007. "Maternal Employment and Child Cognitive Outcomes: The Importance of an Analytic Approach." *Developmental Psychology* 43:1140–55.

Cahn, Naomi and June Carbone. 2010. *Red Families v. Blue Families: Legal Polarization and the Creation of Culture*. New York: Oxford University Press.

Cancian, Francesca M. 1987. *Love in America: Gender and Self-Development*. New York: Cambridge University Press.

Casper, Lynne M. and Suzanne Bianchi. 2002. *Continuity and Change in the American Family*. Thousand Oaks, CA: Sage.

Cherlin, Andrew J. 1992. *Marriage, Divorce, Remarriage*. Cambridge, MA: Harvard University Press.

Cherlin, Andrew J. 2009. *The Marriage-Go-Round: The State of Marriage and the Family in America Today*. New York: Alfred A. Knopf.

Cherlin, Andrew J., Frank F. Furstenberg, Jr., P. Lindsey Chase-Lansdale, K. E. Kiernan, P. K. Robins, D. R. Morrison, and J. O. Teitler. 1991. "Longitudinal Studies of the Effects of Divorce on Children in Great Britain and the United States." *Science* 252 (June):1386–89.

Cohany, Sharon R. and Emy Sok. 2007. "Trends in the Labor Force Participation of Married Mothers of Infants." *Monthly Labor Review*, February 2007, 9–16.

Coltrane, Scott. 2004. "Fathering: Paradoxes, Contradictions and Dilemmas." Pp. 224–43 in *Handbook of Contemporary Families: Considering the Past, Contemplating the Future*, edited by Marilyn Coleman and Lawrence Ganong. Thousand Oaks, CA: Sage.

Conley, Dalton. 2004. *The Pecking Order: Which Siblings Succeed and Why*. New York: Pantheon.

Cooke, Lynn P. 2006. "'Doing' Gender in Context: Household Bargaining and Risk of Divorce in Germany and the United States." *American Journal of Sociology* 112(2):442–72.

Coontz, Stephanie. 1992. *The Way We Never Were: American Families and the Nostalgia Trap*. New York: Basic Books.

Coontz, Stephanie. 2005. *Marriage, a History: From Obedience to Intimacy, or How Love Conquered Marriage*. New York: Viking.

Cotter, David A., Paula England, and Joan Hermsen. 2010. "Moms and Jobs: Trends in Mothers' Employment and Which Mothers Stay Home." Pp. 416–24 in *Families as They Really Are*, edited by Barbara J. Risman. New York: W.W. Norton.

Crouter, Ann C. and Susan M. McHale. 2005. "Work Time, Family Time, and Children's Time: Implications for Youth." Pp. 49–66 in *Work, Family, Health, and Well-Being*, edited by Suzanne Bianchi, Lynne Casper, and R. B. King. New York: Routledge.

Damaske, Sarah. 2011. *For the Family? How Class and Gender Shape Women's Work*. New York: Oxford University Press.

Deutsch, Francine. 1999. *Halving It All: How Equally Shared Parenting Works*. Cambridge, MA: Harvard University Press.

DiMaggio, Paul, John Evans, and Bethany Bryson. 1996. "Have Americans' Social Attitudes Become More Polarized?" *American Journal of Sociology* 102:690–755.

Edin, Kathryn and Maria Kefalas. 2005. *Promises I Can Keep: Why Poor Women Put Motherhood before Marriage*. Berkeley and Los Angeles: University of California Press.

Edlund, Lena and Rohini Pande. 2002. "Why Have Women Become Left-Wing? The Political Gender Gap and the Decline of Marriage." *Quarterly Journal of Economics* 117:917–61.

Epstein, Cynthia F., Carroll Seron, Bonnie Oglensky, and Robert Saute. 1999. *The Part-Time Paradox: Time Norms, Professional Lives, Family, and Gender*. New York: Routledge.

Esping-Andersen, Gosta. 2009. *The Incomplete Revolution: Adapting Welfare States to Women's New Roles*. Cambridge, UK: Polity Press.

Ferree, Myra Marx. 1990. "Beyond Separate Spheres: Feminism and Family Research." *Journal of Marriage and the Family* 52:866–84.

Folbre, Nancy. 2008. *Valuing Children: Rethinking the Economics of the Family*. Cambridge, MA: Harvard University Press.

Friedan, Betty. [2001] 1963. *The Feminine Mystique*. New York: W.W Norton & Company.

Furstenberg, Frank F. 2007. *Destinies of the Disadvantaged: The Politics of Teenage Childbearing*. New York: Russell Sage Foundation.

Furstenberg, Frank F. and Andrew J. Cherlin. 1991. *Divided Families: What Happens to Children When Parents Part*. Cambridge, MA: Harvard University Press.

Furstenberg, Frank F., Sheela Kennedy, Vonnie C. Mcloyd, Ruben Rumbaut, and Richard A. Settersten, Jr. 2004. "Growing Up Is Harder to Do." *Contexts* 3:33–41.

Furstenberg, Frank F., Ruben G. Rumbaut, and Richard A. Settersten Jr., eds. 2005. *On the Frontier of Adulthood: Emerging Themes and New Directions*. Chicago: University of Chicago Press.

Galinsky, Ellen. 1999. *Ask the Children: What America's Children Really Think about Working Parents*. New York: William Morrow.

Galinksy, Ellen, Kerstin Aumann, and James T. Bond. 2009. "Gender and Generation at Home and at Work." New York: Families and Work Institute.

Gerson, Kathleen. 2011. *The Unfinished Revolution: Coming of Age in a New Era of Gender, Work, and Family*. New York: Oxford University Press.

Giele, Janet Z. 1996. "Decline of the Family: Conservative, Liberal, and Feminist Views." Pp. 89–115 in *Promises to Keep: Decline and Renewal of Marriage in America*, edited by David Poponoe, Jean Bethke Elshtain, and David Blankenhorn. Lanham, MD: Rowman & Littlefield.

Goode, William J. 1963. *World Revolution and Family Patterns*. New York: Free Press.

Goode, William J. 1982. *The Family*, 2nd ed. Upper Saddle River: Pearson.

Gornick, Janet C. and Marcia K. Meyers. 2003. *Families That Work: Policies for Reconciling Parenthood and Employment*. New York: Russell Sage Foundation.

Gornick, Janet C. and Marcia K. Meyers. 2009. *Gender Equality: Transforming Family Divisions of Labor*. New York: Verso Books.

Harvey, Lisa. 1999. "Short-Term and Long-Term Effects of Early Parental Employment on Children of the National Longitudinal Survey of Youth." *Developmental Psychology* 35(2):445–59.

Hays, Sharon. 1996. *The Cultural Contradictions of Motherhood*. New Haven, CT: Yale University Press.

_____. 2003. *Flat Broke with Children: Women in the Age of Welfare Reform*. New York: Oxford University Press.

Hertz, Rosanna. 2006. *Single by Chance, Mothers by Choice: How Women Are Choosing Parenthood without Marriage and Creating the New American Family*. New York: Oxford University Press.

Hetherington, E. Mavis and John Kelly. 2002. *For Better or For Worse: Divorce Reconsidered*. New York: W.W. Norton.

Hill Collins, Patricia. 1991. *Black Feminist Thought: Knowledge, Consciousness, and the Politics of Empowerment*. London and New York: Routledge.

Hochschild, Arlie R., with Anne Machung. 1989. *The Second Shift: Working Parents and the Revolution at Home*. New York: Viking.

Hochschild, Arlie R. 1997. *The Time Bind: When Work Becomes Home and Home Becomes Work*. New York: Henry Holt.

Hoffman, Lois, Norma Wladis, and Lise M. Youngblade. 1999. *Mothers at Work: Effects on Children's Well-Being*. Cambridge, UK: Cambridge University Press.

Jacobs, Jerry A. and Kathleen Gerson. 2004. *The Time Divide: Work, Family, and Gender Inequality*. Cambridge, MA: Harvard University Press.

Jayson, Sharon. 2007. "Gen Y's Attitudes Differ from Parents.'" *USA Today*, January 9.

Kefalas, Maria J., Frank F. Furstenberg, Patrick J. Carr, and Laura Napolitano. 2011. "'Marriage Is More Than Being Together': The Meaning of Marriage for Young Adults." *Journal of Family Issues*, February 23.

Kimmel, Michael. 2008. *Guyland: The Perilous World Where Boys Become Men*. New York: HarperCollins Publishers.

Lareau, Annette. 2003. *Unequal Childhoods: Class, Race, and Family Life*. Berkeley and Los Angeles: University of California Press.

Levi-Strauss, Claude. 1964. "Reciprocity, the Essence of Social Life." Pp. 3-14 in *The Family: Its Structure and Functions*, edited by Rose Laub Coser. New York: St. Martins Press.

Li, Allen J. 2007. "The Kids Are OK: Divorce and Children's Behavior Problems." RAND Working Paper No. WR-489.

Lorber, Judith. 1994. *Paradoxes of Gender*. New Haven, CT: Yale University Press.

Luker, Kristin. 2007. *When Sex Goes to School: Warring Views on Sex—and Sex Education—Since the Sixties*. New York: W.W. Norton.

Malinowski, Bronislaw. [1913] 1964. "Parenthood, the Basis of Social Structure." Pp. 51-63 in *The Family: Its Structure and Functions*, edited by Rose Laub Coser. New York: St. Martins Press.

Marquardt, Elizabeth. 2005. *Between Two Worlds: The Inner Lives of Children of Divorce*. New York: Crown.

McLanahan, Sara and Gary D. Sandefur. 1994. *Growing Up with a Single Parent: What Hurts, What Helps*. Cambridge, MA: Harvard University Press.

Moen, Phyllis and Patricia Roehling. 2005. *The Career Mystique: Cracks in the American Dream*. Lanham, MD: Rowman & Littlefield.

Moore, Kristin A., Rosemary Chalk, Juliet Scarpa, and Sharon Vandiverre. 2002. "Family Strengths: Often Overlooked, But Real." Child Trends Research Brief. Washington, DC: Annie E. Casey Foundation.

Newman, Katherine S. 2009. "Ties That Bind: Cultural Interpretations of Delayed Adulthood in Western Europe and Japan." *Sociological Forum* Vol. 23 (4): 645–69.

Newman, Katherine S., and Victor Tan Chen. 2007. *The Missing Class: Portraits of the Near-Poor in America*. Boston: Beacon Press.

Parcel, Toby L. and Elizabeth G. Menaghan. 1994. *Parents' Jobs and Children's Lives*. New York: Aldine de Gruyter.

Parsons, Talcott and Robert F. Bales. 1954. *Family, Socialization, and Interaction Process*. Glencoe, IL: Free Press.

Percheski, Christine. 2008. "Opting Out? Cohort Differences in Professional Women's Employment from 1960 to 2005." *American Sociological Review* 73:497–517.

Pew Research Center. 2007a. "Generation Gap in Values, Behavior: As Marriage and Parenthood Drift Apart, Public Is Concerned about Social Impact." Pew Research Center Social and Demographic Trends Report, July 1.

Pew Research Center. 2007b. *How Young People View Their Lives, Futures and Politics: A Portrait of the 'Generation Next.'* New York: Pew Research Center.

Pew Research Center. 2010. "The Decline of Marriage and Rise of New Families." Pew Research Center, November 18.

Popenoe, David. 1988. *Disturbing the Nest: Family Change and Decline in Modern Societies*. New York: Aldine de Gruyter.

Popenoe, David, Jean B. Elshtain, and David Blankenhorn. 1996. *Promises to Keep: Decline and Renewal of Marriage in America*. Lanham, MD: Rowman & Littlefield.

Porter, Eduardo and Michelle O'Donnell. 2006. "Facing Middle Age with No Degree, and No Wife." *New York Times*, August 6.

Poulin, Colleen and Virginia Rutter. 2011. "How Color-Blind Is Love? Interracial Dating Facts and Puzzles." Council on Contemporary Families Briefing Paper (March).

Powell, Brian, Catherine Bolzendahl, Claudia Geist, and Lala Carr Steelman. 2010. *Counted Out: Same-Sex Relations and American's Definitions of Family*. New York: Russell Sage Foundation.

Presser, Harriet B. 2003. *Working in a 24/7 Economy: Challenges for American Families*. New York: Russell Sage Foundation.

Risman, Barbara J. 1998. *Gender Vertigo: American Families in Transition*. New Haven, CT: Yale University Press.

Risman, Barbara J., ed. 2010. *Families as They Really Are*. New York: W.W. Norton.

Rosenfeld, Michael J. 2009. *The Age of Independence: Interracial Unions, Same-Sex Unions, and Changing American Family*. Cambridge, MA: Harvard University Press.

Rubin, Lillian B. 1994. *Families on the Fault Line*. New York: HarperCollins.

Rutter, Virginia. 2010. "The Case for Divorce." Pp. 159–69 in *Families as They Really Are*, edited by Barbara J. Risman. New York: W.W. Norton.

Shorter, Edward. 1975. *The Making of the Modern Family*. New York: Basic Books.

Skolnick, Arlene. 2006. "Beyond the 'M' Word: The Tangled Web of Politics and Marriage." *Dissent* (Fall):81–87.

Smith, Christian with Kari Christofferson, Hilary Davidson, and Patricia Herzog. 2011. *Lost in Translation: The Dark Side of Emerging Adulthood*. New York: Oxford University Press.

Smock, Pamela. 2000. "Cohabitation in the United States: An Appraisal of Research Themes, Findings, and Implications." *Annual Review of Sociology* 26:1–20.

Smock, Pamela J. and Wendy Manning. 2010. "New Couples, New Families: The Cohabitation Revolution in the United States." In *Families as They Really Are*, edited by Barbara J. Risman. New York: W.W. Norton.

Stacey, Judith. 1996. *In the Name of the Family: Rethinking Family Values in the Postmodern Age*. Boston: Beacon Press.

Stack, Carol B. 1974. *All Our Kin: Strategies for Survival in a Black Community*. New York: Harper and Row.

Stone, Pamela. 2007. *Opting Out? Why Women Really Quit Careers and Head Home*. Berkeley and Los Angeles: University of California Press.

Struening, Karen. 2010. "Families 'In Law' and Families 'In Practice': Does the Law Recognize Families as They Really Are?" Pp. 75–90 in *Families as They Really Are*, edited by Barbara J. Risman. New York: W. W. Norton.

Sullivan, Oriel and Scott Coltrane. 2008. "Men's Changing Contribution to Housework and Child Care." Chicago, IL: Council on Contemporary Families Briefing Paper (April 25).

Swidler, Ann. 1980. "Love and Adulthood in American Culture." Pp. 120–47 in *Themes of Love and Work in Adulthood*, edited by Erik H. Erikson and Neil J. Smelser. Cambridge, MA: Harvard University Press.

Teixeira, Ruy. 2009. "The Coming End of the Culture Wars." Washington, DC: Center for American Progress.

U.S. Census Bureau. 2006. "Current Population Survey Annual Social and Economic Supplement: Families and Living Arrangements: 2005." Washington, DC.

U.S. Census Bureau. 2007. "Single-Parent Households Showed Little Variation since 1994." Washington, DC.

Waldfogel, Jane. 2006. *What Children Need*. Cambridge, MA: Harvard University Press.

Wallerstein, Judith S., Julia M. Lewis, and Sandra Blakeslee. 2000. *The Unexpected Legacy of Divorce: A 25-Year Landmark Study*. New York: Hyperion.

Warren, Elizabeth and Amelia W. Tyagi. 2003. *The Two-Income Trap: Why Middle-Class Mothers and Fathers Are Going Broke*. New York: Basic Books.

Weitzman, Lenore. 1985. *The Divorce Revolution: The Unexpected Consequences for Women and Children*. New York: Free Press.

Whitehead, Barbara D. 1997. *The Divorce Culture*. New York: Alfred A. Knopf.

Whyte, William H., Jr. 1956. *The Organization Man.* New York: Simon & Schuster.

Williams, Joan C. 2000. *Unbending Gender: Why Family and Work Conflict and What to Do about It.* New York: Oxford University Press.

Williams, Joan C. 2010. *Reshaping the Work-Family Debate: Why Men and Class Matter.* Cambridge, MA: Harvard University Press.

CHAPTER 17

Alfano, Sean. 2009. "Poll: Women's Movement Worthwhile," CBS News (Feb. 11, 2009) (http://www.cbsnews.com/2100-500160_162-965224.html).

Alinsky, Saul. 1971. *Rules for Radicals: A Pragmatic Primer for Realistic Radicals.* New York: Vintage.

Amenta, Edwin, Neal Caren, Sheera Joy Olasky, and James E. Stobaugh. 2008. "All the SMOs Fit to Print." (http://www.socsci.uci.edu/~ea3/allthesmosfittoprint.pdf).

Brockett, Charles. 1993. "A Protest Cycle Resolution of the Repression/Protest Paradox." *Social Science History* 17(3):457–84.

Chenoweth, Erica and Maria J. Stephan. 2011. *Why Civil Resistance Works: The Strategic Logic of Nonviolent Conflict.* New York: Columbia University Press.

Cohen, Jean L. and Andrew Arato. 1992. *Civil Society and Political Theory.* Cambridge, MA: MIT Press.

Epstein, Barbara. 2001. "What Happened to the Women's Movement?" *Monthly Review* 53(1):1–13.

Gamson, Joshua. 1995. "Must Identity Movements Self-Destruct? A Queer Dilemma." *Social Problems* 42(3):390–407.

Gamson, William A. 1990. *The Strategy of Social Protest.* 2nd ed. Homewood, IL: Dorsey.

Inglehart, Ronald. 1977. *The Silent Revolution: Changing Values and Political Styles among Western Publics.* Princeton, NJ: Princeton University Press.

Jasper, James M. 1997. *The Art of Moral Protest: Culture, Biography, and Creativity in Social Movements.* Chicago: University of Chicago Press.

Jones, Jeffrey M. 2011. "New High of 55% of Americans Foresee Labor Unions Weakening," Gallup (Sept. 1, 2011) (http://www.gallup.com/poll/149300/New-High-Americans-Foresee-Labor-Unions-Weakening.aspx).

Kurzman, Charles. 1996. "Structural Opportunity and Perceived Opportunity in Social-Movement Theory: The Iranian Revolution of 1979." *American Sociological Review* 61(1):153–70

Kurzman, Charles. 2002. "Bin Laden and Other Thoroughly Modern Muslims." *Contexts* 1(4):13–20.

Lenin, V. I. 1915. "The collapse of the Second International." *Lenin: Collected Works*, Vol. 21. Moscow: Progress Publishers.

Luker, Kristin. 1984. *Abortion and the Politics of Motherhood.* Berkeley and Los Angeles: University of California Press.

McAdam, Doug. 1982. *Political Process and the Development of Black Insurgency, 1930–1970.* Chicago: University of Chicago Press.

McAdam, Doug. 1988. *Freedom Summer.* New York: Oxford University Press.

McCarthy, John D. and Mayer N. Zald. 1977. "Resource Mobilization and Social Movements: A Partial Theory." *American Journal of Sociology* 82:1212–41.

Morin, Rich. 2012. "Rising Share of Americans See Conflict Between Rich and Poor," Pew Research Center (Jan. 11, 2012) (http://www.pewsocialtrends.org/2012/01/11/rising-share-of-americans-see-conflict-between-rich-and-poor).

Morris, Aldon D. 1984. *The Origins of the Civil Rights Movement: Black Communities Organizing for Change.* New York: Free Press.

Munson, Ziad W. 2008. *The Making of Pro-Life Activists: How Social Movement Mobilization Works.* Chicago: University of Chicago Press.

Newport, Frank. 2011. "Blacks, Whites Differ on Government's Role in Civil Rights," Gallup (Aug. 19, 2011) (http://www.gallup.com/poll/149087/Blacks-Whites-Differ-Government-Role-Civil-Rights.aspx)

Olson, Mancur. 1965. *The Logic of Collective Action: Public Goods and the Theory of Groups.* Cambridge, MA: Harvard University Press.

Pew Research Center. 2011a. "More Now Disagree with Tea Party—Even in Tea Party Districts" (Nov. 29, 2011) (http://www.people-press.org/2011/11/29/more-now-disagree-with-tea-party-even-in-tea-party-districts).

Pew Research Center. 2011b. "Frustration With Congress CouldHurt Republican Incumbents" (Dec. 15, 2011) (http://www.people-press.org/2011/12/15/section-2-occupy-wall-street-and-inequality).

Piven, Frances Fox and Richard A. Cloward. 1977. *Poor People's Movements: Why They Succeed, How They Fail.* New York: Vintage.

Roxborough, Ian. 2007. "Counterinsurgency." *Contexts* 6(2):15–21.

Saad, Lydia. 2010. "On 40th Earth Day, Image of Green Movement Still Positive," Gallup (April 22, 2010) (http://www.gallup.com/poll/127484/40th-Earth-Day-Image-Green-Movement-Positive.aspx).

Saad, Lydia. 2012. "'Pro-Choice' Americans at Record-Low 41%," Gallup (May 23, 2012) (http://www.gallup.com/poll/154838/pro-choice-americans-record-low.aspx).

Schwartz, Michael. 1976. *Radical Protest and Social Structure: The Southern Farmers' Alliance and Cotton Tenancy, 1880–1890.* Chicago: University of Chicago Press.

Schwartz, Michael. 2011. "The Egyptian Uprising: The Mass Strike in the Time of Neoliberal Globalization." *New Labor Forum* 20(3):32–43.

Silver, Nate. 2012. "Support for Gay Marriage Outweighs Opposition in Polls," The New York Times (May 9, 2012) (http://fivethirtyeight.blogs.nytimes.com/2012/05/09/support-for-gay-marriage-outweighs-opposition-in-polls).

Skocpol, Theda. 1979. *States and Social Revolutions: A Comparative Analysis of France, Russia, and China.* Cambridge: Cambridge University Press.

Snow, David A. and Robert D. Benford. 1988. "Ideology, Frame Resonance, and Participant Mobilization." *International Social Movement Research* 1:197–217.

Teixeira, Ruy. 2012. "Public Opinion Snapshot: Rich Drawing Away from the Poor and Middle Class," Center for American Progress (June 18, 2012) (http://www.americanprogress.org/issues/2012/06/snapshot_061812.html).

Tilly, Charles. 1986. *The Contentious French.* Cambridge, MA: Harvard University Press.

Walsh, Edward J. 1981. "Resource Mobilization and Citizen Protest in Communities around Three Mile Island." *Social Problems* 29:1–21.

CREDITS

Text Credits

CHAPTER 1 **p. 18:** U.S. Census Bureau.

CHAPTER 5 **p. 118:** *Talk of Love: How Culture Matters,* Ann Swidler is published by University of Chicago Press; **p. 119:** Appadurai, Arjun. 1993. *Modernity At Large: Cultural Dimensions of Globalization.* University of Minnesota Press.; **p. 123:** Appadurai, Arjun. 1993. *Modernity At Large: Cultural Dimensions of Globalization.* University of Minnesota Press.

CHAPTER 10 **p. 268:** Weber, Max. 1978. Economy and Society. Berkeley: University of California Press.; **p. 277:** U.S. Census Bureau 2011; U.S Bureau of Labor Statistics 2012; **p. 277:** Kochlar, Rakesh, Richard Fry, and Paul Taylor. 2011. Wealth Gap Rises to Record Highs Between Whites, Blacks and Latinos. Washington DC: Pew Research Center. **p. 280:** Bureau of Labor Statistics (2011); **p. 280:** Bureau of Justice Statistics (2011); **p. 280:** Digest of Educational Statistics: 2010. (http://nces.ed.gov/programs/digest/d10/tables/dt10_008.asp?referrer=list). Accessed February 22, 2012, National Center for Education Statistics; **p. 280:** "Table 115." Digest of Educational Statistics: 2010. (http://nces.ed.gov/programs/digest/d10/tables/dt10_115.asp?referrer=list).

Accessed February 22, 2012, National Center for Education Statistics; **p. 280:** National Center for Educational Statistics (2011a); **p. 281:** Center for Disease Control and Prevention (2011); **p. 287:** U.S. Census Bureau.

CHAPTER 13 **p. 356:** U.S. Census Bureau, Current Population Survey, 1970, 1980, 1990, 1995, 2000, 2005, 2011 Annual Social and Economic Supplements.; **p. 359:** The Pew Research Center for the People and the Press, http://pewresearch.org/pubs/1802/decline-marriage-rise-new-families; **p. 362:** *Hard Choices: How Women Decide About Work, Career, and Motherhood,* by Kathleen Gerson, © 1985 by the Regents of the University of California. Published by the University of California Press.; **p. 365:** The Pew Research Center, http://www.pewsocialtrends.org/2010/11/18/the-decline-of-marriage-and-rise-of-new-families/5/; **p. 367:** *The Unfinished Revolution: Coming of Age in a New Era of Gender, Work, and Family* by Kathleen Gerson (2011) Fig. 5.3 **p. 122.** By permission of Oxford University Press, Inc.; **p. 368:** The Pew Research Center, http://www.pewsocialtrends.org/2010/11/18/the-decline-of-marriage-and-rise-of-new-families/3/; **p. 371:** Rebecca Ray, Janet Gornick, and John Schmitt, 2009. "Parental Leave Policies in 21 Countries: Assessing Generosity and Gender Equality," Figure 1, page 6. (Center for Economic Policy Research, Washington, DC.

CHAPTER 17 **p. 494:** Gamson, William A. 1990. The Strategy of Social Protest, 2nd edn. Homewood, IL: Dorsey, Wadsworth Publishing Company

Photo Credits

Cover: Jon Helgason / Alamy; **Design Elements:** CVI Textures / Alamy; CVI Textures / Alamy.

CHAPTER 1 **p. 2:** Pearson; **p. 3:** PUNIT PARANJPE/AFP/Getty Images/Newscom; **p. 5 (bl):** Dominic Harris / Alamy; **(br):** Ingolf Pompe/LOOK Die Bildagentur der Fotografen GmbH / Alamy; **(cr):** TIPS/Photoshot; **(tl):** age fotostock / SuperStock; **p. 6 (br):** Photo by Yaroslava/Nik Mills Studio; **(t):** age fotostock / SuperStock; **p. 7:** Oleksiy Maksymenko Photos/Alamy; **p. 10:** Myrleen Pearson/Alamy; **p. 12, (tr):** ZUMA Wire Service / Alamy; **(c):** TIPS/Photoshot; **p. 14 (bl):** Jim West / Alamy; **(c):** jon le-bon/Shutterstock; **p. 15:** A. Ramey / PhotoEdit; **p. 17:** Dominic Harris / Alamy; **p. 18:** Underwood & Underwood/Corbis; **p. 20:** AFP/Getty Images/Newscom; **p. 21:** SHOUT/Alamy; **p. 22:** Deco / Alamy; **p. 23 (t):** Ingolf Pompe/LOOK Die Bildagentur der Fotografen GmbH / Alamy; **p. 24 (tr):** ZUMA Wire Service / Alamy; **(br):** A. Ramey / PhotoEdit; **p. 25 (br):** Ingolf Pompe/LOOK Die Bildagentur der Fotografen GmbH / Alamy; **(cr):** Underwood & Underwood/Corbis.

CHAPTER 5 **p. 110:** Pearson; **p. 111:** Arnaud Chicurel/Hemis/Corbis; **p. 111:** Joson /Corbis; **p. 112:** Zhao Kang/Xinhua/Photoshot/Newscom; **p. 113 (bl):** JoeFox/Alamy; **(tl):** National Geographic Image Collection / Alamy; **(br):** Songquan Deng/Alamy; **(cl):** Neil Emmerson/Robert Harding World Imagery; **(cr):** Frans Lemmens / SuperStock; **p. 114:** National Geographic Image Collection / Alamy; **p. 115:** Paparazzi by Appointment / Alamy; **p. 116 (tr):** David Edsam/Alamy; **(bl):** Science and Society / SuperStock; **p. 119:** Frans Lemmens / SuperStock; **p. 120:** Paul Carstairs/Alamy; **p. 122:** Jim West / Alamy; **p. 125 (tr):** Stuart Bay/Alamy; **(c):** Neil Emmerson/Robert Harding World Imagery; **p. 126:** Russell Gordon/Danita Delimont/Alamy; **p. 128:** Songquan Deng/Alamy; **p. 130:** ANNA ZIEMINSKI/AFP/Newscom; **p. 132:** JoeFox/Alamy; **p. 135:** AF archive / Alamy; **p. 136:** ZUMA Wire Service / Alamy; **p. 137:** Paparazzi by Appointment / Alamy; **p. 138 (tr):** Paul Carstairs/Alamy; **(cr):** Russell Gordon/Danita Delimont/Alamy; **(br):** Songquan Deng/Alamy; **p. 139:** ZUMA Wire Service / Alamy.

CHAPTER 10 **p. 260:** Pearson; **p. 261:** Alix Minde/PhotoAlto/Age Fotostock; **p. 262:** photothek / ullstein bild / The Image Works; **p. 263 (cr):** Malcolm Fairman / Alamy; **(bl):** Peter Casolino/Alamy; **(cl):** AP Photo/Heather Coit; **(tl):** Gino Santa Maria/Fotolia LLC; **(br):** Chuck Fishman / Getty Images; **p. 264:** Gino Santa Maria/Fotolia LLC; **p. 265:** OBAMA PRESS OFFICE/New/Newscom; **p. 266:** Julien McRoberts Danita Delimont Photography/Newscom; **p. 267:** Malcolm Fairman / Alamy; **p. 269:** Philip Date/Shutterstock; **p. 270:** Homer W Sykes / Alamy; **p. 271:** AP Photo/Heather Coit; **p. 273 (r):** Dimj/Shutterstock.com; **(l):** Kim Ruoff/Shutterstock; **p. 275:** AP

Photo/Rogelio V. Solis; **p. 276:** Chuck Fishman / Getty Images; **p. 279:** Jim West / Alamy; **p. 283:** Jim West/Age Fotostock; **p. 284:** Peter Casolino/Alamy; **p. 285:** Daily Mail/Rex / Alamy; **p. 287:** Nik Taylor / Alamy; **p. 289 (br):** Homer W Sykes / Alamy; **(cr):** OBAMA PRESS OFFICE/New/Newscom; **p. 290 (br):** Jim West / Alamy; **(cr):** AP Photo/Heather Coit; **p. 291:** Nik Taylor / Alamy.

CHAPTER 13 **p. 348:** Kathleen Gerson; **p. 349:** Blend Images / Alamy; **p. 349:** Blue Lantern Studio/Corbis; **p. 350:** JuanSharma/Bruja, PacificCoastNews/Newscom; **p. 351 (cl):** Big Cheese Photo LLC/Alamy; **(b):** Jon Arnold Images Ltd / Alamy; **(br):** DK Images; **(bl):** Deborah Davis/PhotoEdit; **(cr):** Wolfgang Spunbarg / PhotoEdit; **(tl):** StockHouse/Shutterstock; **p. 352:** StockHouse/Shutterstock; **p. 353:** rSnapshotPhotos/Shutterstock; **p. 354:** Ariel Skelley/Blend Images / Alamy; **p. 355:** Wolfgang Spunbarg / PhotoEdit; **p. 357:** imagebroker.net / SuperStock; **p. 358:** Big Cheese Photo LLC/Alamy; **p. 359:** Glow Images, Inc/Getty Images; **p. 363:** Mary Steinbacher / PhotoEdit; **p. 364:** DK Images; **p. 367:** keith morris / Alamy; **p. 368:** Deborah Davis/PhotoEdit; **p. 369:** Exactostock/SuperStock; **p. 370:** Jon Arnold Images Ltd / Alamy; **p. 372 (cl):** Design Pics Inc. / Alamy; **(cr):** Tetra Images / Alamy; **(bl):** Richard Kalvar/Magnum Photos; **(tc):** Haruyoshi Yamaguchi/REUTERS; **p. 373:** OLIVIER HOSLET/EPA/Newscom; **p. 375 (cr):** rSnapshotPhotos/Shutterstock; **(br):** imagebroker.net / SuperStock; **p. 376 (br):** keith morris / Alamy; **(cr):** Glow Images, Inc/Getty Images; **p. 377 (cr):** OLIVIER HOSLET/EPA/Newscom; **(tr):** Exactostock/SuperStock.

CHAPTER 17 **p. 474:** Pearson; **p. 475:** Mario Tama/Getty Images News/Getty Images; **p. 476 (cl):** Richard Wareham Fotografie/Alamy; **(tl):** Vespasian / Alamy; **(cr):** akg-images/Newscom; **(br):** Barry Iverson Photography/Barry Iverson/Newscom; **p. 477:** Vespasian / Alamy; **p. 478:** Jim West/Age Fotostock; **p. 479:** JOHN G. MABANGLO/AFP/Newscom; **p. 480:** akg-images/Newscom; **p. 481:** Fred W. McDarrah/Premium Archive /Getty Images; **p. 482:** Richard Corkery/NY Daily News Archive/Getty Images; **p. 486:** ASHRAF AMRA / Demotix/Demotix/Corbis; **p. 487:** Richard Wareham Fotografie/Alamy; **p. 489:** Jim West/PhotoEdit; **p. 490:** Tom Williams/Roll Call/Getty Images; **p. 491 (bc):** Jim West / Alamy; **(cr):** Dennis Van Tine/LFI/Photoshot/Newscom; **(cl):** Rapport Press/Newscom; **p. 493:** AP Photo/Bill Waugh; **p. 496:** Barry Iverson Photography/Barry Iverson/Newscom; **p. 497:** ZUMA Press, Inc/Alamy; **p. 499:** oubeir Souissi/Reuters/Landov; **p. 501:** Image Asset Management Ltd/Superstock; **p. 504 (cr):** Jim West/Age Fotostock; **(br):** Fred W. McDarrah/Premium Archive /Getty Images; **p. 505 (br):** ZUMA Press, Inc/Alamy; **(tr):** Jim West/PhotoEdit.

INDEX

Theories and theorists featured in *The Sociology Project* are highlighted in blue in the index.

Totemism, 511
Townsend, P., 421
Toxic stress, 560
Toyota, 574
Tracking, in education, 433–434
Trade intensity index, 572
"Traditional" families, 352–353, 356
Traditional societies, 510–511
Tragedy of the commons, 528–529
Transfers, 342
Transgendered, 297
Transnational corporations (TNCs), 572–573, 574
Trash, 520
Treadmill of production, 529
Trevelyan, Edward N., 286
The Triumph of the City (Glaeser), 223
Trobriand Islands, 510
The Truly Disadvantaged (Wilson), 217
Trust in the workplace, 190–191
Tucker, M. S, 432
Tunisia, 499, 501
Turkey, 323, 427
Turn taking, 66
Turra, Cassio M., 561
Twitter, 123, 136, 176, 435
Two-dimensional view of power, 145–147, 152
Two Million Minutes, 426
Two-party political system, 160–161
Tyagi, Amelia W., 370
Tyson, Karolyn, 434
Tyson's Corner, Virginia, 206

U

Udry, J. Richard, 308
Ueda, Reed, 218
Uganda, 518, 550
Uggen, Christopher, 281, 465, 469, 470
Ukraine, 323, 573
Unauthorized migrants, 324
UNCTAD (United Nations Conference on Trade and Development), 572
Underemployment, 192
UNDP, 528
Unemployment, 192, 279, 425
Unification (Moonies), 385, 397
Unintentional discrimination, 272
Union Carbide Company, 526
Unions, 19, 191, 193, 246, 419, 491
Unitarians, 396
United Arab Emirates, 323
United Auto Workers, 488
United Church of Christ, 524
United Kingdom. *See also* British Empire

antipoverty programs, 159
as class-bound society, 126
education, 414, 424
end-of-life care, 550
globalization and, 572
healthcare, 555, 557
imagined communities, 123
immigration and, 323
inequality and, 155
poverty, 255
ratio of merchandise trade to GEP, 570
self-employment in, 172
social mobility, 250, 251
support for social programs, 165
United Mine Workers, 488
United Nations, 202, 221, 320, 532, 543
United Nations Conference on Trade and Development (UNCTAD), 572
United Nations International School, 260
United States. *See also* Education; Immigration; Race and ethnicity
agenda setting, 146–147, 160–163
age pyramid, 547, 548
aging and population dynamics, 548
antipoverty programs, 154, 158–160, 252
belief in policies benefiting the powerful, 164–167
border with Mexico, 327
childcare, 372
children in poverty, 159, 228–231, 254–255
consumption in, 236
cultural mobility, 126
death and dying in, 550
family income, 234, 235
fertility and mortality, changes in, 543–544
garment production, 576
Great Migration, 93, 203, 217
healthcare in compared to other nations, 555–557
hegemony, culture wars, or multiculturalism, 120–122
income per-person per capita, 233–234
income share of top 1%, 5%, and 10% of families, 156
inequality in, 243, 251, 423–424, 426
inequality in vs. other nations, 155
intergenerational correlation, 249–250
labor movement, 491, 492

level of support for helping the poor, 165
material power in, 247
money and politics, 161–163
obesity in, 552, 553, 554–555
percentage of poor children pre and post-government actions, 159
physician density, 556
policy and politics in the first dimension, 154–160
politics in the second dimension, 160–163
politics in the third dimension, 164–167
power in, 154–167
preschools and cultural identity, 123, 125
prison population, 466
racial hierarchy, 105
racism in, 274–275
railway lines, 568
rates of poverty vs. other nations, 159
ratio of merchandise trade to GEP, 570
relative and absolute poverty in, 255
spending on education, 424
taxation and economic inequality, 155–158
tax rate on highest-earning Americans, 156
two-party political system, 160–161
work in, 190–191, 193–194
United Steelworkers, 488
Units of analysis, 20
University of California at Berkeley, 442
University of Chicago, 18, 22, 132, 207, 513
UN Wall Chart, 573
Upper-class disunity, 499
Urban areas, 18, 202, 203, 205
Urban change, neighborhoods and, 208–209
Urban diversity, 218–219
Urban ecology, 207–208
Urban farming, 530
Urban ghetto, and concentrated poverty, 216–218
Urbanism, 210–214
Urbanization, 18–19, 202–206
Urban landscape, immigration and, 220–221
Urban neighborhoods, 214
Urban population, growth of, 18
Urban poverty, 219
Urban renewal, 215–216
Urban residents, "differentiation" of, 210
USA Today, 132

U.S. Border Patrol, 329
U.S. Census Bureau, 46, 95, 202, 243, 276, 277, 278, 281, 285, 286, 287, 354, 356, 358, 362, 364, 394, 419, 424, 540, 543, 547
U.S. Commission on Immigration Reform, 341
U.S. Department of Commerce, 577
U.S. Department of Health and Human Services, 52, 281, 549, 553
U.S. Department of Homeland Security, 325, 326, 328
U.S. Department of Labor, 194
U.S. Department of State, 325
U.S. Energy Information Administration, 517
U.S. Immigration Commission, 329
U.S. New Immigrant Survey, 332
U.S. Select Commission on Immigration and Refugee Policy, 330, 341
U.S. Trade Deficit Review Commission, 578
Uzzi, Brian, 176

V

Valdés, Guadalupe, 341
Valencia, California, 206
Valentine's Day, 135
Validity, 39
Vallas, Steven, 188
"Value-added test scores," 45
Values, 34, 115, 117
Van Ausdale, Debra, 274
Vandalism, 71
Van Der Bly, Martha C. E., 123
Vandiverre, Sharon, 356
Vanfossen, Beth E., 433
Van Kempen, Ronald, 221
Vanneman, Reeve, 302
Van Willigen, Marieke M., 420
Variables, 36, 39
Vaughan, Scott, 582
Veblen, Thorstein, 17
Veil, religious, 384
Venezuela, 502
Venkatesh, Sudhir, 218
Veterans of Foreign Wars, 488
Victimization surveys, 467
Video games, 297–298
Vietnam, 286, 497
Vietnam War, 133, 140
Violence, racial, 272
Violence in revolutions, 497–498, 501
Virginia, 557
Visa, 324
Vogl, Tom, 559